police photography
second edition

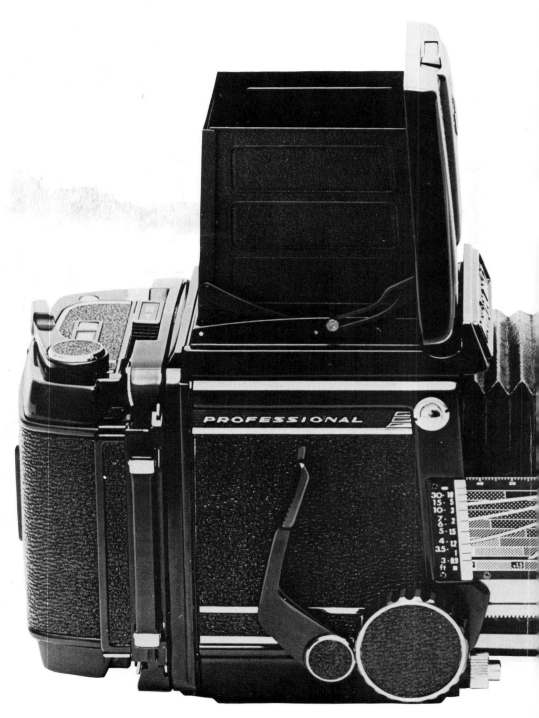

LAW ENFORCEMENT FIELDBOOKS

police photography

second edition

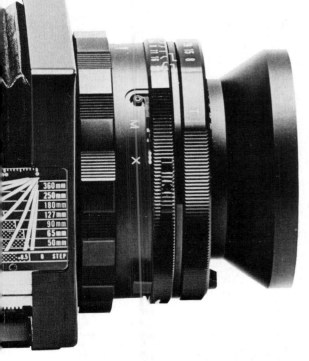

SAM J. SANSONE

Detective Sergeant, Police Photography (Retired)
Shaker Heights Police Department

Former Assistant Professor
Lorain County Community College

anderson publishing co./cincinnati
since 1887

Copyright © 1987 by Anderson Publishing Co.

Second Printing – July 1988

Library of Congress Cataloging-in-Publication Data

Sansone, Sam J.
    Police Photography

    Bibliography: p.
    Includes index.
    1. Photography, Legal. I. Title.
TR822.S26 1987   363.2'5   87-1277

ISBN 0-87084-773-2

This book is dedicated to my late wife, Katherine, for her encouragement and patience during the long and difficult days of preparing the book. And to my daughter, Rosanne, for her assistance in helping me put this book together.

FOREWORD

Scientific and technological changes developed over the past decade have proven to be a mixed blessing to the members of the Nation's police and fire services. Improvements in the methods and instruments used to collect and analyze evidence enable them to pursue their tasks more effectively. These improvements also require that officers have more skills and knowledge and, consequently, create a greater demand for education and training at both pre-service and in-service levels.

Photography continues to grow in its usage in the investigative and reporting activities of police and fire service agencies, criminalistics laboratories and also enjoys wide usage in the private security area. Competency in photography has indeed become a requisite for being able to adequately function in the above areas.

Mr. Sansone's *Police Photography* has been widely circulated and well-received because it presents photographic uses, equipment, techniques and applications using descriptions and illustrations which are straightforward and easily understood by the reader. This latest edition of *Police Photography* covers the very basics of photography and yet still touches all areas of application and the latest materials in both equipment and techniques. The book will be a valuable resource to the pre-service student of the investigative uses of photography, as well as a reference for the experienced professional.

Mr. Sansone's book draws on his extensive experiences as a police practitioner and as a College Instructor in Photography, Police Photography and Criminalistics. In his latest edition of *Police Photography*, Mr. Sansone has succeeded in improving upon a book which has already been judged to be excellent.

CHARLES E. FYE

Chairperson, Division of Public Service
Lorain County Community College
Elyria, Ohio

February 1987

AUTHOR'S PREFACE

Police Photography is designed to teach the fundamentals of photography and their applications to police work. As before, information on planning a darkroom has been included.

The latter parts of *Police Photography* pertain to the application of law enforcement today: what to photograph, and why. They deal with the more specialized aspects of photography used for recording specific types of evidence and for solving crimes.

Students should become proficient in darkroom technique before trying to master the use of the camera. This premise, often ignored in texts of this type, is crucial to the teaching and learning of good exposure and composition.

The logical progression inherent, however, in the photographic process — light is reflected off a subject, refracted through a lens and focused on film — has made necessary that a fundamental discussion of light, the simple camera, and film precede instruction in darkroom technique. Thus, the student can enter the darkroom in the second or third week of the lesson plan with an exposed film and knowledge of how that film came to be exposed.

Once the student has learned darkroom technique, he can study exposure and composition, make mistakes, and profit by those mistakes. It is the hope of the author that the exercises for each chapter will facilitate student and teacher alike in recognizing and analyzing the more subtle of these mistakes.

When *Modern Photography for Police and Firemen* was published in 1971, instruction in photography at the college level, particularly within criminal justice programs, was in its infancy. Now, many schools have courses in police photography and boast well equipped darkrooms. Teaching methods have become established. And, more than ever, students are taking an interest in practical aides to law enforcement. As interest has increased, so has the need for a very special kind of text; I hope that, in transforming *Modern Photography for Police and Firemen* into *Police Photography*, I have satisfied this need.

SAM J. SANSONE

Elyria, Ohio
March, 1987

ACKNOWLEDGEMENTS

Credit is extended

-To Eastman Kodak Company, Rochester, New York for their cooperation in contributing to this book. Without their assistance, this book would have been impossible to write.

-To the United States Naval Department for permission granted to use materials employed in their photographic naval training courses.

-To the Photography and Criminalistic students (Classes 1967-1986) of Lorain County Community College, Elyria, Ohio, for the use of photographs submitted by them in their school projects.

-and to the following companies for their cooperation with photographs or information concerning their products:

General Electric, Cleveland, Ohio
Luna Pro, Kling Photo Corporation, Woodside (New York City) New York, 11377
Minolta Company, New York, New York
Paco Corporation, Minneapolis, Minnesota, 55440
Polaroid Corporation, Cambridge, Massachusetts, 02139
Saunders Photo/Graphic Inc., Rochester, New York, 14611
Simmon Bros., Division of Berkey Photo Inc., Woodside (New York City) New York, 11377
UltraViolet Products Inc., San Gabriel, California, 91778

Special credits are hereby given to the following individuals for assistance with photographs and/or information:

William DiGiovanni, Patrolman, Shaker Heights Police Department, Shaker Heights, Ohio.
Martin G. Johnson, Sgt., Shaker Heights Police Department, Shaker Heights, Ohio.
John E. Kimmet, Jr., Patrolman, Elyria Police Department, Elyria, Ohio.
Jeff Kraynik, Patrolman, Palm Bay City Police Department, Palm Bay City, Florida.
Pete's PhotoWorld, Inc., Cincinnati, Ohio.
Stan E. Puza, Patrolman, Lorain Police Department, Lorain, Ohio.
George Rosbrook, Chairman of Police Science, Lorain County Community College, Elyria, Ohio.
Leon Smith, Lieutenant, Wyoming Michigan Police Department, Wyoming, Michigan.
Michael Tomaro, Patrolman, Pepper Pike Police Department, Pepper Pike, Ohio.

CONTENTS

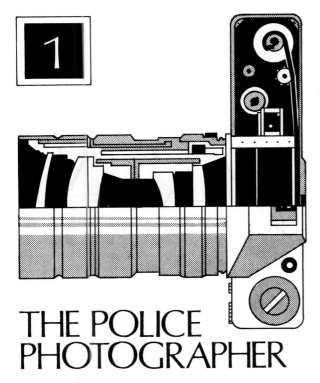

THE POLICE PHOTOGRAPHER

During a routine patrol of a suburban neighborhood, Officer Black receives a call instructing him to investigate a two-car collision some blocks away. He drives to the scene and, before leaving his patrol car, he notes that, while one of the vehicles (a late-model automobile of fiberglass construction) has sustained severe damage, no one seems to be injured.

The drivers of the two cars are arguing heatedly (neither driver, Officer Black observes, seems to have been clearly in the wrong) and nearby a passenger is sobbing. Officer Black calms the drivers, soothes the passenger, records each person's description of the accident (there were no witnesses outside the two cars), radios for a tow truck to remove the damaged vehicle and, before the tow truck arrives and the autos are moved, he takes a few measurements, sketches the scene, and reaches into his glove compartment. Officer Black takes out a tiny pocket instamatic camera, checks to see that it is loaded with film, and snaps four photographs of the accident.

In addition to being a calmer of nerves, an investigator, a law enforcer, an impartial witness (though after-the-fact), an artist, and an agent for the immediate conclusion of a minor catastrophe in the lives of three people, Officer Black is a police photographer. That is not his job description, but then neither is his role as street psychologizer. He may never step into a darkroom, or hold a single-lens-reflex camera in his hands (let alone a video portapak); he may never even change the film in the camera he keeps in the glove compartment of his patrol car. But his function as a police photographer is every bit as important as that of the head of the crime lab in his department who can mix chemicals, change film in the dark with one hand, and who takes photographs in his spare time that could vie with the best of *National Geographic*.

Both Officer Black and the head of his department's crime lab are police photographers; this book is for both of them.

POLICE PHOTOGRAPHY – A Short History

Photography is most obviously useful in police work when photographs serve as evidence that can and often does prove invaluable to investigators, attorneys, judges, witnesses, juries, and defendants. Often, a good photograph can be the deciding factor in a conviction or acquittal when no other form of real evidence is available.

As early as 1859, a photograph was used in the case of *Luco* v. *United States* to prove that a document of title for a land grant was, in fact, a forgery.[1] The first recorded use of accident photography was in 1875; "Plaintiff, in a horse and buggy, was injured when in attempting to go around a mud hole in the center of a road he drove off an unguarded embankment. The photograph was admitted in evidence to assist the jury in understanding the case."[2]

While neither of these early photographs for use as evidence was taken by police photographers, the use of photography in police work is well established in the early annals of photography. In 1841, eighteen years before *Luco* v. *United States*, the French police were making daguerreotypes (an early form of photograph) of known criminals for purposes of identification.

In auto accidents, usually there are injured persons. One of the first cases to hold that a relevant photograph of an injured person was admissible in evidence was *Redden* v. *Gates*[3] in 1879. The photograph was a tintype, a photograph made on a thin iron plate by the collodion process. It showed whip marks on the plaintiff's back three days after the assault. In 1907 in Denver, Colorado, all intoxicated persons were photographed at the police station.

Automobile speeders were being trapped with photographic speed recorders by 1910. In Massachusetts, they approved the use of such devices and gave a full description of their operation. Radar seems to be a more popular device for this opera-

---

[1] See Scott: Photographic Evidence — West — 1969, pp. 2 – 3.
[2] *Ibid.* p. 5.
[3] Iowa – 2 N.W. 1079, 52 Iowa 210 (1879).

tion today.

The use of fingerprint photographs for identification purposes was approved in 1911 in *People* v. *Jennings*,[4] although 1882 was the year in which fingerprints were first officially used in the United States. Mr. Gilbert Thompson of the United States Geological Survey in New Mexico used his own fingerprint on commissary orders to prevent their forgery. In 1902, New York Civil Service began fingerprinting applicants to discourage the criminal element from entering civil service, and also to prevent applicants from having better qualified persons taking the test for them.

The famous Will West case of Leavenworth Prison took place in 1903. When he was received at Leavenworth, Will West had denied ever having been imprisoned there before. Clerks at the prison insisted that West had been there and ran the Bertillon instrument over him to verify measurements. When the clerk referred to the formula derived from West's measurements, they were practically identical and the photograph appeared to be that of Will West. When the clerk turned over the William West record card, he found that it was that of a man already serving a life sentence for murder. Subsequently, the fingerprints of Will West and William West were compared. The patterns bore no resemblance. The fallibility of three systems of personal identification — photographs, Bertillon measurements and names — was demonstrated by this one case. The value of fingerprints as a means of identification was established. There was a great similarity in the photographs of both Will West and William West. An officer has to be very careful when identifying a person from a photograph.

One of the early uses of firearms identification is recorded in a 1902 case, *Commonwealth* v. *Best*.[5] Photographs of bullets taken from the body of a murdered man were put in evidence along with a photograph of a test bullet pushed through the defendant's rifle. This method of obtaining a test bullet is not proper, according to modern authorities, but the use made of the comparison photographs was to be followed in many subsequent firearms identification cases.

Prior to the modern strobe units of today, photoflash bulbs were used, and they were readily accepted by the public in 1930. Prior to the flashbulbs, people used flash powders which were dangerous explosives which produced a great deal of objectionable smoke. The photoflash bulb was a revolutionary development that made possible the taking of many evidence pictures that were otherwise unobtainable. Undoubtedly, their use has contributed greatly to the development of police photography.

Ultraviolet photography was approved in a decision handed down in 1934 in *State* v. *Thorp*.[6] The picture showed footprints in blood on a linoleum floor and brought out distinctive marks of the soles of the shoes worn by defendant corresponding to the marks shown in the ultraviolet photograph.

In 1938, Eastman Kodak Company introduced the Super Six 20 which was a camera featuring a fully automatic exposure control by means of a photoelectric cell which was coupled to the diaphragm of the lens. After 1945, Kodak again introduced cameras which were automatic and in a price range that everyone could afford. Today such features are used in most cameras and are within the price range of most people. You can get an automatic camera that meets almost all of a person's photographic needs. For example, the Minolta Maxxum, once a person learns how to use it, makes police photography very simple.

In 1943, another historic event in police photography happened. The first appellate court case passing upon the admissibility of color photographs as evidence was *Green* v. *County of Denver*.[7]

Eastman Kodak Company introduced a color transparency using sheet film in 1935. Kodachrome quickly became extremely popular, resulting in the widespread use of color photographs in police photography. Then in 1941, a color process known as Kodacolor made it possible to make color slides, color prints, or black-and-white prints from a color negative.

In 1963, a banner event for the police photographer took place. That year the Polaroid company introduced their Polacolor film making it possible to take finished pictures in color in less than one minute. This was one of the most significant developments in the history of photography and has led to the greater use of color photographs as evidence. For police work, Polaroid also puts out many films that can be great tools for the police, such as Type 55 PN., which gives you an instant picture along with a good negative; then there is Type 52, which has an ASA/ISO of 400, giving you all the speed in a film that you would desire. These Polaroid materials are all great tools for the police photographer.

Then in 1965, another great invention was placed on the market. It was the introduction of a fully automatic electronic flash unit making it possible to take exposed strobe flash photographs at distances from two feet to twenty feet without changing the lens opening or shutter speed. Automation was thus achieved by means of the lighting equipment rather than the camera. In 1967, we saw the beginning of the use of video tapes as legal evidence.

Today's cameras are automatic to an extent. The

---

[4]Ill. — 96 N.E. 1077, 252 Ill. 534, 43 L.R. A.N.S.,1206 (1911).
[5]Mass. — 62 N.E. 748, 180 Mass. 492 (1902).
[6]N.H. — 171 A 633, 86 N.H. 501 (1934).
[7]Colo. — 142 P. 2d 277, 111 Colo. 390 (1943).

police photographer can now concentrate more on the subject of his picture than on the intricacies of the camera. Professionals and amateurs now use cameras equipped with semi-automatic or fully automatic controls. With the good cameras of today there is no excuse for a police photographer not getting suitable pictures for evidence.

THE MANY USES OF PHOTOGRAPHY IN POLICE WORK

The modern police department considers photography more than just a way to record evidence or identify a known criminal. Note the role of photography in the following aspects of law enforcement:

Identification files. Criminals, Missing Persons, Lost Property, Licenses, Anonymous Letters, Bad Checks, Laundry Marks, and the Civilian or Personnel Fingerprint Identification Files. In the case of atomic attack or a catastrophe such as an airplane crash, the fingerprints from a civilian file are proving helpful in making positive identifications.

Communications and microfilm files. Investigative Report Files, Accident Files, Transmission of Photos (Wire Photo), Photographic Supplements to Reports. With modern day electrophotography machines, accident reports can be made in seconds and sold to insurance adjusters for nominal fees. An excellent source of revenue for a department is the sale of photographs of traffic accidents to insurance companies and lawyers.

Evidence. Crime Scenes, Traffic Accidents, Homicides, Suicides, Fires, Objects of Evidence, Latent Fingerprints, Evidential Traces. Evidence can frequently be improved by contrast control (lighting, film, and paper filters), by magnification (photomicrography, photomacrography), by invisible radiation (infrared, ultraviolet, soft x-rays and hard x-rays).

Offender detection. Surveillance, Burglar Traps, Confessions, Reenactment of Crimes, Intoxicated-Driver Test. One of the newest applications of police photography is to record on motion picture film arrests in which the suspect offers resistance. The practice has been instituted by at least one metropolitan law enforcement agency to counter charges of police brutality.

Court exhibits. Demonstration Enlargements, Individual Photos, Projection Slides, Motion Pictures.

Reproduction or copying. Questionable Checks and Documents, Evidential Papers, Photographs, Official Records and Notices.

Personnel training. Photographs and films relating police tactics, investigation techniques, mob control, and catastrophy situations.

Crime and fire prevention. Hazard Lectures, Security Clearance, Detector Devices, Photos of Hazardous Fire Conditions made when fire prevention inspections are made.

Public relations. Films pertaining to safety programs, juvenile delinquency, traffic education, public cooperation and civil defense.

In general, then, there are four primary ways of using photography in police work: (1) as a means of identification; (2) as a method of discovering, recording, and preserving evidence; (3) as a way to present, in the courtroom, an impression of the pertinent elements of a crime; and (4) as a training and public relations medium for police programs.

PUBLIC RELATIONS

Aside from the obvious uses of photography in police work, the photographer must be aware of the importance of police photography in public relations. A recent report stated that less than one percent of reported burglaries are solved. The inability of police departments to catch these particular criminals is, of course, founded in the elusiveness of the criminal, his ability to literally slip into the dark; the public, however, regards this rather poor percentage as ineptitude on the part of the police. Careful and thorough photography of a burglary scene can go a long way toward dispelling this and other misconceptions of the public.

POLICE PHOTOGRAPHY AND ARSON

Of all the crimes listed in the code book, the least investigated is arson. Why? A raging controversy exists as to who should investigate it. Should it be the police, who have extensive knowledge and experience in interrogation? Or should it be the fire department which has much more knowledge about the causes of fires? In large cities, this problem is solved because they have their own arson investigation units. But in the smaller towns, this is not the case; neither department wants to get involved in this problem so it goes unsolved.

No matter who photographs a fire for investigation, their chief role is to document a fire from its origin to its completion. Another aspect of his job would be to document aspects of the operation for the training of new firemen, to show both correct and incorrect procedures for future study. Another angle, often overlooked, is the many accidents which fire trucks have on the way to and from a fire. It is helpful if the photographer is right there and can immediately start taking the pictures of the accident because he looks at a fire truck accident with a different perspective than that of the policeman.

As with the police photographer, the fire photographer can play a great role in public relations for his department. This is a big job with any large company. If the police and firemen are going to advance in the eyes of the public, they must do a super job of public relations.

The primary principle to remember in police photography is that a finished photograph must be accurate. As a means of evidence, a photograph can be factual *and*, in many cases, revealing. In other words, the essence of photography lies in its ability to both record and clarify. To use the camera to its fullest advantage, then, it is necessary to learn the fundamentals of the photographic process — to learn and understand the techniques of, and wide range of possibilities for, photography in law enforcement.

FUTURE OF PHOTOGRAPHY

From my experience of teaching police photography, I gave my students an experiment to photograph an automobile accident, shoot the accident on a 35mm camera in black-and-white, develop the negatives and print the twenty-four pictures, all within a two hour period. This was accomplished rather handily by these students. So, if my students can do this, there is no reason why the police cannot do it. I have seen too many departments, lately, call in professional photographers to shoot their accidents for them. This is not necessary, and the continuity of the accident investigation is broken. There is nothing like having real police officers testify in court that they shot the accident and also developed the photographs. You gain a great deal of admiration from the court by showing them that the police can do many different jobs, besides writing traffic tickets.

Astounding developments are being made in photography that are going to lead to even greater use of police photography. Years ago, people laughed when they thought that you could produce any desired size form almost immediately without the use of a darkroom. Polaroid can be had today in sizes 35mm, 2¼ x 3¼, 4 x 5, and 8 x 10. We have been using these materials at the college for the past eighteen years, and I have found them to be very good. The traditional darkroom as we know it in its present form is going to disappear. Photographic evidence will be produced not only more quickly but more economically, and, of course, at the same time will be of excellent quality.

Because revolutionary changes are in process and are happening so quickly, it will be most difficult to keep up with them. During my time, I have seen film speeds go from ASA/ISO 64 to ASA/ISO 4000. The police photographer of today has so many better photographic materials to work with than did his predecessors. Even though photography will go electronically, and most pictures are recorded and stored on video tape, the basic principles of photography will not change. We will still have the basic laws of perspective, correct tone reproduction and so forth. Photographic processes after all are but a means to an end, and police are primarily concerned with whether the final photographic exhibit is a fair representation of a subject rather than how it was reproduced.

In the future it will be possible to obtain color pictures and have them finished in less than one minute. Color photographs will virtually supplant black-and-white in all but certain scientific branches of police photography in which color would have no advantage. Today I have seen where it is practical to make tape recordings of the oral testimony and investigations. The video recordings preserve both the words and the appearances of the witnesses. Video tape recordings of depositions are commonplace today. Already photographic evidence is an important specialty, a powerful tool recognized as indispensable in the proof of facts in court. The opportunities for use of photographic evidence in the future will be limited only by our ability to grasp, understand, and appreciate the power of the photographic picture and to comprehend its limitless value.

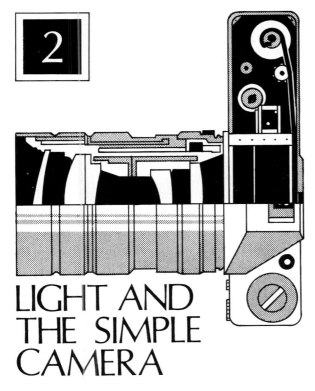

LIGHT AND THE SIMPLE CAMERA

others in wavelength. Radiant energy can be identified by its wavelength and listed on a number line called the *electromagnetic spectrum*.

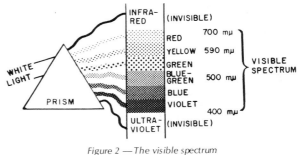

Figure 1 — *The electromagnetic spectrum*

The portion of the electromagnetic spectrum that affects the sense of sight in humans is called the *visible spectrum* and is limited to radiations of extremely short wavelength. These radiations are seen as colors, the longest of which is seen as "red," the shortest seen as "violet." Photography is concerned with these radiations and with those lying adjacent to red and violet, but outside the visible spectrum — infrared and ultraviolet.

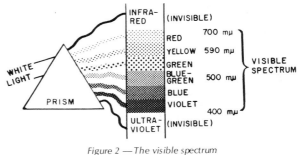

Figure 2 — *The visible spectrum*

A photograph is the result of a manipulation, recording, and, in some cases, creation of light. The entire science of photography is concerned with light manipulation and recording. The camera and its parts (shutter, diaphragm, focus) filter light; the enlarger manipulates light; and film, photographic paper, and exposure meters record light. Flash creates light.

Light is radiation. When an atom in a light source is changed physically (the cause of the physical change is here irrelevant), it emits a *photon* (electromagnetic radiation) which behaves like a wave and, at the same time, like a particle. For the purposes of photography, light may be discussed as photons which behave like waves.

Light can be compared to a ripple over a pond. If a stone is thrown into a smooth-surfaced pond, a series of concentric ripples can be seen which radiate from the source. The concentric ripples are formed because the energy from the disturbance is radiating in straight lines and in all directions over the surface of the pond. A cross section of the ripples in the pond would show that the energy moving across the pond has formed waves which are characterized by their peaks and troughs.

The distance from peak to an adjacent trough in a wave is called the *wavelength* of the wave. The number of waves per unit of time is called the *frequency* of the wave.

Light, heat rays, X-rays, and radiowaves are all forms of radiant energy, each differing from the

When all wavelengths of the visible spectrum are radiated by a light source in equal amounts, the mixture is seen as "white" light. In places where no radiations from any light source can be seen, the absence of light is called "black." Whenever any wavelength of light is present in greater abundance than others, the resulting light is colored.

Light travels through a vacuum and through the air at a speed of 186,000 miles per second but can be slowed by dense mediums such as glass or water. Mediums which merely slow the speed of light but allow it to pass freely in other respects are called *transparent* objects.

Objects which divert or absorb light, but allow no light to pass through are called *opaque*. Thick metal, stone, and wood are opaque.

There are some objects which allow light to pass through them in such a way that the outline of the light source is not clearly visible. These objects are spoken of as *transluscent*; a few examples are opal glass, ground glass, and oiled paper.

Light sources, such as the sun, flames, white-hot metals, and stars emit radiations within the visible spectrum and are called *luminous* objects. All other objects, called *non-luminous* objects, are visible because they reflect light from luminous objects.

Reflection occurs whenever an object changes the direction of a light wave but does not allow the wave to pass through it. Reflected light can be either *specular* or *diffuse*. Practically all surfaces reflect both specular and diffuse light — smooth surfaces reflect more specular light and rough surfaces reflect more diffuse light. Diffuse light is more common than specular light; most objects are seen and photographed by diffuse light reflected from their surfaces.

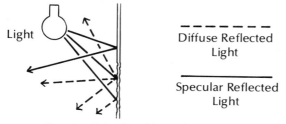

Figure 3 — Light reflected from a sheet of pitted glass

All surfaces vary in their ability to reflect light. A black cloth will reflect scarcely any light, whereas a white handkerchief reflects much light.

REFRACTION

When light passes through a piece of glass, the light is slowed from its normal speed of 186,000 miles per second. If the light passes through a sheet of flat glass, such as a modern window pane, it will resume its normal speed when it has passed through but it will have changed direction. Flat glass, because of its physical properties, corrects the change in direction of the light and no change is readily noticeable.

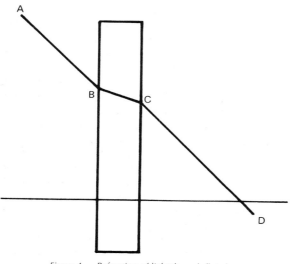

Figure 4 — Refraction of light through flat glass

If a piece of glass is made with sides that are not parallel, the glass will not self correct the bending of the light; in fact, the glass may intensify the change of direction. A prism is a good example of this.

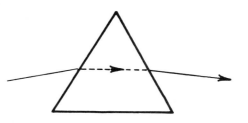

Figure 5 — A prism bends a ray twice

A lens is simply a piece of glass that has been constructed so that all the light rays which pass through it are bent toward or away from one point which is determined by the maker of the lens.

Light rays which meet at one point after they pass through a lens *converge*; those which bend away from a given point *diverge*. Lenses which cause light rays to converge are usually thick in the center and thinner at their edges; these are called *convex* lenses. Lenses which are thin at the middle and thick around the edges are *concave*; these usually make the light rays diverge.

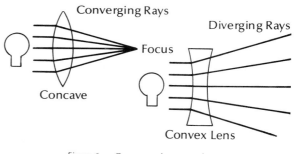

Figure 6 — Convex and concave lenses

The point at which light rays converge is called the *focus*. For any lens, this point is not the same for a subject ten feet away as it is for a subject twenty feet away. The farther a subject is from the lens, the closer the focus will be to the lens. Subjects more than 600 feet away from a lens, however, will focus at very nearly the same distance from the lens. The difference between the focus of a subject 600 feet from the lens and another subject 1000 feet from the lens is nearly negligible.

Distances of 600 feet or more are called *infinity*. In order that the lens maker can describe the properties of a lens that he has made, he can say that the lens will focus subjects at infinity at a certain distance from the lens. This distance is called the *focal length* of the lens.

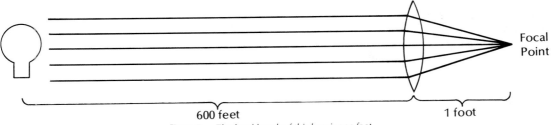

600 feet   1 foot

Figure 7 — The focal length of this lens is one foot

LIGHT

For the police photographer, photographs are statements of what he saw. The eye sees a photograph and translates the image to the mind; the mind then reacts and within itself it equates, evaluates, and responds to the photograph.

We become capable of describing photographs with words, but more important, develop the ability to describe words with photographs. This is what it is all about — communicating with photographs — the verbal picture.

Objectively, photography is a combination of the following tools:

1. Light
2. Camera
3. Lens
4. Film
5. Paper
6. Chemistry
7. Composition

OUR MOST IMPORTANT TOOL

There is little doubt that *light* is our most important tool. Light brushes on the lines, sculpts our subject, provides shadows, highlights and middle light values, emphasizes, subdues, lifts out, hides, and dramatizes our subject. Light can flatter, or be terribly brutal to our subject.

All cameras are essentially boxes to support the lens and contain the film.

All lenses are optics. They vary in characteristics and optical quality.

The variety of film material available on the marketplace is limited. The same is true of photographic papers.

Chemical processing in color photography is very rigid, almost totally inflexible. In black-and-white a limited choice still exists.

Another tool, composition, is a Pandora's box. One group in photography bases its approach on the rules of classic composition while another boldly claims photography must stand on its own. Composition is a series of principles accepted or not. In police photography we are not striving for

the beautiful or perfect picture to adhere to the rules of composition. We are interested in getting all the true facts of the case, so we can present them to the jury. The police officer must make use of the seven rules for good composition, which are:

1. Simplicity
2. Rule of thirds
3. Lines
4. Balance
5. Framing
6. Mergers
7. Factual

Summarizing the above, we find we have a limited number of cameras, lenses, film paper, and chemistry to work with.

Light then remains alone as the tool of greatest selection. Here the possibilities are enormous and the selection is ours.

INTENSITY OF LIGHT

One important aspect of light is its intensity as it reaches the subject, and how it is reflected by the subject. This is very important for the police officer to understand, because the intensity of light on a subject varies considerably when the distance between the light source and the subject of the film is changed. The relationship of intensities is governed by the inverse square law which is shown graphically in Figure 8.

If an object, such as a card, is placed one foot from a light source, the light striking the card will be of particular intensity. If it is then moved two feet away from the light, the intensity of the light falling on the card will be one-fourth as great. As the card is moved farther away, the intensity of the light reaching the card further decreases as the square of the distance from the source increases. This property of light is very important to the police photographer especially when shooting vehicle accidents outdoors at night with flash or flood. The officer's failure to correct the exposure as the subject moves farther from the light source, will result in badly underexposed negatives due to the inverse square law. This function is also important in the darkroom. If, for example, you have made a satisfactory 5 x 7 enlargement, then decide to make an 11 x 14 enlargement from the same negative, there should be an approximate increase of four times in the exposure. If the importance of this inverse square law is not recognized in the darkroom, disappointment and poor quality prints will result.

follows these simple rules can take good photographs with a box camera:

1. The lens of a simple camera should be set so that objects from ten to fifteen feet from the camera will be in focus. As subjects get closer to the camera than ten feet, or farther than fifteen, they get progressively fuzzier.

2. Whenever possible, color film should be used

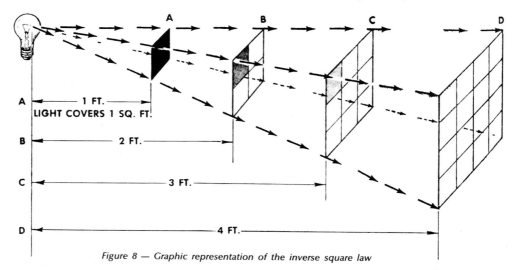

Figure 8 — Graphic representation of the inverse square law

THE SIMPLE CAMERA

A camera is simply a box which has been designed to keep out all light except for such light as the photographer may wish to have enter. Inside the camera, the photographer places a sheet of acetate. The acetate is coated with a chemical which changes when light hits it — hence the reason for making the box light tight.

To take a photograph, the photographer must let a certain amount of light through a small opening in the box. This light will strike the acetate and change the chemicals. When enough light has been let in, the photographer shuts out any more light. The light which did enter is then recorded on the acetate.

The simple camera, also known as the box camera, is little more than a pinhole camera (see below) to which has been added a lens and a shutter. The lens cannot be moved in relation to the back of the camera, nor can the time the shutter is open be changed.

But photographs — often *good* photographs — can be made with the simple camera. Who has not been in the following situation? A group of people are huddled around a pile of photographs. Someone (it never fails) says, "These are beautiful pictures. What kind of camera did you use?" Invariably, the answer is, "a Brownie," "an Instamatic" or "a Pocket Instamatic." How can a cheap camera make good pictures? Anyone who

in a box camera. It is difficult to make a bad color picture.

3. Pictures should be taken outdoors in sunlight or indoors with the flash suggested by the manufacturer of the camera. The subjects of photographs taken indoors with flash should be between ten and fifteen feet from the photographer.

4. The camera should be held steady. Any movement of the camera at the time the shutter is open will result in a blurry picture.

The simple camera is much too limited to be used by a practicing police photographer; but for learning about film and the darkroom, it is an excellent tool.

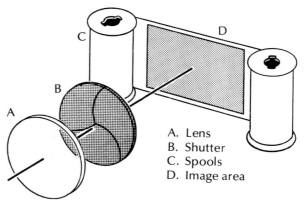

A. Lens
B. Shutter
C. Spools
D. Image area

Figure 9 — The simple camera

A PINHOLE CAMERA

If he wants to make a picture, the photographer must do more than record light with his camera; the light must be organized so that the respective shapes, colors, lights and darks are recorded on the acetate in such a way that they look like the real thing.

This is done by giving the opening for light a shape which will sort out the light while it is passing through. A pinhole will serve this purpose. The pinhole does not actually bend or refract light the way a lens does, but rather (because light travels in a straight line) it allows only a tiny bit of light which has been reflected from any point on the subject to pass through.

When the light, properly sorted out, has been recorded on the acetate, the record is called an image.

DISADVANTAGES OF THE PINHOLE CAMERA

The pinhole image is not a focused image, although it is reasonably sharp. For this reason, the image can be made large or small, depending upon how far the acetate is held from the pinhole.

The farther the acetate is held from the pinhole, however, the less bright it will become. Added to the fact that the pinhole itself lets in very little light, the pinhole camera is not very good for gathering a lot of light and organizing it in the very short amount of time (often one/one hundredth of a sec-

ond) that is necessary for making a good picture.

ADDING A LENS

By adding a lens to the camera in place of a pinhole, the photographer is able to gather much more light to be recorded. In exchange for the light gathering capability, however, he must now focus the lens for the various distances of subject-to-lens. This can be avoided, as it is in many budget cameras, by setting the lens-to-image distance so that subjects ten to fifteen feet from the lens are in sharp focus. In cameras with adjustable focus, the lens is moved closer to or away from a stationary back.

ADDING A SHUTTER

To control the light that enters the camera, the photographer must have some kind of door which he may open and close at will. The door can be as simple as a finger held over the pinhole of a pinhole camera, or as complicated as the focal plane shutters of expensive cameras. However it is constructed, the door is called a *shutter*. Most shutters are spring loaded and open and close automatically when a button on the side of the camera is depressed. For most pictures, the shutter need only be open for a fraction of a second — enough light is gathered by the lens and let in the camera by the shutter in this very short time to make the necessary chemical changes which will form an image.

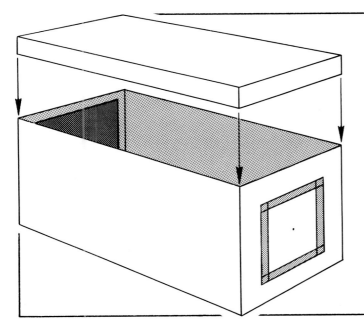

Making a Pinhole Camera

To make a pinhole camera, use a shoe box with a tightly-fitting lid. Paint the inside of the box flat black, and cut a square hole at one end. Tape a piece of aluminum foil over the hole and pierce it with a pin.

In a darkroom, tape a piece of film opposite the pin hole. Cover the box, tape it shut around the edges, and cover the pinhole with your finger. Now carry the box out of the darkroom, finger over the pinhole, and aim it at a stationary subject. Expose for one minute, carry the box back into the darkroom (cover the pinhole!) and remove the film. Place the film in a light-tight package until it can be developed.

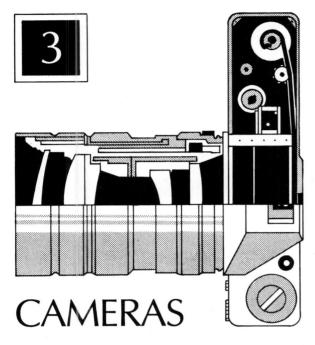

CAMERAS

More than almost any other art, photography requires equipment. The basic piece of equipment for taking photographs is, of course, the camera. Yet a camera itself will not produce a photograph. The camera must be loaded with film and requires a photographer to manipulate it. The film must be the right size for the camera — it must be *compatible* — and the photographer must know how to manipulate the camera. These three items — camera, film, photographer — working together constitute a system of photography.

The system, and therefore the capabilities of the system, may be enlarged with the addition of various pieces of equipment (each of which must be compatible with the system) and the thoughtful use of the many films which are available. For instance, a simple box camera, loaded with film and manipulated by a photographer, is a very limited system which may be enlarged and adapted to indoor use by adding a compatible flash attachment.

As demands upon the photographer are increased, he must refine the capabilities of his system by adding pieces of equipment, replacing pieces of equipment, simplifying his operation of equipment, and by enlarging his knowledge of photography. He should choose a particular camera and organize all his photographic work and equipment around that camera. The camera should be designed to serve all the needs of the photographer so that one camera can be employed for most, if not all, facets of his work. Then, the photographer must set up his darkroom with all the accessories and equipment necessary to complete the system.

The camera must be compatible with the photographer's needs, his abilities, and his budget. The various film sizes and their uses should play a large role in the choice of a camera. But with the current proliferation of cameras, particularly those which use 35mm film, the photographer is given a wide choice of cameras which vary in performance, complexity and price.

Size of film, nevertheless, is the variable which needs first consideration; camera and system should be planned around one film size.

110 AND ULTRA MINIATURE CAMERAS

Ultra miniature cameras, or "spy cameras" as they were often called, have been on the market for many years. Most notable of these cameras is the Minox B, though Minolta and Yashica also produced popular ultra miniatures. The films used in these cameras were not standardized and were very small, making darkroom work difficult at best. Also, the cameras were expensive.

Kodak revolutionized the ultra miniature market with its popular 110 film and "Pocket Instamatic" cameras, placing the conveniently sized ultra miniature within the budget of any photographer. Refinements of the original pocket instamatic include a camera with a built-in telephoto lens as well as various forms of flash.

The cameras are simple to operate; each is equipped with a fixed-focus lens. Most objects between four feet and infinity will be in focus, but the instruction pamphlet recommends that ten to fifteen feet will yield the best result. The cameras are not adjustable; they are merely aimed at a subject and their shutters are then depressed.

The small size of the camera makes it easy to carry; the cartridges are easily loaded. The light weight of the camera and its odd shape, however, make it unstable when shooting. The manufacturers recommend that the shutter be "squeezed" in order to lessen vibration which will cause a blurred image.

This camera is designed solely for ease of operation, not for accuracy. Also, because 110 film is so small and difficult to work with in the darkroom, this camera is almost wholly unsuited for police work.

126 CAMERAS

The large commercial success of the 126 camera is evidence that, to sell more cameras, one need only make the simple box camera simpler. This was done by designing a method of loading and advancing film so that operation of the camera is nearly fool-proof. 126 film is packaged in a plastic cartridge that is dropped into the back of the camera; neither the film nor its paper backing is ever handled by the photographer when changing film. A lever replaces the normal winding mechanism, and also serves to cock the shutter so that double exposures are impossible.

The 126 camera comes in a large range of types and prices, many with built-in exposure control.

While 126 film is similar in size to 35mm film, and therefore is handled similarly in the darkroom, it rapher to compensate without attachment, although this becomes difficult when using a telephoto lens.

The chief disadvantage of the rangefinder type camera arises when it is used in the laboratory. Because the main lens of the camera and the viewfinder are independent, the photographer becomes faced with the problem of parallax (parallax is defined as an apparent displacement of an object as seen from different points. See Fig. 2) which causes difficulty when attempting to center or focus on an

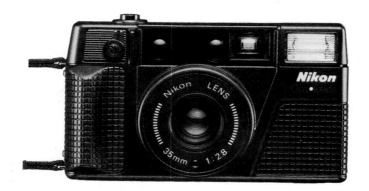

Figure 1 —The Nikon One Touch 35mm camera (left)

Figure 2 — This cross-section of a rangefinder type camera shows the separation of optical systems (below)

would be incorrect to expect from a 126 system the full range of photographic capabilities that are needed in police work.

THE 35mm ADJUSTABLE CAMERA

There are two types of 35mm cameras in wide use: the rangefinder and the single-lens-reflex (SLR). Both offer such features as interchangeable lenses, adjustable focal plane shutters, adjustable diaphragms and motor drive. They differ mainly in how a subject is viewed and focused.

The rangefinder camera has a viewfinder which, like most instamatic cameras, is independent of the main lens of the camera. The viewfinder presents a miniature view of the subject; focusing is aided by a split-screen rangefinder which is coupled to the main lens. The view through the viewfinder is fixed and the photographer must compensate for changed view when using other than a standard lens. This is accomplished by attaching a correcting lens to the viewfinder. Some viewfinders are etched with cross-hatches which allow the photog-

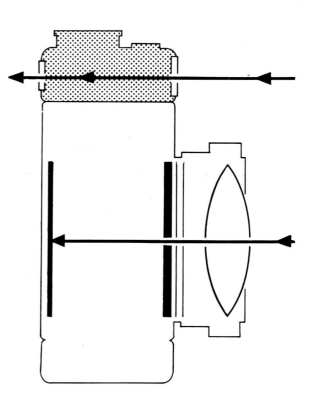

object closer than three feet. It is nearly impossible to photograph through a microscope with a rangefinder type camera. These difficulties are completely solved by the single lens reflex camera.

The single lens reflex, or SLR, camera allows the photographer to view a subject through the main lens of the camera. The image seen through the viewfinder window is a *replica* image; when using a standard lens the image is similar in size and appearance to the scene before the unaided eye. The optical system for viewing the system is comprised of: the main lens; a mirror for diverting light away from the film and into the rest of the system; a prism for reversing and inverting the image as reflected (upside down and reversed) from the mirror; a focusing screen; and a viewfinder. Thus, a change in lenses will automatically cause a change in the optical system; no compensation by the pho-

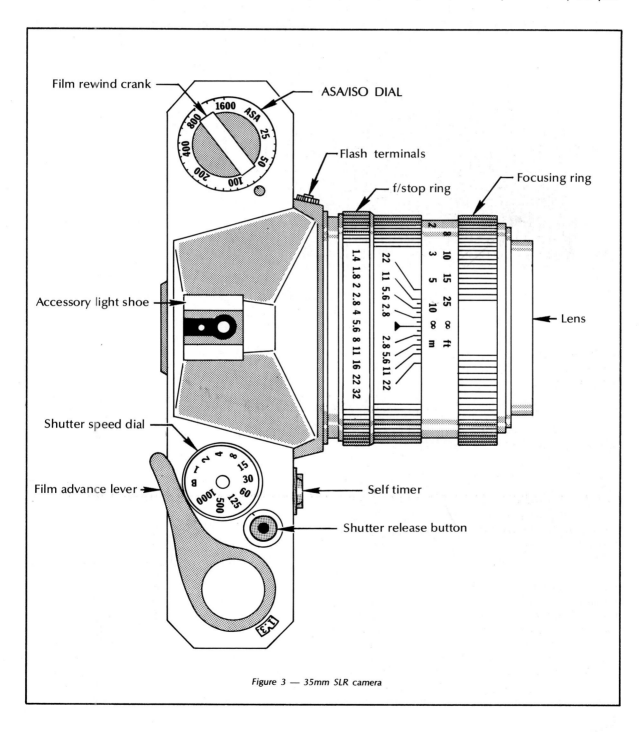

Figure 3 — 35mm SLR camera

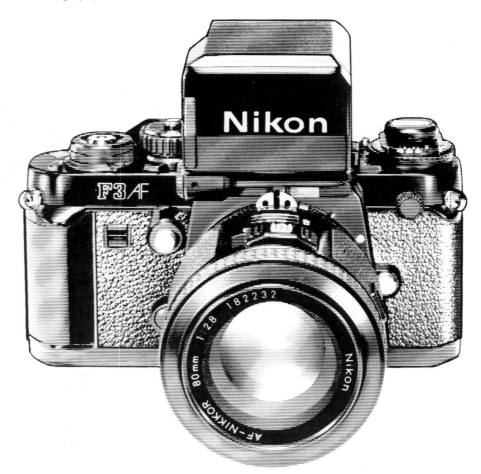

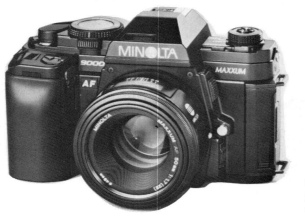

*Figure 4 — Nikon F3AF with DX-1
Finder and 80mm. f2.8 ED AF-NIKOR LENS.
Minolta Maxxum Autofocus SLR.*

tographer is necessary. Also, parallax is eliminated — there is only one point from which to view.

The mirror is mounted on a hinge and flips up and down automatically before and after the shutter opens and closes, blocking out the viewfinder only at the instant of the exposure. The majority of standard, wide angle, and moderately long-focus lenses are fitted with an automatic iris control so that the lens is always wide open for focusing and viewing but closes down to the preselected shooting aperture when the shutter is released.

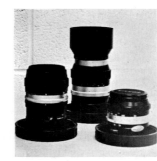

Figure 5 — Nikon accessories (right and far right) and cross-section of SLR optical system

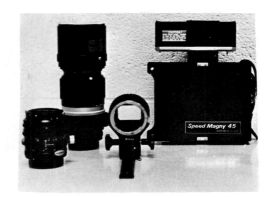

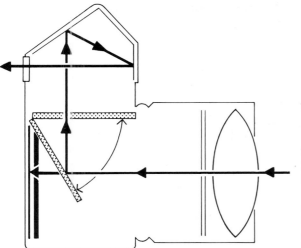

THE 2¼ CAMERA

As with the 35mm camera, there are two basic types of 2¼ cameras, or cameras which use 120 size film. These are the Twin-lens Reflex camera and the SLR.

The Twin-lens Reflex (TLR) camera is equipped with two identical optical systems, one of which focuses on the film when the shutter is opened. The other reflects a similar image up toward the top of the camera and focuses it upside down and reversed, on a ground glass screen. Because both lenses on a TLR are linked, correct focus on the viewing screen will guarantee correct focus through the main lens. As with viewfinder cameras, however, parallax may become a problem when photographing a subject closer than three feet.

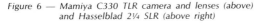

Figure 6 — Mamiya C330 TLR camera and lenses (above) and Hasselblad 2¼ SLR (above right)

Special purpose lenses are available in a limited variety for TLR cameras but they are expensive because two lenses must be changed.

The 2¼ SLR camera is similar in principle to the SLR 35mm camera. Most 2¼ SLR's, like the TLR's, have viewing screens which show a reversed and inverted image. The cameras are held at chest or waist level for viewing. Eye level viewing is made possible if a prism finder is attached. Some of the better 2¼ SLR cameras are the Hasselblad, Bronica, and the Mamiya Professional RB67.

One advantage of the 2¼ camera over the 35mm is the larger negative size for work in the darkroom. Also, changeable backs are available for cameras, such as the Mamiya Professional RB67, which allow negatives of 2¼" x 2¼" or 2¼ x 2¾." These sizes permit highly acceptable enlargements. However, the 2¼ camera is much bulkier than the 35mm and often heavier; they are also priced higher than comparable 35mm cameras.

THE 4 × 5 CAMERA

The one system which most closely meets all the requirements for police photography is the 4 × 5 system. The advantages of the 4 × 5 system are: (1) it is relatively inexpensive, (2) it can be easily ser-

viced, and (3) it is very versatile. Almost every aspect of police photography can be covered by this one camera with the use of attachments. For example:

1. With the addition of an adapter roll back, the photographer can use 120 roll film to shoot either black-and-white or color film.
2. A 545 or 500 Polaroid adapter back allows the photographer to shoot many of the 4 × 5 film packets manufactured by Polaroid. Polaroid 55 P/N is especially useful in police photography; the photographer can immediately examine his photograph, make any necessary corrections, and retain a negative from which he may make further prints in the darkroom.
3. A split back adapter will convert a 4 × 5 into a "mug shot" camera.
4. With the addition of a Faurot Foto-Focuser, the 4 × 5 becomes an excellent fingerprint camera for use in small police departments. This, used with a 545 Polaroid back, can be a very effective system.
5. The 4 × 5 makes an excellent copy camera.

The photographer may take as many or as few photographs as he wishes with the 4 × 5 camera without changing film rolls or having to wait until a roll is completely filled. In police work there are a

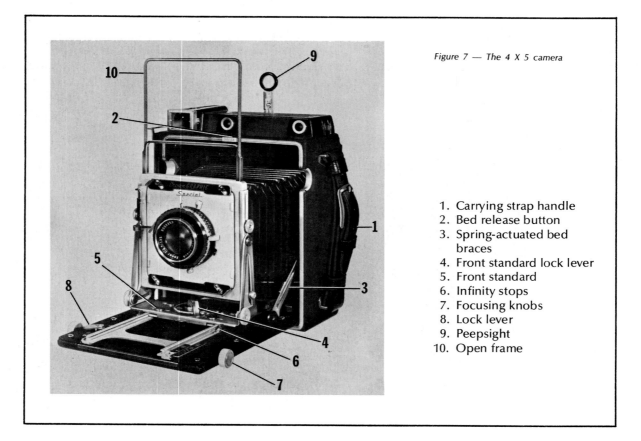

Figure 7 — The 4 X 5 camera

1. Carrying strap handle
2. Bed release button
3. Spring-actuated bed braces
4. Front standard lock lever
5. Front standard
6. Infinity stops
7. Focusing knobs
8. Lock lever
9. Peepsight
10. Open frame

great many times when a job calls for only two or four photos.

The large 4 × 5 size of the negative is the most convenient to work with in the darkroom. A photograph as large as 16″ × 20″ or even 20″ × 24″ is often needed for courtroom presentation; the 4 × 5 negative offers high resolution for enlargements of this size. In order to produce such a large negative, the camera itself must be large. This poses no problem for the policeman, since the camera is stored in the darkroom or carried in the trunk of the car and removed only when needed.

One of the best features of this camera is the abuse that it can take with very little maintenance. The cameras are built to withstand the rugged handling that is often the case in police photography. About once every four years, however, the camera should be sent back to the factory even if there is nothing wrong with it. The factory will completely inspect the camera and put it in good working condition for a minimal amount of money.

ROLL FILM ADAPTERS FOR 4 × 5 CAMERAS

For the 4 x 5 camera with a Graflok back, you can obtain a roll film holder to suit your needs. You can add 120 or 220 roll film to your present system by simply taking off your Graflok back and adding the roll film adapter to your camera. (See Figure 8.) The Graflex roll film holders feature automatic exposure counter and dark slide for inserting or removing holder from camera at any time.

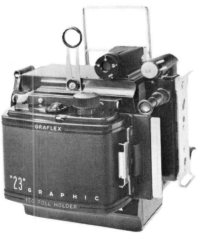

Figure 8 — Roll film adapter

The Rapid-Vance roll film holders come in different models: RH 8 for 8 exposures 2¼ × 3¹/₁₆″; RH 10 for 10 exposures 2¼ × 2¾″; RH 12 for 12 exposures 2¼ × 2¼″; RH 20 for 220 roll film, 20 exposures 2¼ × 2¾″; and a RH 50 for 70mm films, 50 exposures, 2¼ × 2¾″.

POLAROID LAND 4 X 5 SYSTEM AND FILM

The Polaroid Land 4 × 5 photographic system is built around the Land film holder which is usable in

Figure 9 — Five easy operating steps allow you to take all the pictures you want without removing the holder from the camera

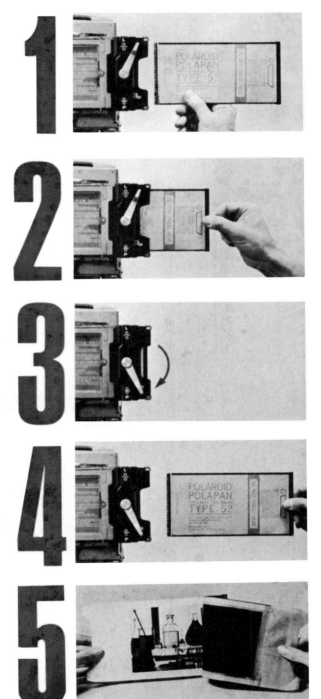

most 4 × 5 cameras (those with Graphic, Graflok, and similar backs). It instantly adapts these cameras to on-the-spot photography without any alteration of the camera focusing system. Just slide it into position and it is ready to use.

Pictures taken with the Land film holder are processed in the packet outside the holder so the photographer may shoot as many as he wants, one after the other, without having to wait for development. Instead of developing them as they are taken, the packets can be set aside and processed later. Once a packet is exposed and processed, development takes place immediately.

All cameras are basically alike. Each is a box with a piece of film at one end and a hole at the other. The hole is there so light can enter the box, strike the chemically sensitized surface of the film, and make a picture. Every camera from the most primitive to today's sophisticated cameras work this way. Many of today's camera designs are based on the slogan, "You press the button we do the rest." Automatic and computerized modern cameras try to make picture taking as easy as possible by choosing the shutter speed or aperture for you or by presetting the focus.

Today's 35mm Maxxum from Minolta does practically everything for you. It focuses, picks the aperture, loads automatically, advances itself, and even sets the ASA/ISO for you; so there is no reason today for a police photographer not to be able to take a good picture. He can make choices even though the cameras are fully automatic, and he has a multitude of things he can do with today's cameras and film. He can, if he wants, freeze the motion of a speeding car or let it race by in a blur, bring the entire accident scene into sharp focus or isolate a single vehicle. You can exaggerate the distances of the vehicles in an accident or show the right perspective as to the distances between the vehicles.

THE 35mm SLR

In the past, most police photographers used the 4 X 5 camera. Today with the great improvement of lenses, camera and film, it is no longer necessary to use a 4 X 5. In the past they said that the larger the negative, the less grain you would get on the negative. With the great improvement in the lenses, you can do just as well with a 35mm camera as you can with the old 4 X 5. I am not saying that a 35mm camera can do everything for the police photographer. There are many jobs inside the lab where a universal camera like the 4 X 5 has a big advantage. You can put a polaroid adapter on it, and use the many different kinds of film that Polaroid puts out, especially their type 55 PN film where you get a positive and a negative. Their type 52 film is a good film because it has a rating of ASA/ISO of 400, and is a fast film.

For most of the on-the-job crime scenes, auto accidents, and other police functions, you can do very well with the 35mm cameras, especially since today's better cameras have many more functions than the cameras of the past. There are shutter speeds of up to ASA/ISO 4000, and with an automatic electronic flash compatible to that camera, you can use it and shoot electronic flash with the Minolta (Maxxum) 7000's microprocessor circuitry to solve a common daytime flash exposure problem. When the Maxxum 7000 is set to program mode, flash duration and aperture adjustment are automatically controlled to provide optimum subject illumination.

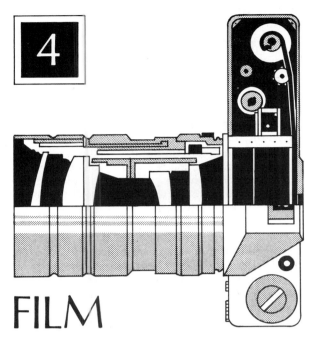

FILM

The primary function of film is to record the image focused upon it by the lens of the camera. The recorded image is called a *latent image* because it is not visible on the film; exposed film cannot be visually distinguished from unexposed film. But the film has changed physically during exposure and that change can be made visible if the film is treated chemically. The chemical treatment which causes a latent image to become a visual image is called *development*. When the chemical change has taken place the film is called a *negative* and the visual image is called a *negative image* because the tonal values of the visual image are the inverse (hence negative) of the tonal values of the subject. Black becomes white, white becomes black; dark objects appear light on the negative and light objects appear dark.

THE EMULSION

An *emulsion* is the light-sensitive part of the film; it is the medium through which the physical and chemical changes from latent to negative image take place. In an emulsion, grains of *silver halide* are suspended in a thin layer of gelatin. Silver halides are sensitive to light; their characters are altered when they are exposed to light. When the altered silver halides are treated chemically during development, they are converted into a black metallic silver which remains attached to the base of the film. Silver halides which have not been exposed to light do not form this metallic silver and are washed away from the base in the development process.

A minimum amount of light is required to effect the change in the grains of the silver halide and form a latent image. This minimum amount of light alters only a few of the grains near the surface of the emulsion and produces a barely perceptible silver deposit upon development. If less than this minimum amount of light reaches the emulsion, the silver halides are not affected, and they cannot be changed into metallic silver by development. As the quantity of light acting upon the emulsion increases above the minimum necessary to produce a change in the grains near the surface, it penetrates deeper into the emulsion to expose additional grains, and also makes them subject to development into metallic silver. The thickness or *density* of the silver deposit in the negative is increased when the amount of exposure is increased. In any negative which records a subject that has varied lights and darks, there will be a variation of densities. The aggregate of these variations is called the *brightness range*.

THE BASE

The film bases in general use today are cellulose acetate and other acid esters such as triacetate. Cellulose acetate films are usually called safety bases since they have the advantage of low flammability. Bases may be transparent, translucent, or opaque, depending upon how the recorded image is to be used. Generally, films are made on a transparent base whether they are used as negatives or as positives, as in the case of motion pictures, color transparencies, and lantern slides.

The photographer has a variety of emulsions and bases from which to choose. Emulsions vary in color sensitivity, speed, graininess, contrast, sharpness and acutance. Film manufacturers have created and marketed a number of films which combine these variables in such a way that, while a given film may not have a perfect combination of these variables, the photographer may obtain a film which closely satisfies his needs. The choice of emulsion type is a trial and error business; guidelines can be given and film type may be suggested, but the photographer should use and experiment with many films before he can know which film is best for a given job. The choice of a base, however, is more easily determined.

Bases differ in chemical composition, size, and package. The composition of a base plays little or no role in choice of film; package is determined almost wholly by size. Size, however, is very important. The size of a film is determined by the size of the camera for which it is made (width) and by the number of exposures that are possible on one piece of film (length). For example, 35mm film is 35mm wide. It can be used only in 35mm cameras, and can be purchased in lengths which allow twenty or thirty-six exposures.

The choice of film size is dependent upon its use. On the whole, small cameras are simpler and more convenient to use than are large cameras; thus, film of small size, which has been designed for use in a small camera, is simpler and more convenient to expose than is large film. However, this generalization about size, simplicity, and convenience becomes reversed when the film is taken into the darkroom. A large film will yield a large negative. Larger negatives produce better results, particularly in the enlarging process, than do smaller negatives.

Not all emulsions are available in all sizes of film. Therefore, some compromise must be made by the photographer when choosing a film. The photographer will want a film that is convenient to shoot, convenient to process, and produces as closely as possible the desired result. If one must work with a given camera or darkroom, as have police photographers in the past with the 4 × 5 camera, the choices are greatly simplified.

BASIC FILM SIZES

110 film has many advantages for the small police department with a limited budget. The cameras which have been designed to use 110 film are small

and lightweight. However, 110 film is very small and it is difficult to enlarge to courtroom specifications. Thus, its use is limited.

The primary advantage of 110 film is its simplicity of loading. 110 film is packaged in a *cartridge* — a self-contained plastic envelope which stores the film before and after exposure in dual storage spaces. A printed, opaque paper backing protects the film from unwanted exposure in the camera and permits the photographer to note at a glance the number of exposures which he has made.

Among the disadvantages of 110 film are the cameras which are designed to use the film, and the small negative which it yields. The tiny 110 camera is portable in the extreme, and inexpensive so that each patrolman may carry one in his shirt pocket or glove compartment. This camera need only be pointed at a subject, its trigger depressed, and the film advanced. Thus, taking pictures is simple, but deceptively so. The 110 camera is so small that it is difficult to stabilize — shaky hands can easily render an entire roll of film worthless and the manufacturers of the cameras warn in their instruction booklets that the shutter must be "squeezed" to produce a presentable photograph.

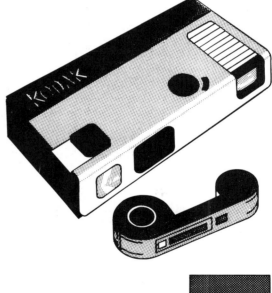

Figure 1 — 110 camera and film cartridge (above), negative (right), and print from 110 negative

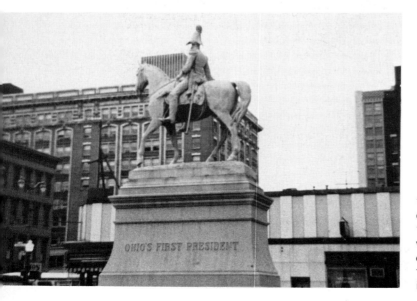

The tiny 110 negative cannot be enlarged to more than 5 × 7 size and it is difficult to enlarge to standard 3 × 5 snapshot size. The enlarger used for a 110 enlargement must be dust-free to a tolerance which, for the most part, is outside the capabilities of any lab but one specifically designed to process 110 film, that is, a commercial processor. However, it is not advisable to send a film to an outside studio for development and enlargement because the chain of evidence will be broken. Police work demands custody of this vital chain.

126 film is the same width as 35mm but is packaged in a cartridge of a design similar to 110, thus combining some of the advantages of 110 film with some of the advantages of 35mm. Few good cameras are made to accept 126, and the photographer must be satisfied with all-purpose emulsions.

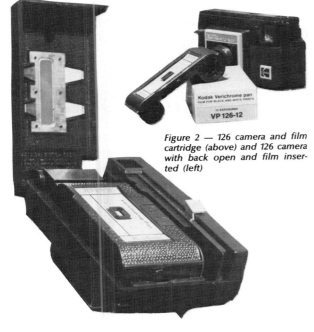

Figure 2 — 126 camera and film cartridge (above) and 126 camera with back open and film inserted (left)

35mm film for 35mm adjustable cameras is probably the most widely used film today. 35mm is primarily a compromise between the needs of the photographer in the darkroom and those of the photographer with camera in hand. But at best, 35mm is a compromise and should be treated as such. Film manufacturers, in recognizing that 35mm is the best compromise, have made it available in many different emulsion types and speeds.

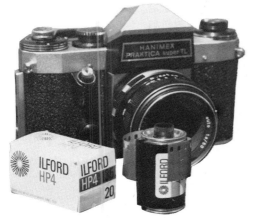

Usually 35mm film is purchased in cassette form. The *cassette*, a metal or sometimes plastic container allows for simple loading, is light-tight, stores the film before and after exposure, and obviates the need for paper backing. Unlike the film cartridge in which 110 and 126 film is packaged, the cassette has a single film storage space; film is wound out of the cassette and onto a roller in the camera and must be wound back into the cassette before film can be removed from the camera. Because 35mm film has no paper backing, the accounting for remaining exposures must be done mechanically. All 35mm cameras have a provision for exposure counting.

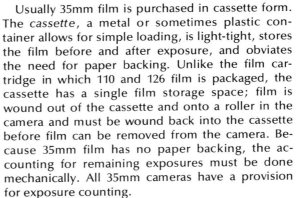

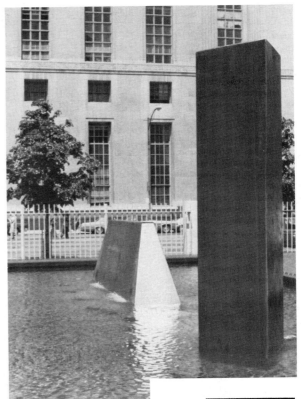

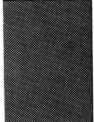

Figure 3 — 35mm camera and film cassette (left), negative (right) and a print from the negative (above)

35mm film can be bought in 12, 24 and 36 exposure cassettes, and in bulk rolls — usually 100 feet — which allow the photographer to load his own cassettes. A bulk loader may be purchased for this task.

DX FILM

In 1888, the Eastman Kodak Company adopted the slogan, ''You press the button, we do the rest,'' to describe their Kodak roll-film cameras. Today's photographers, raised on the visual media, expect perfectly focused and exposed pictures under any amount of light and darkness. Consequently, manufacturers have dropped the idea of simplification and followed instead one of automation. The police photographer today has all the controls that the professional has.

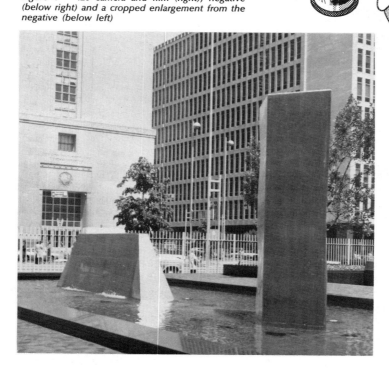

Figure 4 — 120 camera and film (right), negative (below right) and a cropped enlargement from the negative (below left)

In the quest for the automated camera, most of the action today is in the 35mm camera. The increasing miniaturization of computer circuits has allowed the development of automatic exposure and automatic focusing systems that perform beyond the abilities of most photographers. Many new cameras (35mm) have built-in motors that advance the film automatically between shots, rewind the film at the end of the roll, and provide a degree of automatic loading.

The weak link in 35mm photography was the film magazine. At its introduction in the twenties, it was a definite improvement over roll film, but it remained what it was at the beginning: A tin can loaded with motion picture film. It has always proved a challenge for camera manufacturers to design a loading system for the 35mm that wasn't awkward, and until recently there was no film speed coding at all on the magazines.

In 1963, Kodak introduced the 126 film cartridge, the first of the familiar plastic cartridges that slip easily into the back of the camera. The 126 cartridge, or something similar, might have been the logical successor to the 35mm magazine. The film was physically the same size as the 35mm film, but provided a larger negative because it didn't have the 35mm's two rows of sprocket holes to take up space. The cartridge was encoded to set the film speed automatically, and it had a film ID that could be seen through a window in the back of the

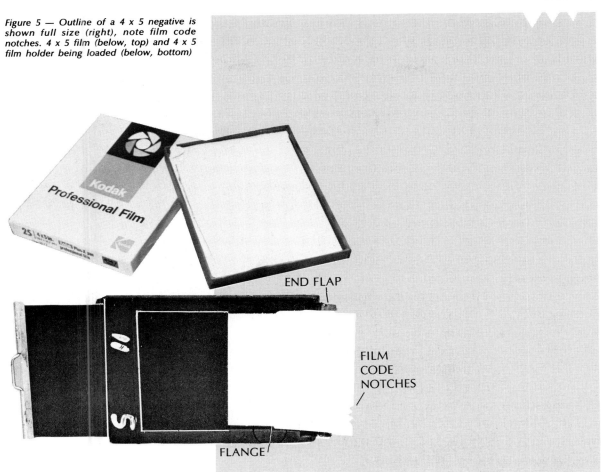

Figure 5 — Outline of a 4 x 5 negative is shown full size (right), note film code notches. 4 x 5 film (below, top) and 4 x 5 film holder being loaded (below, bottom)

END FLAP

FILM CODE NOTCHES

FLANGE

camera — two features that are now available to 35mm with the DX code.

As Kodak found out, once you have established a standard you are stuck with it. With the tremendous proliferation of the 35mm cameras in the seventies, all that was left was to try to improve the film can without changing it radically, and that's where DX came in.

The DX system comprises five separate chunks of information: four codes and a small, one line film ID. The most obvious of the codes, and the one that will affect you most directly, is the Camera Auto Sensing Code. This is a checkerboard pattern of up to 12 squares of bare metal and black insulation. Probes in the film chamber of the camera press against these patches forming a simple circuit board that tells the camera three things: Patches two through six indicate the film speed in 24 increments from ISO 25 to ISO 5000; patches eight, nine, and ten indicate the number of exposures, and eleven and twelve indicate the exposure range of the film. Patches one and seven are common electrical contacts.

The value of the CAS code should be clear. Primarily it will save most of the vast amount of film

that every year is accidentally rated at the wrong film speed. With DX there is no need to check the ISO dial every time you change film, just pop the film into the camera and you're ready to go. The only hitch here is that people often *intentionally* rate their film differently from the manufacturer's ISO. It's common, for example, to overrate transparency film slightly and overrate Kodak's Tri-X significantly. If you own a DX-reading camera that doesn't allow you to override the encoded ISO, and many of them don't, you will have to resort to taping over the CAS code on the film can or the pins on the camera. If your camera has no way to set the ISO manually, and some of them don't, you are out of luck.

The other two functions of the CAS checkerboard are less crucial than the film speed setting. The frame number information may permit the camera to signal you when it nears the end of the roll, or trip an automatic rewind at the appropriate moment, although the rewinding can easily be done without the DX code.

The information about the film range will theoretically permit the exposure of a film with a wide range in situations where cameras currently signal improper exposure or prevent exposures altogether. The picture would be misexposed, but the camera would know that you could get an exposure of some kind.

The second feature of the DX code that will directly affect the photographer is the information panel on the opposite side of the canister from the CAS code. This film ID is placed so that a camera with a small window in the back (and these are beginning to appear) will permit you to see what

Figure 6 — Film names, sizes, color, sensitivities and speeds

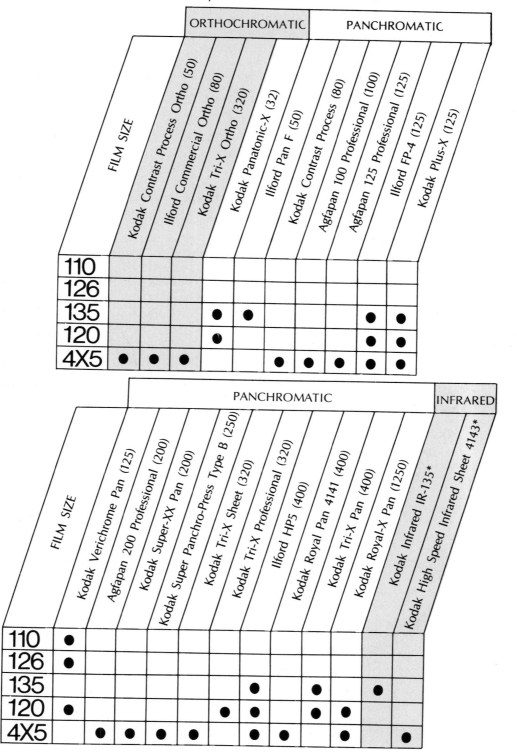

FILM SIZE	ORTHOCHROMATIC			PANCHROMATIC						
	Kodak Contrast Process Ortho (50)	Ilford Commercial Ortho (80)	Kodak Tri-X Ortho (320)	Kodak Panatomic-X (32)	Ilford Pan F (50)	Kodak Contrast Process (80)	Agfapan 100 Professional (100)	Agfapan 125 Professional (125)	Ilford FP-4 (125)	Kodak Plus-X (125)
110										
126										
135				●	●				●	●
120				●					●	●
4X5	●	●	●			●	●	●	●	●

FILM SIZE	PANCHROMATIC										INFRARED	
	Kodak Verichrome Pan (125)	Agfapan 200 Professional (200)	Kodak Super-XX Pan (200)	Kodak Super Panchro-Press Type B (250)	Kodak Tri-X Sheet (320)	Kodak Tri-X Professional (320)	Ilford HP5 (400)	Kodak Royal Pan 4141 (400)	Kodak Tri-X Pan (400)	Kodak Royal-X Pan (1250)	Kodak Infrared IR-135*	Kodak High Speed Infrared Sheet 4143*
110	●											
126	●											
135						●			●		●	
120	●				●	●		●	●			
4X5		●	●	●	●	●	●		●			●

type of film you have loaded into the camera. The ID window is much more convenient and reliable than the old technique of sticking the end of the film box in the clip on the back of the cover, but it does seem to be a potential source of light leaks if things aren't fitting properly.

The remaining three DX codes are for the benefit of the lab. The bar code is the thing that looks like the universal product code you see at the supermarket. It and the raster code, a series of up to 12 holes arrayed in the film leader, will assist in identifying the length of the film and getting it into the correct developing solution. The latent-image bar code, printed every half frame along the length of the film, will identify the film during printing for automatic color balance.

Kodak introduced the DX film code in 1983 with confidence that other film and equipment manufacturer's would adopt it, and they have. One reason that Kodak is *giving* the code away, no fees involved, is an effort to broaden the appeal of the 35mm photographer. Most manufacturers do not yet use the DX code, although interest is there. When they do go on line with DX-reading machines, it will mean, if not better prints, at least faster prints. One hour photo labs will be replaced by, say, 45 minute labs.

120 and 220 roll film is an adequate film for police work. This film requires a bulky camera, but yields a 2¼" negative which is easily enlarged. Excellent courtroom presentation photographs are possible. Fewer emulsion types are available in the 120 size than in 35mm.

120 film is packaged on a roll in a printed light-tight paper backing and allows 8 or 10 exposures; 220 differs only in length, allowing 16 or 24 exposures.

4 × 5 film is losing favor in police work, but anyone who has used it can appreciate its size. Very sharp photographs are possible with 4 × 5 film because the large negative size requires less magnification in enlarging. Many film types are still available in the 4 × 5 size, and though the Graflex Company of Rochester, N.Y., has stopped making 4 × 5 cameras, it is not difficult to procure a new or used 4 × 5 camera from the Calumet Co., Chicago, Illinois.

4 × 5 film, often called sheet film, is an individual piece of film which must be loaded into a holder before it can be exposed in the camera. Most types of sheet film have a reference notch in one corner to allow identification, in the darkroom, of the emulsion side and the type of film. The size, shape, and number of notches vary with each film manufacturer and with type of film. They are standardized, however, as to their location.

The choice of a film size, with the exception of 35mm, will limit the photographer in his choice of emulsion type. There is, for example, only one black and white emulsion available in 110 size – Verichrome Pan. In film sizes which allow a choice of emulsions, it is well to know and understand the characteristics of each emulsion before experimenting with them. The ability to choose the correct emulsion for a given job depends upon the photographer's knowledge of each type *and* his experience with them.

Different emulsion types react to subject light in different ways. For instance, some emulsions are more sensitive to specific colors than others.

COLOR SENSITIVITY

The final image obtained from black and white negative emulsions consists of a series of gray tones varying in brightness and ranging from light to dark gray. These tones represent the color of the subject; different emulsions represent subject color with varying degrees of acceptability. The extent to which this representation of colors as shades of gray is acceptable is called the *color sensitivity* of the film.

Pure emulsions, composed only of silver halides, reproduce only blue, violet, and visible ultraviolet regions of the visible spectrum. Thus, pure emulsions are *color-blind*. The addition of dyes to ordinary silver halide emulsions can increase their sensitivity to approximately the same spectral region as that which is seen by the human eye. The combinations of dyes used influences the color sensitivity of the emulsion.

Emulsions are divided into four general types according to the way in which they render color differences as brightness differences. These four classifications are monochromatic, orthochromatic, panchromatic, and infrared. All emulsions are sensitive to ultraviolet radiations; a separate emulsion for ultraviolet photography is not necessary.

Monochromatic film, because of its limited color sensitivity, has no use in regular photography. It is used primarily for copying.

Orthochromatic films are sensitive to the ultraviolet, violet, blue, green, and yellow-green portions of the spectrum. They do not accurately reproduce the relative brightness of a subject as seen by the eye. Orthochromatic film is available in sheet film only and is not used in regular police photography.

Panchromatic films are sensitive to all the colors of the visual spectrum. To assist in the selection of the correct film for any kind of work, panchromatic films are divided into two general classes, and the classifications are based on color sensitivity.

The first of these classes is Type B Panchromatic, a black-and-white film which reproduces the various tones and hues of the subject in tones of gray with a brightness range approximately the same as that seen by the eye. The major difference between the various Type B Panchromatic films is their speed.

Type B film may be divided into two sub-classes, long scale and short scale, according to their inherent contrast. Long scale films, such as Kodak Plus-X and Kodak Panatomic-X are used in portraiture, press, illustrative, continuous tone copy, general outdoor and indoor photography. Short scale films, generically called Process Pan, are used for copy work when complete tonal separation is required, Kodalith Pan and Reprolith Pan are shortscale Type B films.

Type C panchromatic film has greater sensitivity in the red end of the spectrum than Type B film. Type C films, Ilford HP4, and Kodak Tri-X, are useful for tungsten-light photography, flash or flood photography, and for outdoor photography in the early morning or late afternoon hours of sunlight. Each of these light sources are predominately red in available light.

Infrared films have a band of color sensitivity in the ultraviolet and blue, little or no sensitivity in the yellow-green portions of the spectrum, and a second band of greatly increased sensitivity in the visible red and infrared. These films can be of great value to the police photographer in criminalistics (see Chapter 15).

There is no special film for ultraviolet photography. Most light-sensitive films respond to the longer ultraviolet radiations, but the gelatin in the emulsion absorbs some of the longer wavelengths and all of the invisible ultraviolet band. Thus, only the visible ultraviolet region of the spectrum can be used for photography when using normal untreated light-sensitive films.

A subject can be illuminated with ultraviolet light and reproduced by using normal photographic film and procedure, if the film used has high blue sensitivity and good tonal separation properties. Therefore, the films selected should be a noncolor sensitive process or commercial type.

All films are sensitive to ultraviolet radiations, but in regular photography they are considered insensitive to these wavelengths because glass lenses and the gelatin in normally coated emulsions absorb a large portion of these radiations. When it is desired to use all of the ultraviolet light band photographically, a special lens made of quartz is used which transmits ultraviolet light. The film used must have a very thin emulsion coating — that is, much less gelatin is applied than is used for regular emulsions.

Emulsions differ not only in color sensitivity but in speed, graininess, contrast, sharpness and acutance. The most important of these remaining variables is speed.

SPEED

Film *speed*, or emulsion speed, is determined by the degree of sensitivity of an emulsion to light. This degree of sensitivity is called the *light sensitivity* of the emulsion. Emulsion speed has a direct bearing on the amount of light required by an emulsion to produce an acceptable negative image.

Some emulsions are rated as "slow" because they need more light in order to yield an acceptable image than do other relatively faster emulsions which are rated "fast." The American Standard Association (ASA) has assigned a numerical rating to each emulsion that is manufactured. Ostensibly, the scale begins at zero and the numerical ratings increase as film speed increases. Thus, a film speed with an ASA of 400 (Tri-X) is faster than one of ASA 125 (Plus-X). This rating is called the Exposure Index of a film.

The Exposure Index, or "ASA" of an emulsion is used to calculate the amount of light needed to produce an acceptable negative image. The method of calculation is discussed in Chapter 9.

GRAININESS

A negative image is composed of grains of metallic silver which adhere to a transparent base. To the eye these grains appear as a continuous deposit. However, when the image is enlarged a few diameters, a granular effect becomes apparent. This granular appearance of the enlarged image is called *graininess*. With greater enlargement the granular structure of the image can be seen.

The graininess of an emulsion depends upon the size of the silver halide crystals in the emulsion and upon clumping of the silver grains during development. As a general rule, slow emulsions are fine-grained and fast emulsions are coarse-grained. The tendency of silver grains to clump during development can be reduced by using a fine-grain developer. Therefore, an image which is to be greatly enlarged should be recorded on a fine or normal-grain emulsion, and developed in a fine-grain developer. Any reduction in graininess as a result of using a fine-grain developer is also accompanied by a loss in effective emulsion speed and in contrast.

CONTRAST

The difference in the densities of various areas in

the negative is known as *contrast*. A bright area in the subject reflects a great amount of light, causing a corresponding heavy density in the negative. This dense portion of the negative is referred to as a *highlight*. A dark area, such as a shadow, reflects very little light, resulting in a correspondingly thin density in the negative. The subject brightness between the lightest and darkest areas is also recorded on the negative in corresponding densities which are termed *halftones*. The difference between the darkness of highlights and the brightness of shadows in the negative is called contrast. Normal contrast is represented by a full range of densities, including highlights, halftones, and shadows. High contrast does not exhibit a full range of densities, and consists of only highlights and shadows, with little or no intermediate tonal gradation. Low contrast shows very little difference in densities.

Film is manufactured with varying degrees of inherent contrast; that is, it may have either a long scale or a short scale emulsion. High contrast or short scale films are used to record a short range of tones like black and white, such as is used for copying line drawings. Medium and low contrast or long scale films are used to record a wide range of tones as employed for commercial or portrait photography. The proper selection of the film to be used should be governed by the contrast of the subject and the rendition desired.

SHARPNESS AND ACUTANCE

The *sharpness* of a negative refers to the precision with which a boundary between areas of varied contrast are reproduced. Grains of silver halide, because of their crystalline structure, tend to scatter light which they have not absorbed. This scattering, called *diffusion*, can cause nearby silver halides to be effected by light which has not been focused upon them by the lens of the camera. Diffusion can also be caused by the reflective properties of the film base. Thus, highlights will tend to encroach upon shadows in a negative image. Maximum sharpness, then, depends upon minimum diffusion.

Sharpness is the perception of minimum diffusion; *acutance* is a measure of the tendency of an emulsion to diffuse light. An emulsion of high acutance will produce a very sharp image; emulsions of lesser acutance will produce negatives which are less sharp.

HANDLING FILMS

Film should be handled carefully to prevent damage. A broken package admits moisture and light. Moisture accelerates the deterioration rate of these materials, which shortens their expected useful life. Accidental exposure to light completely ruins them. Careless handling can also damage rollfilm and spools, magazines, and film packs beyond use.

Condensation of moisture on the surfaces of cold film can be avoided by removing film packages from cold storage and allowing them to reach room temperature before they are opened. The time usually recommended for large film packages is 24 hours, but small boxes of films should come to room temperature within 2 to 4 hours. If the package is taken from cold storage, opened, and subjected to rapid temperature changes, as from cool dry air to warm moist air, moisture or dew forms on the film surfaces. Moisture on an emulsion caused by condensation leaves marks that have every appearance of watermarks on processed film. A sufficient tempering period is necessary.

Films should be removed from their containers in a room which is used for this purpose. The room must be lightproof, clean, and dust free. The bench or table on which the film handling operations are performed should be cleaned with a damp cloth. The hands must be clean, dry, and free from perspiration. Individual films should be handled only by the edges. Handle films carefully, avoid contact with the emulsion surface, and touch the base side near the edges only.

Care in handling prevents fingerprints, abrasions, and scratches caused by holders, hangers, or other darkroom gear coming in contact with the film surfaces. Dust should be removed from darkslides, film holders, and magazines by brushing them with a soft brush. This should be done outside of the handling room.

Film should be handled in total darkness or under suitable safelight illumination for all operations including loading, developing, and fixing.

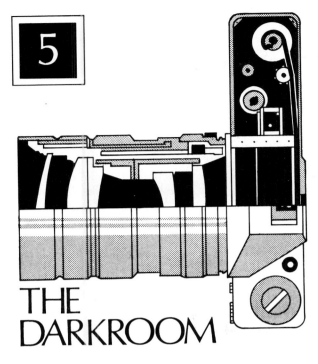

5

THE DARKROOM

The processing of film and the enlarging of negatives can only be done in a properly equipped darkroom. A darkroom is, literally, a room which is dark and in which light-sensitive materials may be handled without fear of accidental exposure.

Below are described the design characteristics of a basic darkroom. The student may have the use of a college darkroom while the police photographer will have use of a department lab. The characteristics described below should serve to orient both the student and police photographer to an environment which, when being used, is not seen or not seen well.

The basic components of the darkroom are: the room; work areas; storage areas; plumbing; electrical outlets and lighting; and ventilation. The photographer must become as familiar with these components and their requirements as possible so that touch and memory serve the purposes of sight when the room is dark.

THE ROOM

The location of the darkroom depends on the available space of the building and the type and amount of work to be accomplished. A small room that is well arranged is more than adequate; a large, rambling place is time consuming. The size of the darkroom is dependent on the size of the department. A small department may have to do film developing, printing and the finishing process in one room. A large department, on the other hand, may

have three separate rooms: one small room for film developing, a small room for enlarging and printing, and a larger room for the finishing process. The three-room set is good because it keeps all three processes separate and allows more than one person to work at the same time. This is impossible in the one-room set up, since all three procedures require a different amount of lighting.

The approximate minimum-size room that can serve as an efficient darkroom is about 6 by 8 feet, width of passages between working areas should be at least three feet, but if it is anticipated that several people will normally work in the darkroom at the same time, wider passages are desirable.

Figure 1 shows an example of a darkroom arrangement used by the Shaker Heights Police Department, Shaker Heights, Ohio.

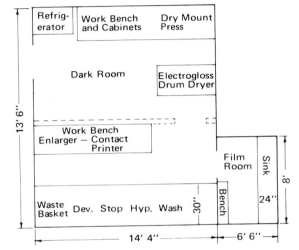

Figure 1 — Darkroom design for Shaker Heights Police Department, 1957 Shaker Heights, Ohio. Doorway from darkroom leads to identification bureau.

WORK AREAS

Bench-top height should be approximately three feet from floor level. Bench width should be about two feet. Underneath the dry working area there is usually room for one or more cabinet units with drawers, shelves, or combinations of both, as desired.

Bench tops should be chemically inert, watertight, and fairly resistant to abrasion. Good-quality, solid-color linoleum is an economical topping material.

When planning the space to hold the enlarger, if you make it 25 inches from the floor, you will find that you can sit down and work while doing the enlarging. (See Figure 2.) If you are going to do any amount of work in the darkroom, you will find this position less tiresome.

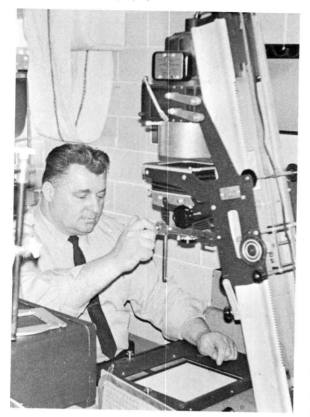

STORAGE

Wall shelves or overhead cupboards above the benches provide convenient storage space. The bottom of these units should be at least two feet above the bench top. Shelf width of about twelve inches is adequate.

Many of these furnishings are commercially available in wood or metal from suppliers of laboratory

furniture. Similar units sold for kitchen installation often will serve the purpose, also, and are available in semiassembled, unfinished form at quite reasonable prices.

PLUMBING

An adequate and reliable supply of reasonably pure, clean water should be provided.

Processing sinks should preferably be of stainless steel, but, with care, quite serviceable stoneware, lead-lined, and even wooden sinks can be constructed.

To minimize future maintenance problems, drain plumbing should preferably be of stainless steel or Duriron, neither of which is impaired by the flow of photographic waste through it. Normal piping materials will serve for many years, but eventually, in constant photographic service, they will require replacement.

Plumbing installation is most economical and efficient when all sinks and drains are located along outer walls of the darkroom area so that a common raceway can be utilized for all. This offers the additional advantage of making internal partitioning simpler and more flexible.

Long runs of uninsulated, exposed piping should be avoided in order to minimize temperature fluctuations of the water supply.

Thermostatic mixer valves for regulating the water temperature are a great convenience and time saver.

In warm climates where the "cold" water supply averages 80° to 90°F. for long periods of the year, some thought should be given to providing refrigeration facilities for cooling the water.

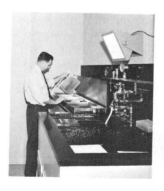

Figure 2 — Enlarger base (top) is 25 inches above the floor, so one may work seated

Figure 3 — Darkroom sinks. The sink at right is constructed of stainless steel

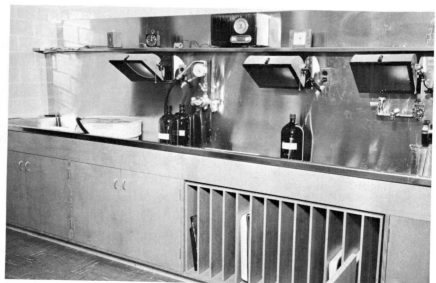

All pipe fittings to stainless steel sinks should be made with brass or copper fixtures extending at least 4 inches from the sink.

ELECTRICAL OUTLETS AND LIGHTING

All electrical circuits should be designed for 30-ampere loads, and the number of these circuits must be dictated by the total load of the electrical equipment which may eventually be used in the darkroom. Film and print driers, mounting presses, and copying lights all constitute large power drains which should be anticipated and provided for.

The switch for the general illumination safelight should be installed within easy reach, next to the entrance to the darkroom, at a height about 4½ feet above the floor. The switch for the white light should be located much higher (about 6 feet) and can be provided with a coverplate or mechanical or electrical interlock to prevent its being turned on inadvertently.

Safelights should be provided on the basis of one for every five linear feet of bench or sink working space. They should be located not less than four feet above the working level and, at this distance, 15-watt bulbs should be used. If the darkroom is adjacent to the identification room, its electrical circuits should be separate from those of the studio

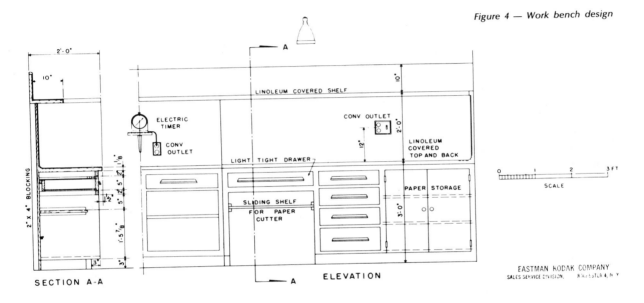

Figure 4 — Work bench design

Electrical circuits should be provided with reset type circuit breakers in preference to replaceable fuse links which may not be readily available when needed. In addition, the control panel should be located as close to the darkroom as possible so that service can be restored quickly after an interruption without the necessity of going to another part of the building to replace the fuse or reset the circuit breaker.

The lighting circuit should be separate from the equipment circuit in order to prevent safelights and room lights from being extinguished when equipment overloads interrupt the supply.

Convenient outlets should be located in the walls at chair-rail height, immediately behind the apparatus which they are to serve. This eliminates the hazard of trailing wires on the floor, and it also places the outlets far enough above the floor so that there is little danger of their being accidently splashed with spilled solutions or with water when the floor is mopped.

so that changing equipment loads in the darkroom will have no effect on the output and color temperature of the flood lamps. Conversely, the use of separate circuits will prevent varying lighting equipment loads from affecting printing exposures and drying times in the darkroom.

Constant voltage controllers for enlargers and printers are desirable for minimizing the effects of random voltage fluctuations in black-and-white printing. If color printing is anticipated, voltage stabilization is practically mandatory.

If possible, both 100- and 220-volt service outlets should be provided in all rooms.

VENTILATION

Clean fresh air should be pumped into the darkroom. This is preferable to using an exhaust fan because it produces a positive static air pressure in the darkroom and by causing air leakage currents through cracks and crevices to move outward rather than inward, helps to minimize the dust problem.

Glass fiber furnace-type air filters may be used over the air intake to lessen the amount of dust brought into the darkroom.

Lightproof louvers (nesting W type) are commercially available in a variety of sizes and can be utilized as exit ports for the air flow.

The ventilating system should provide a volume of air sufficient to change the air in the darkroom from 6 to 10 times per hour. More may prove "drafty" and less, inadequate.

A definite pattern of air flow should be planned so that the fresh air is brought in at the "dry end" and exhausted from the "wet end." Thus, vapors from open trays and sinks will be quickly exhausted without traveling the length of the darkroom.

Film and print driers which give off heat and water vapor should be provided with individual external vents to prevent their raising the temperature and humidity of the whole darkroom area.

The room should be clean and well ventilated. The arrangement of a darkroom should be convenient, with a place for everything and everything in its proper place. Sinks should be of adequate size

proximately 70°F. is the most comfortable temperature. The well-equipped darkroom contains the following items: waterproofed aprons to protect clothing, a supply of clean towels, a thermometer, a timer, and the necessary film hangers, trays or tanks. All darkrooms should be well stocked with prepared chemicals and their containers must be correctly labeled. In general, good photographic work demands that all operations be conducted in a clean, orderly and systematic manner.

DARKROOM EQUIPMENT

SAFELIGHTS

Safelights are enclosed light sources equipped with a filter. The function of a safelight is to transmit a maximum amount of light which is of a color that will not damage sensitized materials. Because the color sensitivity of sensitized materials varies with different emulsions, the color transmission of the safelight must vary accordingly to be safe.

The Kodak Wratten N. OC (light amber) and DuPont S-55X (orange/brown) safelight filters are generally preferred for printing because of their high safety factors (photographic papers are predominantly blue-sensitive) and the good working light they provide.

Table 5 — Darkroom safelight recommendations

Safelight filter	Type of paper		Lamp wattage	Safe working distance
	Contact	Projection		
KODAK:				
Series #O	Safe	Safe	25	3 ft
Series #OO	Safe	Unsafe	25	3 ft
Series #OA	Safe	Safe	25	3 ft
Series #OC	Safe	Safe	15	4 ft
Series #10	For panchromatic emulsions		15	4 ft

and constructed so they drain thoroughly. Duckboards are recommended to keep trays and tanks above the bottom of the sinks. There should be adequate and correct safelights placed at recommended working distances. Sensitized materials other than those in actual use should never be stored in the darkroom. The temperature of the laboratory should be maintained as closely as possible to the normal processing temperature — approximately 70°F. is the most comfortable tempera-

Film, because of its greater color sensitivity, must be handled in total darkness; thus, no safelight is truly "safe" when developing film. However, if the sensitive materials can be viewed at a distance under their illumination without fogging for the period of time that is normally required to expose and process them, the safelights adequately serve their purpose. As the sensitivity of the material increases, less exposure to the safelight is required to produce fog. If specific safelight instructions are lacking for a given type of paper, the best plan is to make a test using the paper under the questionable light source. Such a test is simple and only involves exposing portions of a sheet of the paper for various times — 2, 4, 6, 8, and 10 minutes, for example — at a normal working distance from the safelight. Then, after developing the paper, if a fogged appearance is noticeable beginning with the 8-minute exposure, the test shows that 6 minutes is the limit of permissible safe exposure under the existing conditions. Leave a strip of paper unexposed so that you may compare the strips made at the various times to see if they are fogged.

There are two remedies for an unsafe light. One is to increase the working distance from the safelight to the sensitized materials being used; another is to replace the bulb in the safelight with one of lesser wattage.

Wherever possible, the walls of the darkroom should be painted a light color to reflect the maximum amount of (safe) light and thus improve visibility.

TRAYS

Trays, though once made of enameled metal, are now constructed of plastic. The darkroom should be equipped with a minimum of four trays of a size larger than the materials to be processed.

TANKS

It is more convenient to develop rollfilm in a small tank than in a tray. The results are usually better, and the possibilities of damage to the film are minimized. Design detail and construction differ somewhat among the various manufacturers' models of rollfilm tanks, and obviously there are corresponding differences in details of loading, manipulation, agitation, etc.

The Nikor equipment which is constructed of stainless steel, is unbreakable and easily cleaned. The basic unit is composed of a spiraled and grooved reel to hold the film and a tank with a light-tight cover. Each reel is constructed for a specific size rollfilm such as a 35mm, 127, 120, etc. The tank cover has a light trapped pouring hole with a leakproof cap to allow solutions to be poured in and out of the tank during processing. Larger Nikor tanks are made which hold a number of reels stacked vertically, but these tanks do not have the light-trap opening. (See Figure 6)

Eastman Kodak Company has available the Kodacraft miniature rollfilm tank for developing 135, 828,

Figure 6 — 35mm and multiple roll Nikor tanks

120, 620, and 127 rollfilms. These tanks are made of tough, chip-proof Tenite plastic. They hold 16 ounces of solution. They are quick-loading and easy to use. There are two film aprons included with each tank. These tanks are very good for black and white developing, but when developing color film, the Nikor tank is recommended. These Kodacraft tanks are inexpensive and sturdy. (See Figure 7.)

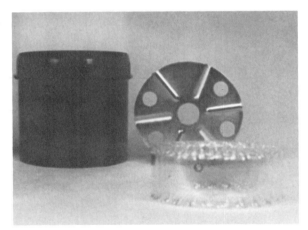

Figure 7 — Kodacraft miniature roll-film tank and aprons

Other tanks are manufactured, usually of plastic, for developing rollfilm. Most are unsuitable for quality work.

MECHANICAL WASHERS

Mechanical washer designs vary to accommodate the type of printing accomplished, but their general function is to wash prints in a continuous and changing water bath.

The recommended class of mechanical print washers consists of a tublike tank and a perforated cylindrical drum which revolves in the tank. Fresh water is circulated in the tank and through the drum by an inlet and an overflow outlet. The power for rotating the drum is supplied by the force of the water entering the tank from the bottom and hitting the fins and making the tubular inside tank turn around. The drum has a locking hinged door for convenience in loading and unloading prints. (See Figure 8.)

is pressed and the printing paper is exposed. When making a number of prints from one negative, this timer is invaluable in giving each print exactly the same exposure. A FOCUS button is usually provided on the various timers to permit the operator to turn on the printer light and view the image to be printed.

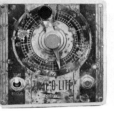
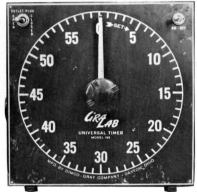

Figure 9 — Interval timer (left) and Gra-lab timer (right)

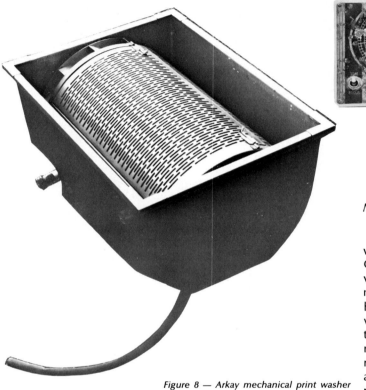

Figure 8 — Arkay mechanical print washer

MECHANICAL GLOSSY PRINT DRYERS

There are several models of machine dryers which dry prints to a ferrotyped or glossy finish. Glossy print dryers are equipped with a wide conveyor belt which carries the prints around a chromium or stainless steel-plated, highly polished, heated, slowly revolving drum. (See Figure 10.) The washed prints are placed on the apron portion of the conveyor belt *emulsion side up*. The belt carries the prints between the polished drum and a rubber squeegee roller. The pressures of the drum and the roller squeeze the surplus water off the prints and roll them into smooth contact with the polished surface of the drum. The cloth belt holds the prints in firm contact with the revolving drum.

Figure 10 — Floor model dryer (courtesy of Pako Company, St. Paul, Minn.)

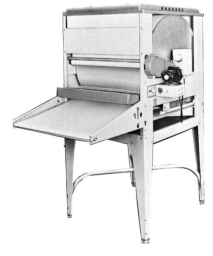

TIMERS

Most darkrooms contain two types of timers — a large wall clock with a sweep-second hand and interval timers connected to the contact printers and enlargers. (See Figure 9.)

The wall clock timer most often used has a black background with white numerals and hands. The dial has 1-second graduations and a large sweep-second hand. It is mounted on a shelf convenient to the developing tray. It should be sufficiently illuminated so that the photographer can accurately time the development of the print.

There are a number of models of interval timers used to time the exposure when printing. Some are built into the printer or enlarger and others are connected electrically. All work on the same principle. The exposure time is set by moving a pointer to the desired time on the dial; the EXPOSE button

The speed and temperature of the drum can be regulated so the prints are completely dried with one cycle of the dryer. When the prints have traveled one revolution around the drum, they fall off the drum into the print tray.

Machine glossy dryers have a capacity for drying many prints per hour. Good results can be obtained when the emulsions of prints are properly conditioned, and if the drum is kept clean and well polished. Sometimes prints that are dried glossy are found to have drying marks, which are termed oystershell markings. These marks are caused by uneven drying. The dryer should be operated so the prints are dried slowly and completely with one revolution of the drum to prevent drying marks and to reduce curling and wrinkling.

The polished surface of the drum should be cleaned periodically with a mild soap and hot water to remove any gelatin, residue, or dirt which may have collected. Then wipe the surface thoroughly dry and repolish the drum with a soft cloth.

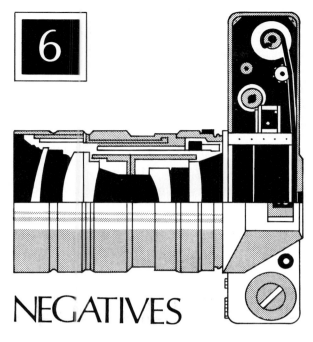

NEGATIVES

After the camera work is done, getting to the final picture is generally a two-step process:

1. Production of the negative from the exposed film.
2. Production of the positive, or print, from the negative.

Both operations, if performed in the usual manner, require a darkroom. Its equipment need not be elaborate, but the room must be truly dark for handling today's films, which are often sensitive to light and are usually *panchromatic*, which means they are sensitive to all colors of light. Years ago, we were able to use a red light in the darkroom, and we could look at the film to see how it was developing. If it needed more time in the developer, we could look at it and then put it back in the developer. This cannot be done today. Basic equipment should include a tank for developing films, trays for print processing, an accurate thermometer, a timer, a graduate for measuring liquids, bottles for storing solutions, a safelight, a printing frame or printing box, and if enlargements are wanted, and they usually are, an enlarger.

A timer for the enlargements is not essential, but it is handy and desirable. Some timers will function as both an interval timer for negative development and as an enlarger lamp control for printing exposures.

FILM DEVELOPMENT

The beginning police officer should start with one of the many excellent prepared developers that come as liquids to be diluted with water or as mix-tures of powdered chemicals packaged in cans, boxes, or packets and need only be poured into water and dissolved according to instructions on the label. Start with a developer recommended for the film you have exposed. Film comes packaged with development recommendations and these should be followed, unless other reliable and reasonable instructions are available. Do this until enough experience has been accumulated which will make experimental changes meaningful and productive. Recommendations from film manufacturers and developer suppliers are based on both scientific knowledge and practical tests. These recommendations are, of course, intended for average conditions, and it makes sense to alter procedures only if experience proves the need. So that we can learn to recognize and meet this need, it is important in the beginning to adhere to one film and one developer. For any one film-developer combination, the results (leaving exposure aside for the moment) depend on three factors:

1. Temperature
2. Time
3. Agitation

Control of these three factors reduces film development to the approximate level of making french toast for your breakfast. It is possible to guarantee a predicted result by developing the film for a known time at a fixed temperature with controlled agitation.

TEMPERATURE

The ideal temperature for most standard developers is 68°F or 20°C (Sixty-eight degrees Fahrenheit, twenty degrees centigrade or Celsius). It is best to develop at the recommended temperature, if possible, but most of the popular developers will perform well over a fairly wide range of temperatures, from 65°F to as high as 80°F if the time factor is altered in an inverse relationship; that is, the lower the temperature, the longer the development time. How much time change is needed to compensate for abnormal temperatures is best determined by consulting a time-temperature chart for the film-developer combination involved. See the printed data sheet packaged with the film. It is inadvisable to develop at a temperature higher than 80°F because the possibility of damage to the emulsion layer becomes great. High temperatures may soften and swell the emulsion gelatin of the film and thus make it especially susceptible to damage. At temperatures substantially less than 65°F, the developer solution may not function properly.

Accurate measurement of the developing solution temperature is important. The laboratory thermometer must be accurate. It should be checked regularly with a second standard thermometer or with a medical thermometer kept just for that purpose. Inaccuracies in darkroom thermometers are not uncommon.

Ideally, all solutions in black-and-white processing, including the final rinse wash water, should be kept near the same temperature as the developer. Generally this means ± 5°F, although some darkrooms attempt to hold ± 2°F. Variations in temperatures between solutions, if relatively large, may cause what is called reticulation, a cracking of the emulsion, and, in the case of small negatives, a quite small degree of reticulation seems to show up as a grainy print. However, without a temperature control device on the water tap, maintaining close temperature tolerances is difficult, and you will find that reticulation is not a major danger except when temperature changes are sudden and in excess of 10°F.

TIME

The time factor is variable, depending primarily upon the particular film-developer combination involved. Here again, we must refer to recommendations supplied with the film and/or the developer, and even these are only guides; they are not absolute values. There is no such thing as a correct development time for all workers under all circumstances. The variables are personal preference, equipment, and agitation.

We can, however, begin with the recommended times and modify them as experience dictates to meet individual requirements. A rough guide for alterations: If negatives consistently emerge with too much contrast, cut the development 20 to 30 per cent; if they are consistently too soft (lacking in contrast), boost the development time about 25 per cent. The longer the development time, the more silver is formed and the blacker the image. Contrast, or the difference between highlights and shadows, also increases with time, but only up to that point where chemical fog level begins to overtake the increase in the highlight density; then flatness or low contrast results.

AGITATION

Careful and consistent agitation is as important as time and temperature. It is often neglected. Fresh developer must be worked into the emulsion layer while the exhausted developer and by-products of the development reaction are swished out and away from the surface of the film. Agitation also keeps the solution uniform so that streaks on the negative caused by exhausted solution flowing across the emulsion do not occur. Agitation should begin the moment the film is placed in the developer and should continue for the first 5 seconds of the development period. After that, agitation is usually advisable for about 5 seconds out of every 30 seconds for the remainder of the time.

Some photographers, however, agitate less than this, perhaps only for 5 seconds out of every minute, or only twice, once at the beginning and again midway through the development period. Generally, the less agitation, the lower the contrast, but some photographers contend that reduced agitation also gives less graininess in the image. You may want to experiment to establish your own preference.

GENERAL PURPOSE DEVELOPERS

A developer for general purpose work should develop quickly to gammas of 0.8 to 1.1 and produce a clear density readily, with fog-free images of moderate grain. Since, in most photographic laboratories, tank development is common and the developer is used continuously, the keeping properties of the solution, the staining tendencies, and the rate of exhaustion are important factors.

In most general purpose developers the developing agent is a combination of Metol and hydroquinone, and an alkali such as borox, sodium carbonate, or sodium metaborate (Kodak). This combination produces a clean, fog-free, normal density negative. Some of the more popular developers of this type are listed below:

Ansco 42	Kodak DK-50
Ansco 47	Kodak DK-60A
Ansco 48 M	Kodak D-76

WATER RINSE

I. Properties: The water rinse is just what it says, plain tap water.

II. Function
   A. When a negative or print is removed from developing solution, there is a small amount of developer both in the emulsion and on the surface of the film which must be removed or neutralized to stop the action of the developing solution.
   B. A water rinse bath helps retard the action of the reducing agent and removes the excess developer.

III. Importance
   A. If the developing solution is not removed or

neutralized it may cause stains on the negative.

B. If the negative is not rinsed, the developing solution may contaminate the stop bath and fixing bath.

C. To remove developer, immerse the negative in rinse bath of water.

STOP BATH

I. Properties
A. Stop bath is a very weak acid solution.
B. Acetic acid or a solution more commonly known as vinegar is an example of a weak acid.

II. Function
A. Stop bath instantly neutralizes the action of the developer and stops any further development.
B. It neutralizes the alkalinity of the developer and prolongs the useful life of the fixing bath.
C. It reduces the defect known as pinholes.
   1. It is advisable to use a weak acid rinse between development and fixation of all thin base films.
   2. The strong acid in the fixing bath has a tendency to form carbon dioxide gas bubbles in the emulsion when the film is taken from the developer and placed directly into the fixing bath.
   3. These bubbles very often break small round holes in the emulsion which are sometimes mistaken for pinholes like those caused by dust particles settling on the emulsion prior to the camera exposure.

III. Precautions
A. The acid rinse must be weak.
B. If the acid rinse or stop bath is too strong, it will cause blister formation on the emulsion. This negative defect is known as blistering.

IV. Names of recommended stop baths
A. Edwal stop bath
B. Kodak indicator stop bath

FIXING BATH

When a light-sensitive material is removed from the developing solution the emulsion contains a considerable amount of silver salts which have not been affected by the reducing agents. These silver salts are still sensitive and, if they are allowed to remain in the emulsion, light will ultimately darken them and obscure the image.

The fixing bath is employed to prevent this discoloration and to assure the permanency of the developed image. Thus, the purpose of the fixing bath is to fix the photosensitive materials by removing all of the unaffected silver salts from the emulsion.

The fixing bath for films contains the following five ingredients:

1. Fixing agent or fixer
2. Preservative
3. Neutralizer or acidifier
4. Hardening agent
5. Antisludge agent

A fresh fixing bath will have the distinct pungent odor of acetic acid and will feel grippy to the fingers.

An exhausted fixing bath may have the following characteristics: milky in appearance, sulfurous odor, and slippery feeling. The large bubbles that form in an exhausted fixing bath during agitation do not disappear. An exhausted bath may become discolored and produce stains.

HYPO-CLEARING BATH

In various parts of the country there is what is termed hard water and soft water. Water contains chemicals and minerals. In order to reduce the washing time and remove the scum from the negative, the next step is to immerse the negative in Kodak hypo-clearing agent.

WASHING

Thorough washing is necessary to remove the fixing agent, which if allowed to remain, will slowly combine with the silver image to produce brownish-yellow stains and cause the image to fade. Water containing iron should not be used for any photographic procedure.

I. Temperature
A. The temperature of water used for washing should be 68°F.
B. Water at temperatures higher than 75°F can cause the emulsion to frill or reticulate.

II. Rate and Time
A. The rate of washing depends upon the degree of agitation and the amount of fresh water that comes in contact with the emulsion.
B. The minimum washing time for negatives in running water is twenty minutes, in a system which completely changes the water.

DRYING

The final step in processing a negative is to dry the wet film.

I. Removal of surface water

   A. Upon completion of the washing, the film should be gently sponged on both surfaces with a wet viscose sponge or wet absorbent cotton. This removes all dirt sludge.

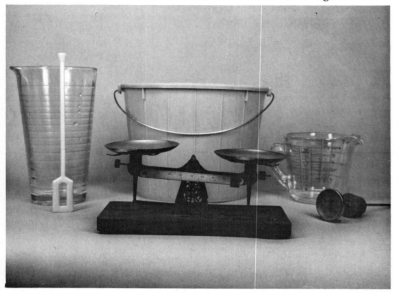

Figure 1 — Mixing utensils

   B. Following the sponging, rinse the film and remove the water from its surface with either a sponge, chamois or cotton.

   C. A wetting agent such as Kodak Photo-Flo may be added to the final rinse water. Wetting agents are used to break down the surface tension of water. The water will penetrate faster and drain more evenly. It reduces the drying time and helps prevent drying spots.

II. Evaporation

   A. The film should be attached to a line with a film clip or the holder.

   B. It should hang by one corner or one end in a good circulation of dry air and be allowed to dry without being disturbed.

   C. It should be dried in a place as free of dust as possible.

III. Rate

   A. The drying rate of films depends upon the humidity, temperature and amount of air circulated over the film surface.

   B. Shortening the drying time may be done by soaking the film in ethyl alcohol, which evaporates more readily than water.

MIXING UTENSILS

Chemicals should be mixed thoroughly. To do this you will need a mixing rod. There are several different types of stirring rods on the market. Eastman Kodak has a thermometer which indicates temperature and can also be used gently to stir. Most camera stores sell mixing rods made of plastic which are quite inexpensive (Figure 1). A *Holloway* electric mixer is a handy gadget to have, since it can cut down considerably the amount of time you spend mixing chemicals.

There are available good plastic buckets that can be used to mix chemicals. It is a good idea for police departments to buy the two-gallon buckets made out of plastic because they are inexpensive. Another handy plastic container would be the plastic diaper pail, approximately two gallons in size, with a lid which on occasions may be useful.

Most camera stores also offer mixing buckets made out of stainless steel; however, these, in addition to being more expensive, may develop holes and have to be discarded.

PROCEDURES

PROCESSING PROCEDURE

Most processing of roll film and 35mm is done in tanks. In tanks, the film is rolled loosely around a spool and is kept in total darkness as long as the tank is closed. Spools vary in construction — Kodak spools are, in fact, not spools at all, but aprons — and in loading style; the photographer must learn how to load his film onto the type of spool he is using.

Film must be loaded into tanks in total darkness, but once the film is inside and the tank is sealed, the processing procedure may continue under white light.

HOW TO DEVELOP FILM

35 mm film.

   1. Prepare your working place. Have tank and solutions properly placed for immediate action. Measure, with water, the amount of solution your tank will hold and make a notation of the amount. Load your bottles with the proper amount of solutions (1) Developer; (2) Stop Bath; and (3) Fixer (Hypo).

   2. In complete darkness, pry off the flat end of the 35mm cassette with a bottle opener, a Capro film cartridge opener, or a magazine/cassette opener for 35mm film. A screwdriver should not be used.

   3. Push the spindle on which the film is wound out of the cassette. Discard the cassette. With scissors, cut off the leader so that the film is square, discarding the leader. Pull the film off

the spindle so that it rolls up in your hand. The end of the film is connected to the spindle with masking tape and must be cut or, preferably, pulled off. Discard the spindle.

4. Loading the film onto the reel or apron should be done very carefully.

   With an apron, hold the wound film in the palm of your hand. With the other hand, let the apron roll down to its full length. Holding the round riveted end with both your index finger and thumb, begin to roll the film onto the apron. When completed, place it into the tank. Put the lid on the tank, and you are now ready to develop the film.

   If you are using a center-loading reel type tank, hold the film by its edges and press slightly so that the film buckles in the center.

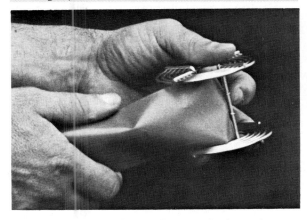

Figure 2 — Loading a Nikor center-loading reel

Secure the end of the film to the reel by catching it in a spring clip. Continue buckling the film with one hand as you rotate the reel with the other, checking with your fingers to make sure the film is going into the grooves correctly. Continue this operation until you have wound the complete film onto the reel.

   If you are using an edge-loading type reel, start the film onto the open end groove of the reel, using both hands and twist the two sides of the reel back and forth alternately. The film will automatically wind itself into the reel. Be sure that this type of reel is perfectly dry before using. Place the reels into the tank.

5. Working at a sink, have three beakers with working solutions of developer, stop bath and fixer ready. Set your timer for the desired time. Make sure that the developer is close to 68° by measuring it with your thermometer.

   Once the film is in the tank, you can turn your white light on and the remaining procedures can be done with the lights on.

   If your tank holds 16 ounces of solution, pour the 16 ounces of developer into the tank.

This must be done quickly so you will not get any streaks in the development of your film. Agitate the tank at 30 second intervals for the remainder of the development time. Agitate a tank like the Nikor stainless steel tank by turning it upside down gently. Tanks without a sealed top can be gently agitated by turning left and right in a swirling motion. You can also place a piece of sponge rubber on your sink and hit the sponge gently with the tank.

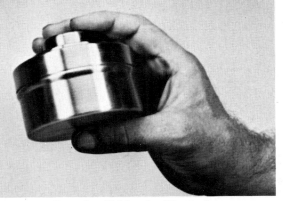

Figure 3 — Holding the Nikor tank

Be sure to agitate evenly. Many problems can arise if you don't. After completing the prescribed time in the developer, empty the developer back into the bottle (it can be reused).

6. Pour some water into the tank, and agitate every 30 seconds for about two minutes. Pour the water out and pour in your stop bath solution, agitating again every 30 seconds for about two minutes. Pour the stop bath out and rinse again for two minutes with water.

7. Pour in your fixer (hypo), agitating every 30 seconds, for about 5 to 8 minutes. When this step is completed, save the fixer for this can be reused.

8. Wash your film. Take the lid off the tank, put a hose into the tank, and let the water run into it. Wash the film for 15 to 20 minutes. Then put the film in a wetting agent or photoflo for about two minutes. Pull it out of the wetting agent. Squeegee with a good squeegee brush and hang the film to dry in a dust-free film-dryer.

Shaded areas indicate that the proceding is to be done in complete darkness.

120 film

If you know how to develop one type of film, the others are also done the same way, with minor variations. 120 film is processed with developer, stop bath and a fixer (Hypo). The only difference in procedure is in the size and packaging of the film. 120 film comes on a spool, wrapped with paper. Be careful not to develop the paper, instead of the film. This mistake should not occur if you feel the film, which is smoother. 120 film is usually a thinner film, and it requires more care when being wound onto the reel. The beginner should use an apron type tank. Another type of tank which is good for the beginner, is the adjustable type tank, for which you can adjust the reel to fit your film.

Be sure that both your hands and the reel are absolutely dry, and that your hands are clean. You may want to wear a pair of surgical rubber gloves so that you will not get any fingerprints on the film.

1. *Be Prepared*. Have your tanks and solutions ready. Developer, Stop Bath, Fixer (Hypo).

2. Break the seal on the roll of film and start unrolling the paper leader. When you come to the film, it will not be fastened to the paper leader. Avoid touching the inner part of the film. Continue unrolling the paper backing; the film will roll itself as you unroll the backing.

3. Let the film unwind and hold it by its edges in the palm of your hand. Hold both apron and film by their edges and insert the end of the film onto the riveted loop of the apron. Roll the film onto the apron. If you are using a load reel, pick up the reel with either your left or right hand and feed the reel into the outermost groove, emulsion side in, so that the natural curl of the film follows the spiral of the grooves in the reel. Avoid touching the emulsion side of the film; *always hold the film by its edges*. Walk the remaining film into the reel with back and forth motion of the reel, gently if you must hold the edge of the reel, that it will not slip back.

4. Put loaded reel into tank and put the top on. *Now you can turn your room lights on*.

5. Pour the correct amount of developer into the tank, so that it will cover the entire reel.

6. Agitate constantly, but not violently, during the first minute, then for 5 seconds every 30 seconds until complete development time has been completed. These steps should all be done with strict adherence to the timer. The developer is the critical time in the making of negatives.

7. After complete development, rinse with water by filling the tank at least three times with fresh water.

8. Pour out the water and add your stop bath.

Agitate gently for two minutes, then pour out the stop bath. Rinse again with water.

9. Pour the fixer into the tank, and agitate for 5 seconds every 30 seconds for 8 to 10 minutes. If your film is milky when you open the tank, reimmerse it in the fixer for a few more minutes.

10. Take the top off the tank and put a hose into the center of the tank. Let fresh water run into the tank, emptying the tank at least 15 to 20 times, so that fresh water is constantly running into the tank. You may want to use a coffee can with holes punched in the bottom so that the sludge can come out the bottom. You can pour water directly into the coffee can if you do not have a hose. Wash for 10 to 15 minutes with water at about 68°.

11. After proper washing, remove the film from the reel or apron and hang it to dry. While hanging, run a squeegee or a brush over the film to remove the excess water.

12. When dry, cut the film in sizes of three or four images and place them in an envelope or in plastic sleeves for storage.

13. Filing can be done by subject matter, job material, cases, alphabetically by name, or by name of individual involved.

TRAY PROCEDURE

1. Remove one film from its holder and place it face down (emulsion side down) on the paper or cardboard. Remove the second film and place it face down on the first. Continue until all the films to be developed have been placed in a loose pile on the space provided for them. Do not attempt to develop more than four or six films for the first several processes.

2. Submerge the films one at a time in the tray of water which should have the same temperature as the other processing solutions. Pick up the film on top of the pile with the left hand (keep the left hand dry until all films have been placed in the water), drop it emulsion side down into the water, and immerse it quickly with the right hand. Pick the film up immediately, turn it over (emulsion up) and push it back under the solution. Place the wet film, emulsion side up, at one end of the tray. Immerse the next film in the same manner. Stack it on top of the first film, and continue with this procedure until all the films are stacked in a pile at one end of the tray. The left hand should follow the last film into the tray to assist in the agitation of the films. Wet film may be handled with wet fingers. Extreme care should be taken to keep wet fingers *off* dry films. Slight pressure with the balls of the

fingers is not harmful to a wet emulsion unless it becomes swollen excessively.

3. The films should be agitated or shifted constantly to prevent the individual sheets from sticking together. Agitation is accomplished by moving the first film from the bottom of the stack and placing it on top, or by starting a new stack at the other end of the tray. Continue agitating the films from bottom to top until they become completely saturated with water — between 1 or 2 minutes is sufficient. After the emulsion is completely saturated, the danger of films sticking together is no longer a problem.

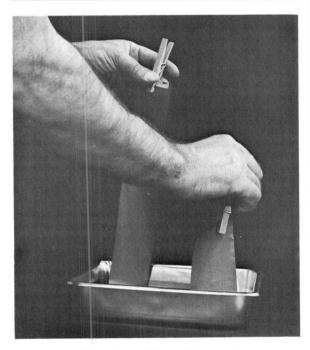

Figure 4 — Agitating rollfilm in a tray

NOTE: Presoaking the films in water prevents them from sticking together in the developer. If sticking occurs in the developer, it causes streaks and uneven development. Presoaking assures even developer absorption by the emulsion. It also causes a slight increase in the time required for normal development because complete saturation of the emulsion by the developer is delayed. Compensation for this increase in time should be made when determining the developing time. Presoaking is an optional step.

4. Remove the films one at a time from the water rinse and immerse them in the developer (DK-50). Place the films in the developer emulsion side up, slide them under the surface of the solution quickly, and agitate them vigorously to eliminate any possible air bells. Start the timer just before the first film is placed in the developer. Use the left hand to remove all films from the water, and be careful not to get the water contaminated with developer. The left hand should follow the last film transferred from the water into the developer to assist with the agitation.

NOTE: It is important to be able to quickly locate the first film placed in the developer. Align the long dimension of all subsequent films at a right angle to the first film placed in the developer.

The films are immersed emulsion side up in the developer to minimize the possibility of damage, which might occur if the emulsion, already softened by presoaking, is allowed to come in contact with the bottom of the tray. Be careful not to dig or drag the corner or edge of any subsequent films into the emulsion surface of the film below it. Do not allow the fingernails to touch the emulsion at any time. Stacking the films by aligning their edges against sides of the tray helps prevent scratches and abrasions.

Agitate the films constantly. Move the film from the bottom of the stack, place it carefully on top, and press it down gently to assure a flow of solution over its surface. Tray development is considered to involve constant agitation, and the development time is approximately 20 percent less than if the same film were being developed with intermittent agitation. If the films are agitated very slowly, or if the number of films being developed is so large that an appreciable interval exists between the handling of each film, the agitation should be considered intermittent, and the developing time should be adjusted to the frequency of agitation.

5. When the timer rings, remove all the films from the developer one at a time, in the same order in which they were placed in the developer, and submerge them in the stop rinse bath.

The right hand should go into the stop bath with the first film, and stay there to handle each film as it is transferred from the developer by the left hand. Use the left hand only to transfer the film in order to avoid contamination of the developer and spotting of the film. A few drops of developer does not mate-

Shaded areas indicate that the proceding is to be done in complete darkness.

rially affect the stop rinse bath, or a fixing bath, but a few drops of either of these baths ruins a developing solution.

6. After all the films have been shifted several times in the stop rinse bath, they should be transferred individually to the fixing bath or hypo. It is necessary to agitate vigorously in both the stop bath and the hypo, because gases are released in these solutions and there is danger of gas bells forming on the film surfaces. If these gas bells or bubbles are allowed to form, they cause dark spots. This is due to the continued action of the developer under the bubbles. Shift the films several times in the fixing bath, as agitated in the developer, and then safelights or the white lights may be turned on. Continue shifting the films until they lose the cloudy or creamy appearance and turn dark all over. Note the time required for this change to occur because it is just half of the total required fixing time. Shift the films several times during the second half of the fixing time. Continuous agitation is not necessary.

7. After fixing is complete, transfer the negatives to the wash water where agitation should be continued unless a regular film washing tank or tray is available. The negatives may be put in regular film hangers for washing. If so, the hangers should be loaded underwater to avoid scratching the films with the dry hangers. Usually, however, when developing is done by tray, the washing also has to be done by tray.

8. Wash the negatives thoroughly and give them the sponging treatment previously described. Then hang them to dry.

NEGATIVE PROCESSING CONTROL

Any practicing photographer realizes that the mere composing and exposing of a scene is no assurance of a prize winning photograph. The quality of the finished print is dependent to a great extent on the processing of the exposed film. A beautifully exposed negative is useless if it is fogged, scratched, or reticulated during processing.

Frequently, a photographer tends to become careless in his work. Also, in many cases he becomes so familiar with the equipment and procedures of film processing that safety precautions, tricks, or hints of procedure, and similar points are completely forgotten.

PREDEVELOPMENT WATER RINSE

The use of a water rinse before immersing the film in the developer is optional, but its use has several advantages. A water rinse prevents formation of air bubbles which usually occurs when the dry film surface is immersed in a solution. If the film is immersed directly in the developer, these air bubbles will likely cause trouble. In the water rinse they can be removed by agitation without harmful effect.

The water rinse also softens the emulsion so that, when placed in the developer, the developing solution is able to work uniformly on the emulsion. This helps prevent development streaks on the film.

The water rinse also removes the antihalation backing dye, which interferes with the action of some developers. It also brings the temperature of the film and the film hangers to the same temperature as the processing solutions. This is of considerable value when attempting to maintain constant temperatures in the processing solutions, and helps in the obtaining of more uniform results.

To use the water rinse, the film is immersed in a tank of clear water, which should be at the same temperature as the processing solutions. The film is agitated in the water for a period of approximately 2 minutes, after which it is removed from the water, drained, and then processed in the usual manner.

AGITATION

If a film is placed in a developer and allowed to develop without any movement, the chemical action soon slows down because the developing power of the solution in contact with the emulsion of the film becomes exhausted. If the film is agitated, fresh solution is continually brought to the film surfaces, and the rate of development remains constant. Agitation also has an important effect on the degree of development. An even more important effect of agitation is that it prevents uneven development. If there is no agitation, the exhausted solution, which is contaminated with bromide from the emulsion, may flow slowly across the film from the dense highlight areas and produce uneven streaks.

For consistent and uniform results, proper agitation of the film in the developing solution must be adhered to. There are two types of agitation: constant and intermittent.

Constant agitation usually refers to tray development of films, in which two to six films are placed in the tray in a pile and agitated constantly by moving the bottom film to the top continuously.

Intermittent agitation applies to tank development of 35 mm and rollfilm in small tanks, and the processing of sheet film in hangers. For 35 mm and rollfilm, the proper method is to agitate the film for 1 minute continuously after it is placed in the developer, and for 5 seconds each minute thereafter. Sheet film in hangers should be placed in the solution in a group, tapping the hanger bars on the top of the tank several times to dislodge any air bells. Next, allow the hangers to remain undisturbed for 1 minute. At the end of the minute, lift them clear of the solution, drain 1 to 2 seconds from each corner, replace smoothly in the solution and separate the hangers. Repeat at 1-minute intervals.

CLEANLINESS

Cleanliness in the chemical mixing room and the negative processing darkroom is of paramount importance in all types of photographic work. Mixing vessels, trays, tanks, ledges, and sinks should be cleaned and washed frequently. Chemical dust produces spots on films. The chief sources of chemical dust are leakage from containers and accidental spilling of dry or wet chemicals. It is a good idea, whenever possible, to store chemicals in one room, and do the actual negative developing in another room. If it is not possible to do this, photographic work can still be done in the same room in which the chemicals are mixed if care is used to keep the room clean.

The developing darkroom should be kept clean and well ventilated. Shelves, bottles, walls, and floors spotted with chemicals that have been spilled and allowed to dry are detrimental to good work. There should be aprons, preferably waterproof, to protect clothing. There should be a supply of clean towels available. In general, good photographic work demands that all operations be conducted in a clean, orderly and systematic manner.

SAFELIGHTS

Essentially, safelights are filters. The safelight's function is to transmit the maximum amount of light which may properly be used for visibility without damage to the sensitized material. Since color sensitivity varies with different emulsions, the color-blind emulsions may be developed under a Series No. OO, No. O or No. OA safelight. Orthochromatic emulsions should be processed under a red Series No. II. Panchromatic emulsions should be processed under a Series No. III safelight, with caution. The general practice is to process panchromatic emulsions in total darkness. If the Series No. III is used, the film should not be exposed to it until at least 50 percent of the developing time has elapsed, and then examined only momentarily at a distance of about 36 inches from the safelight.

Any safelight is most efficient when its output of illumination is indirect or by reflection. If the safelight is not constructed on the indirect principle, the light should never be pointed straight at the sensitized material, but should be placed so that the light beam is away from or at an angle to it.

A good guide to correct development and a safe procedure when developing negatives by safelight inspection is to examine the silver densities from the back, or base, side of the negative by reflected light. If a highlight or dark area can be seen and very little of the halftones, the negative is underdeveloped. When the highlights and halftones appear and the shadows are barely visible, the negative is normally developed. The above directions should be considered approximate. The principle may be used, and after some practice, negative density for both average and very thin films can be judged with a considerable degree of accuracy.

USEFUL LIFE OF SOLUTIONS

The useful life of developing solutions depends on the type of container in which they are stored, the type of film processed in them, the temperature at which they are stored, and the amount of agitation used while developing.

The action of the silver in the negative on the chemicals in the developing solution results in a depletion of the chemicals' actions. As the developer is used, it becomes less efficient. This loss of efficiency is characterized by a loss of effective emulsion speed and gradation of the photographic image.

The rapidity of developer exhaustion is influenced by the type of negatives being developed. When the average density of the negatives being developed is high, exhaustion is faster. When average density is low, exhaustion occurs more slowly.

The useful life of a developer is shortened by oxidation caused by contact with air. Exhaustion characteristics therefore depend greatly on the age and manner in which the solution is used.

A normal negative developer, such as Kodak D-76, Kodak DK-50, Ansco 17, Ansco 47, etc., can safely develop approximately 96 sheets of 4 × 5 inch film per gallon, if compensation in developing time is made as the solution is used. On the basis of a gallon of developing solution, the increase in developing time amounts to approximately 10 percent for every 16 sheets of film developed.

REPLENISHMENT

In large-scale developing, it is not economical to attempt to use a developer to the practical exhaustion point and discard it. Usually, the quality of the image falls off seriously long before the exhaustion point of the developer is reached. For this reason a replenisher may be used. The strength of the replenishers is usually adjusted so that they may be added to the tank to replace the developer carried out on the processed films; thus it is only necessary to maintain the level of the tank at a fixed point to maintain the activity of the developer at its normal level.

Replenishment is also used in small-scale work with low-energy fine-grain developers which fall off markedly in strength even with intermittent use. With this method, as very little developer is lost in processing, the replenisher is added to the stock bottle before the developer being used is poured back in, and any excess developer is discarded. This method keeps the developer at a constant strength from one processing to another.

The exact strength and quantity of replenishment required varies with different formulas. Specifications for the recommended formulas and their recommended use is found after each formula in the Photo-Lab Index, or prepared replenishers can be purchased.

Use the replenisher without dilution and add to the tank to maintain the level of the solution. It is frequently advisable to discard some of the developer before adding the replenisher to maintain proper negative quality. The life of the developer D-76 is at least 5 times as great with the use of this replenisher.

Replenishment of the developers cannot be carried to an extreme, due to the accumulation of silver sludge, dirt, and gelatin in the solution. Working developers should be discarded at the first sign of stain, fog, or instability.

STORING CHEMICALS AND SOLUTIONS

All liquids should be stored on the bottom shelves. If a container should break, its contents will damage only the bottom shelf and the floor.

Chemicals that react violently with each other should be stored separately to prevent explosion or fire. Large bottles and cans should be stored on the lower shelves because of the greater ease in handling.

All chemicals and solutions should be labeled for safety and accuracy.

SAFETY PRECAUTIONS

All chemicals should be regarded as poisons and handled with caution!!

1. Acids and caustics may cause severe skin burns.
2. The fumes from acids and caustics may cause irritation to the throat.
3. Acids and caustics may start fires when in contact with certain other materials.
4. Always add the chemicals to the water.
5. Never mix an acid with a cyanide; a lethal gas is released.
6. Wear protective clothing such as aprons and make sure there is adequate ventilation in the darkroom.
7. Avoid unnecessary contamination of the hands. Use tongs, clips, and hangers. If the skin is extremely sensitive use rubber gloves.

NEGATIVE QUALITY

A normal negative is one that will produce a pleasing print or reproduction of the original scene when printed on a normal printing material. If a negative is normally exposed on a film of normal qualities and developed for a normal time in a developer of normal strength, it will be a normal negative. The basic characteristics of negative quality will always be in accordance with the conditions under which a negative is made. It is necessary to learn the normal appearance of the following characteristics in order to recognize any departure from normal.

1. General negative density or opacity to light.
2. Image highlights or areas of greatest density.
3. The shadows or areas of least density.
4. Contrast, or the differences between highlight density and shadow density.
5. Tonal gradation, or the range of grays, between the highlights and the shadows.

DENSITY

Density determines how much of the incident light falling upon a negative will pass through the image. If very little silver is present in the negative, the image appears thin (transparent) and it is said to have a low density. If there is a large amount of silver present, very little light will pass through the image, and the negative is said to have a high density, or may be called a heavy or even dense negative.

A dense negative is more easily printed by contact than by enlarging; and a thin negative is much easier to print by enlarging than by contact.

HIGHLIGHTS

The highlights or dark areas of a negative for most purposes should not lack detail. If any detail is missing, the highlights are termed too dense, choked up or blocked out. The highlights in a negative will lack sufficient detail if they are too dense.

The detail will be missing in both the highlights and the shadows if the negatives are thin.

SHADOWS

The shadows or the more transparent areas of the negative should also contain detail. If these areas are so thin and weak that the outlines of the image are lost, the shadows are termed lacking in detail or blank. The need of detail in both the highlights and the shadows for photographs of most subjects cannot be stressed too strongly.

CONTRAST

Contrast is the difference in density between the highlights and the shadows. If this difference is great, the negative is said to have great contrast. If the negative has less contrast than the scene from which it was made, the negative is described as having reduced the scene contrast.

TONAL GRADATION

The middle tones are the variations of the range of grays between the highlights and the shadows; that is, the densities which are not highlights or shadows are termed middle tones, or halftones, for identification. They are also termed the intermediate tones of the image. The brightness between the highlights and shadows of a subject should be correctly reproduced as density variations by the middle tones of a negative. However, the middle tones vary with the type of film and with subject contrast, and may be omitted in the evaluation of negatives of some subjects.

NEGATIVE DEFECTS AND CORRECTION

● *Appearance*: Abrasion marks or streaks appear as fine lines usually resembling pencil scratches and running in the same direction.

Abrasion marks or streaks

● *Cause*: They are caused by friction on the emulsion of the film which may be due to improper handling or storage at some time between manufacture and development.

● *Remedy*: Great care should be taken in the storage of the film. The boxes containing such supplies should be stored on end in order that no pressure is exerted on the surface of the emulsion. Care should be taken not to rub or drag a piece of sensitized materal over a rough surface, either before or after development.

● *Appearance*: When an air bell occurs during development it is seen as a small transparent spot. Sometimes a minute, dark streak leads from the spot. When the negative is rocked in a tray, the streak projects from each side of the transparent spot in the direction the tray is rocked. If the tray is rocked in two directions, the streak forms a cross with the transparent spot in the center. When the air bells occur in tank development, the dark streak usually forms at the lower edge of the transparent spot. When the air bells occur in the fixing bath, they show as small, round, dark spots.

Air bells

● *Cause*: The transparent spots which occur in the developer are caused by bubbles of air on the surface of the emulsion. These prevent the developer from coming into contact with the emulsion. The darkened streaks are the result of the excess oxidation of the developer, caused by air in the bubble. The dark spots which occur in the fixing bath are caused by the pocket of air holding the fixing bath away from the emulsion. This allows a slight continuation of development.

● *Remedy*: Immerse film carefully and thoroughly in the developing and fixing solutions; move film during development and fixation in order to break up and prevent air bells. Water always contains some air and, when there is a rise in temperature, this air is expelled and gathers in the form of small bubbles on the inside of the tank and also adheres to the surfaces of film during the preliminary stages of development. The water needed for development may be allowed to stand for several hours at the temperature required for use before beginning development operations.

Blisters

● *Appearance*: Blisters on negatives resemble the familiar ones which arise on the human skin from slight burns.

● *Cause*: Blisters are caused by fluid or gas, formed between the emulsion and the film support when the solution has become too warm and has loosened the gelatin from its support. They are also produced by a developer and fixing bath that are both strongly concentrated. In changing a film from one bath to the other, there may be a formation of gas between the emulsion of the film and its support. Blisters are frequently caused by insufficiently rinsing the film after development and placing it directly into a fixing bath having strong acid content. Another common cause of blisters is allowing water from the faucet to flow directly on the emulsion side of the negative.

● *Remedy*: The description of the causes of blisters indicates the manner in which these defects may be avoided.

Blurred negative

● *Appearance*: Indistinctness or lack of definition in the negative image is typical of a blurred negative.

● *Cause*: The subject was not properly focused on the film; there was movement of the camera or the subject; or through lack of proper adjustment, a portion of the film was not flat on the focal plane of the camera when the exposure was made. A blurred effect is sometimes produced by moisture or haze on the lens or by a dirty lens.

● *Remedy*: Care must be taken in focusing and in holding the camera, keeping the camera in proper adjustment and the lens free of moisture or dirt.

Brown spots

● *Appearance*: These appear as brown or sepia-colored spots or small areas on the negatives.

● *Cause*: Brown spots are produced by an oxidized developer or by fine particles of chemicals settling on the film prior to development. This defect may also occur during the washing, resulting from rust or other impurities in the wash water.

● *Remedy*: Avoid an exhausted or oxidized developer. Do not use the developing room for the mixing of chemicals. Filter the water used for washing.

Crystalline surface

● *Appearance*: The surface of the negative emulsion possesses a crystalline appearance suggesting frost on a window pane.

● *Cause*: There was insufficient washing after fixing. Hypo remains in the film and crystallizes.

● *Remedy*: Use sufficient final washing.

Dark lines

● *Appearance*: These lines must be divided into two distinct classes; those dark lines which run from dark areas to the more transparent areas of the negative, and those lines which run from the more transparent areas to the darker areas. In both cases the lines are wider, not as clean cut and nearly as parallel as abrasion marks.

● *Cause*: The first class is caused by insufficient agitation of the negative in tank development. The cause of the second class is thought to be of an electrolytic origin.

● *Remedy*: For the first class, more frequent agitation of the negative during development is needed. The remedy for this class aggravates the defect in the second class. The only known remedy is to remove all the film hangers from the tank four or five times during the developing period, holding the hangers in a bunch, and allowing the corner of the bunch of negatives to rest on the edge of the developing tank for 10—15 seconds.

Fading tendency

● *Appearance*: Fading appears as sepia or yellow-colored stains or areas in the negative.

● *Cause*: Incomplete fixation, or insufficient washing will cause fading. Remnants of the fixing bath left in the emulsion continue their action and in time this defect appears.

● *Remedy*: Always fix and wash the negatives fully and properly. Final washing is as important as any other operation in negative processing.

Fingermarks

● *Appearance*: Imprint of fingers shows up on the negative.

● *Cause*: Caused by impressing wet or greasy fingertips on the emulsion side of the film before or during development and fixation. If the mark is merely an outline of the finger, it was caused by water or grease on the finger; if darker it was caused by developer; and if transparent or light is was caused by the fixing bath.

● *Remedy*: Keep the hands clean and dry when handling film. There is sometimes enough natural oil on the fingertips to cause the grease marks referred to above. Handle film by edges. When the fingers have become wet with water or solution, wash and dry them before attempting to handle film. Keep the hands out of the fixing bath as much as possible; but whenever it becomes necessary to place them in the solutions always wash them thoroughly before handling the film.

Fog (aerial)

● *Appearance*: Fog shows up as a slight veiling of the negative or parts of the negative exposed to air during development.

● *Cause*: Fog is caused by exposure to air during development, especially when hydroquinone is used as a developing agent. It occurs most frequently in freshly mixed developers, especially those containing excessive amounts of hydroquinone or alkali.

● *Remedy*: Add potassium bromide to developer or add used developer to fresh developer.

Fog (dichroic)

● *Appearance*: This type is usually a fog of little density, consisting of finely divided particles of silver. When viewed by transmitted light it is pinkish; when viewed by reflected light, it is a reddish-green.

● *Cause*: Using ammonia as an accelerator causes dichroic fog. The presence of hypo or an excessive amount of sulfite in the developer may also be the cause.

● *Remedy*: The fog can easily be removed by treating the negative in a weak solution of potassium permanganate. The prevention is obvious from the list of causes. Further prevention is assured by using clean trays for developer and fixing baths.

Frilling

● *Appearance*: In frilling, edges of the gelatin become detached from the base. The detached edge of the emulsion may either break off or fold over. When the latter happens, it is sometimes possible to partially remedy the damage by smoothing out the emulsion when the negative is placed to dry.

● *Cause*: Frilling is caused by: careless handling; using solutions that are too warm; insufficient hardening of the emulsion due to insufficient fixation; a spent fixing bath or one containing an insufficient amount of hardener; and/or excessive washing. Frilling is usually caused by the combination of careless or too frequent handling of the film and any mistake that renders the emulsion of the film soft.

● *Remedy*: To remedy, handle film carefully and not too much; have all working solutions sufficiently cold and of proper freshness or strength. Wash film sufficiently, but not excessively.

Gas bells

● *Appearance*: These bells appear as minute pimples or blisters.

● *Cause*: Bells are developed by transferring a negative from a strongly concentrated developer to a strongly acid fixing bath without thoroughly rinsing the negative after removing it from the developer and before immersing it in the fixing bath. In warm weather, gas bells may appear in developing and fixing solutions of normal strength if the rinsing between development and fixation has been insufficient.

● *Remedy*: To remedy, use an intermediate hardener rinse bath.

Halation

● *Appearance*: Halation appears as a dark band or area extending from the negative record of an intensely bright object, suggesting a double image, and appearing in the print as a halo or band of light around the object.

● *Cause*: Halation results from photographing an intensely bright object that is surrounded by dark objects. The intense light penetrates the emulsion and is reflected back by the negative support.

● *Remedy*: To remedy, use antihalation film and avoid pointing the camera at bright sources of light.

Pit marks

● *Appearance*: These marks show up as fine holes or pits in the emulsion.

● *Cause*: An excessive amount of alum in the fixing bath, sulfurous precipitation from the fixing bath when negatives are fixed in a tray, and too rapid drying of the film are causes.

● *Remedy*: The best remedy is proper fixing and drying.

Pinholes

● *Appearance*: Minute transparent spots in the negatives.

● *Cause*: These holes are caused by dust on the film before exposure.

● *Remedy*: Proper handling of the film.

Reticulation

● *Appearance*: Leatherlike graininess of wrinkling of the emulsion.

● *Cause*: Too great a difference in the temperature of the baths or between final wash water and air in which negative is dried is a cause. Due to the temperature of a solution of wash water, the gelatin of the emulsion may become badly swollen and upon shrinking contracts irregularly due to the metallic silver incorporated in the emulsion. Reticulation is also caused by excessive softening of the emulsion followed by a strong hardening bath or a highly alkaline treatment followed by strong acid.

● *Remedy*: Keep all solutions cool and at uniform temperatures. The reticulation effect may sometimes be removed by placing the negative in a 10% solution of formaldehyde for a few minutes and drying rapidly with heat. Use ample ventilation in drying negatives treated in formaldehyde.

Streaks

● *Appearance*: Streaks and patches, in the case of spots, may be dark, white or transparent.

● *Cause*: Dark patches or streaks may be due to uneven development caused by not flowing the developer evenly over the film, by not rocking the tray, or by not moving the film in the developer. They may also be due to a splash of developer on film before developing, a dirty tray or tank, using a fixing tray or tank for developing, or light fog. If the edges of the film are clear, the trouble is in the camera; if the edges are fogged, it is due to manipulation in the darkroom. White or transparent patches may be due to an obstruction in the camera, which prevented the light from acting on the film, a "resist" in the form of oil or grease, which prevented the action of the developer, a splash of hypo, or touching the film with hypo-soaked fingers before development. The hypo dissolves away some of the emulsion so that, on developing, the portion touched appears lighter than the rest. Drying marks in the form of teardrops or white patches are caused by splashes of water on a dry negative or by leaving spots of water on the film before drying, especially if the film is dried in warm air.

● *Remedy*: Precautions to be taken to avoid streaks suggest themselves when the cause of the streak is traced.

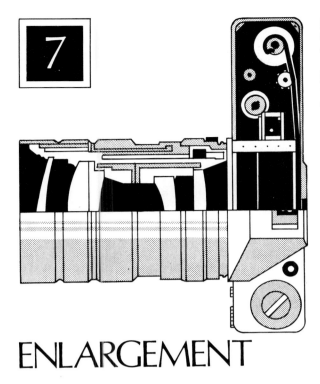

7

ENLARGEMENT

The final process in making a photograph is called *printing* or, more often, enlarging. When the photographer makes a print, he is making a negative of a negative, thus creating a *positive*. Two wrongs, in this application of photography, make a right.

There are two methods for making a positive image: contact printing and enlarging. In both methods, light passes through the negative and exposes a sheet of photographic paper. The dense, dark areas in the negative allow little light to pass through; less dense areas permit more light to reach the paper.

In contact printing, the negative is in contact with the paper; the resulting print is equal in size to the negative. A small negative yields a small print; larger negatives yield larger prints. Contact printing has it uses in darkroom work (see p. 56) but in order to prepare a presentable photograph, corrections of the negative image are often necessary. These corrections are easily made while enlarging the negative.

An enlargement is the result of projecting a negative image through a lens onto photographic paper. Enlarging allows the photographer to make a print of any size *within the limitations of the negative*. Enlarging is a very adaptable and versatile process in which considerable control can be exercised. Although the main advantage of enlargement over contact printing is that large size prints can be made, there are several other important advantages. Among these are the ease with which local printing control can be accomplished, various special effects may be obtained, and the fact that both composition and perspective can be improved.

The quality of the image on prints can be varied by the choice of printing materials, exposure, and processing. The results can actually correct many of the deficiencies which may exist in the negative. Because of this, it is important for the photographer to have a working knowledge of all the materials, equipment, and procedures employed in order to produce the desired results. There are many similarities between the two printing methods, especially in the papers, chemicals, and processing procedures involved.

RESIN COATED (RC) PAPERS

Today the resin coated (RC) paper is very good for the police officer to use, for it does not require any expensive equipment to dry. All you have to do is hang it up to dry. You can buy it with a glossy finish or a matte finish. The police do not need a photograph to last a lifetime. After they get through using it in court, there is not much use for it later. If the occasion arises that they may need another print, they have the negative, and it is a simple matter to make another. The big objection they have against RC paper is that it is made of a plastic; it is not a good conductor of heat. Usually police pictures are put away in files, which would be no problem for the resin coated paper. At the college I have seen photos made five and ten years ago, and they still look good. Resin coated (RC) papers require less washing time than fiber base papers.

PAPER STORAGE

Paper storage is important because stray light fogs paper, giving it an over-all tinge of gray. Time and heat do the same. Store paper in a light-tight box in a cool dry place. Open a package of paper only under darkroom safelight. Most papers last about two years at room temperature, considerably longer if kept in a refrigerator.

PHOTOGRAPHIC PAPERS – EMULSIONS

Prints are made by exposing a sensitized photographic paper which records, much as does film, a latent image. When the paper is developed, fixed, washed and dried, the image becomes visible and permanent.

Photographic paper is in many ways similar to film; in photographic paper, light-sensitive silver compounds are suspended in gelatin to form an emulsion. This emulsion, unlike that of film, is coated on a white paper base which is opaque. Photographic papers, like films, are manufactured in a variety of types which differ in physical and photographic properties. A knowledge of these properties will help the photographer to select an appropriate paper for a given job.

There are three types of emulsion used on photographic paper: silver chloride, silver chlorobromide, and silver bromide. These emulsions are much slower than those used on film. High sensitivity is not needed; in fact, it is undesirable. Often, it is necessary to manually manipulate the light which exposes the paper; this requires seconds, not parts of a second, of exposure.

When the photographer is manually enlarging several prints from the same negative, there is bound to be some degree of variation between exposures. This variation is not good when trying to make several match prints, but for most work the generally low speed of paper tolerates small variations by lessoning their effects. A fast paper, however, requires a shorter exposure and variations become much more serious.

To state an absolute speed for papers, one which would correspond to the Exposure Index of films, is impractical. Even general figures are impractical and should be regarded as no more than approximate guides because the speed of paper emulsions tends to vary from batch to batch and with climate, age and storage conditions. Certain tests, such as the test strip (see p. 61), are therefore an important step in printing process; exposure values for individual situations must be found by trial.

EMULSION TYPES AND CONTRAST

Silver chloride papers, with their relatively slow emulsions, are used primarily for contact printing.

Silver bromide papers are approximately 100 times as sensitive as papers with a pure chloride emulsion. Because of their high speeds, pure bromide papers have a limited use in enlarging.

Silver chlorobromide papers are coated with an emulsion that combines silver chloride and silver bromide. Depending upon the mix chosen by the manufacturer, chlorobromide papers vary in sensitivities from slightly faster than chloride papers to slightly slower than bromide. Medium speed chlorobromide papers are suitable for contact printing or enlarging.

Because it is not always possible to produce negatives that are exactly normal in tonal range and contrast, contact and projection papers are made in several grades or degrees of inherent contrast. There are low-contrast papers for printing contrasty negatives, normal-contrast papers for normal negatives, and high-contrast papers for flat negatives. The contrast grades are designated by numbers and each manufacturer uses a similar series of numbers.

The degree of contrast control that can be exercised during the positive process — exposure and development — is very small. It is important to use the correct grade of paper as the contrast control. The wide range of contrasts available in development papers is difficult to appreciate without studying actual comparison prints. A series of prints from the same negative, each one on a different grade of paper, shows the effects of increasing contrast with paper grade as the paper is changed from the softest towards the hardest grades. The comparison also illustrates how a negative of practically any degree of contrast can be printed to a pleasing contrast when a suitable grade of paper is chosen.

PAPER BASES

The paper used as the base for emulsions is the highest grade of paper available. The most stable papers are made from high grade sulfite woodpulp and processed to be as free as possible from chemical and metallic contamination. Sulfite woodpulp withstands alkaline and acid solutions, handling while wet, and thorough washings. Furthermore, its chemical purity prevents chemical reactions with the solutions it encounters during processing. The color or tint of paper emulsions is controlled by mixing dyes or other materials with a barium sulfate coating. A few of the emulsion tints available are white, ivory, and cream.

Ansco, Du Pont, Ilford, AGFA, and Eastman Kodak produce several different thicknesses of paper bases, classified according to weight. There are also some special purposes papers which do not fall within these base weight classifications.

Lightweight paper (abbr. LW.) is furnished in a thin or lightweight stock and is intended for purposes which frequehtly involve folding. Part of the weight and stiffness of photographic papers is due to the baryta coating applied to increase the reflecting power of the paper base. This coating is not applied to lightweight paper. By omitting this coating, a much thinner paper is produced, and folding is possible without cracking the emulsion. For the above reasons, photocopying papers are made on similar thin base stock without the baryta coating.

Single-weight paper (abbr. SW) is relatively thin. It is about half as thick as double-weight stock, and it is used for all ordinary photographic purposes. Single-weight papers may be processed more rapidly, and they are much less bulky than double-weight.

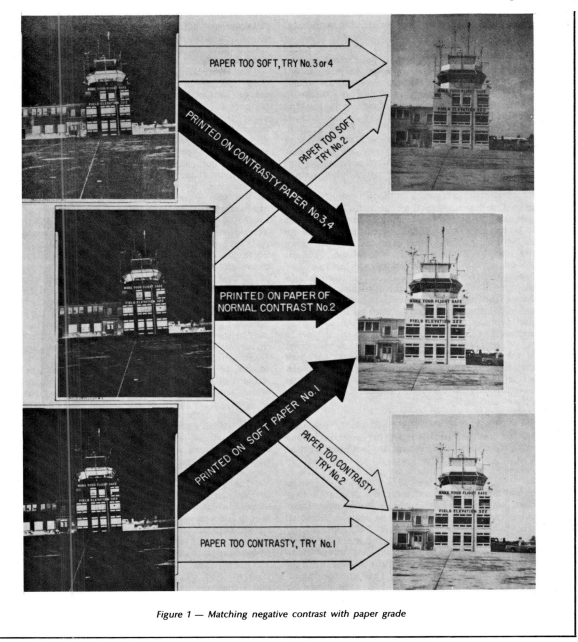

Figure 1 — Matching negative contrast with paper grade

These papers are best suited for print sizes 8 × 10 inches and smaller, and for larger prints that have to be mounted. Most all of the common glossy surface prints are on single-weight papers.

Double-weight paper (abbr. DW) is thicker than the average heavy postcard. It is the heaviest stock normally used for photographic paper. However, there are emulsions supplied on a cardboard-weight base for making postcard prints.

Double-weight papers are generally used for large prints because they stand up better under rough treatment. Heavy stock is usually employed for all prints that are exposed to much handling.

Heavy papers are also recommended for portrait and exhibition photographs. Double-weight papers have several different surface textures.

Water resistant papers (abbr. RC) have an acetate coating applied to the back of the base to prevent the absorption of processing solutions, which cause the expansion and contraction of the paper. The coating reduces shrinkage and the time required for washing, since solutions do not soak into the base. Special low-shrinkage papers are available in single and double-weight.

Papers with water-resistant bases serve two important purposes: first, they are used to produce photographs which require the positive print to have a minimum shrinkage; and second, water-resistant bases are useful where quick production of a few prints is necessary. When the processing schedule for these papers is strictly observed, their bases will not absorb solutions or water and therefore the time required for processing, washing and drying is reduced.

Papers having this special base are not actually waterproof. Excessive soaking or washing allows liquids to seep between the paper base and the emulsion, causing separation of the emulsion from the base. This practice should be avoided, especially at temperatures above 68° to 70°F.

PAPER SURFACES

The effect of a print depends a great deal upon the surface of the paper upon which it is printed. Papers are made with a wide variety of surfaces, thus permitting the selection of a surface that contributes the most to the purpose for which the print is intended.

Different surface textures are formed on the paper bases by passing them between large rollers. Papers having smooth surfaces are passed between smooth surfaced rollers under extreme pressure, while the rougher surfaces are pressed very lightly. Special surfaces such as silk, linen, and burlap are made by passing the paper stock between high-pressure embossing rollers which have that particular pattern on their surfaces.

Glossy surfaces give maximum detail and brilliance. They have no pattern. This glossy paper can be highly polished or have a semigloss effect. Smooth papers are recommended for small prints which require good definition. The requirements of police photography place the emphasis on maximum detail and brilliance, so smooth glossy, white papers are best suited for these purposes.

Matte surfaces are softer and less glaring. They are preferred for pictorials, portraits, landscapes, and other views not requiring a great deal of detail and brilliance. The rougher bases have a noticeable texture. The rougher surfaces subdue fine detail in proportion to the degree of roughness.

PAPER SIZES, PACKAGING AND STORAGE

Photographic paper may be purchased in many sizes; postcard, 5 × 7, 8 × 10 and 11 × 14 are among the most often used. Prints may be cut to any size and the dimensions of a print are not limited to the dimensions of the paper as long as the paper used is larger than the intended print.

Paper is usually purchased in quantities of twenty-five or one hundred sheets, and is packaged

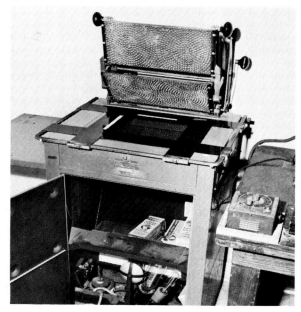

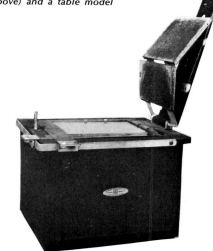

Figure 2 — A floor model contact printer (above) and a table model (below)

in double light-tight envelopes or boxes.

Photographic paper is perishable and deteriorates with age. It must be protected from the harmful effects of heat, moisture and physical damage. Heat and moisture, particularly, hasten deterioration of paper and shorten its usable life.

Do not keep paper under refrigeration once the sealed package has been opened unless storage conditions can be held at 50 to 60 percent relative humidity. Refrigerators containing food or unsealed containers of liquids are generally areas of high relative humidity, and are unsuitable cold storage spaces for paper. Paper removed from cold storage areas must be brought back gradually to room temperature before the packages are opened in order to prevent condensation.

Store individual packages of paper on end so that the weight of the contents is on the edges of the paper.

THE PRINTING ROOM

The printing room should contain the following materials and equipment, arranged so that the flow of work moves slowly from one stage to another: contact printer or frame, enlarger, safelight, trays for the solutions, a graduate for measuring and mixing solutions, a thermometer, at least two pairs of print tongs, and a timer or a wall clock with a sweep second hand.

MAKE A PROOF SHEET

Making a proof sheet is an optional step in the process of making a finished print. With experience, it becomes possible to select and judge a negative without seeing a positive beforehand. But at first the photographer will find that a proof sheet is a convenient and effective way to inspect his negatives before going to the enlarger.

A proof sheet is a contact print of one or (usually) more negatives. An entire roll of 35mm or 120 film can be printed on one sheet of 8 × 10 paper, thus giving the photographer a permanent record of all the photographs on one roll of film.

To make a proof sheet:

1. Prepare the darkroom. You will need a contact printer or printing frame and a source of white light if a printing frame is used. Solutions (developer, acid stop bath, and fixer) should be ready in trays large enough to accommodate the size of paper which you will be using (8 × 10). A safelight with series No. O or No. OA filter should be turned on.
2. Select a paper. You may want to write on the proof sheet; a matte paper will accept pencils or pens, but glossy paper can be written on with a white or black grease pencil or wax crayon. A chloride paper, such as AZO, is more than adequate for contact printing. The paper should be slightly larger than the area of the negatives to be proofed. If the negatives have not been cut, cut them to fit in the printer or printing frame but *no more than is necessary*. Place the negatives against the glass in the frame or printer with the emulsion side away from the glass, arranging them so that they will all be covered by the paper.

3. Turn off the general illumination. Allow a few moments for your eyes to adjust to the illumination of the safelight. You are now ready to begin printing.
4. Remove a sheet of paper from its package and *close the package before proceeding*. If the paper is considerably larger than the area to be printed you may wish to cut the paper to size.
5. Place the paper over the negatives in the printer or frame with the emulsion side of the paper in absolute and uniform contact with the emulsion side of the negatives. (You can determine the emulsion side of the paper by touch.) Press the back of the printing frame in place or close the door of the printer.
6. Expose the paper for fifteen seconds. This may be done by turning on the contact printer and switching off after exposure time or, if the printer is connected to a timer, setting the timer for fifteen seconds. For printing with a frame, the general illumination of the darkroom may be turned on or the light from the enlarger may be used.
Because papers vary in speed, an exposure of more or less than fifteen seconds may be necessary. Whether more or less time is needed will be determined after the print has been developed.
7. When the exposure has been made, remove the paper from the printer or frame.
8. Immerse the paper, emulsion side down, into the developer. This is best accomplished by sliding the paper rapidly into the solution and pushing it under the surface. (Kodak Dektol is used for the routine development of prints. It should be diluted one part developer to two parts water.) After the initial immersion, grasp one edge of the sheet lightly, lift it out of the solution, and turn it over. Replace the print, emulsion side *up*, on the surface of the solution, push it under the surface again and leave it under during the remaining developing time. The average developing time for contact prints is 60 seconds, but actual developing time ranges from 45 to 120 seconds.
The print must be immersed rapidly and evenly to prevent the formation of air bubbles on its emulsion surface and to insure that all of the emulsion is wet with developer

Shaded areas indicate that the procedure is to be done under safelight.

in the shortest possible time. Agitation for the remaining developing time should be constant. Stir the solution gently, either by rocking the tray or by stirring slowly with print tongs.

The image will form slowly over the surface of the paper. Because the proof sheet is made without any masking of the negatives, large areas of the paper will have been exposed completely. These areas will become black and will be visible before the images of the negatives. Although it is difficult, at first, to judge tones under the illumination of only a safelight, these completely exposed areas may be used to help judge whether the print is fully developed. When positive images from the negatives are fully visible and the unmasked areas are completely black, the print is fully developed. Over-development will cause darkening of the lighter areas of the print and should therefore be avoided.

9. Lift the print out of the developer, drain it briefly, and place it in stop bath (Kodak Indicator Stop Bath is best) for a minimum of 10 seconds or in a plain water rinse for 30 seconds. Lift the print and drain it briefly.

10. Place the print, emulsion side up, in the fixing bath (Kodak Rapid Fixer or Kodak Ektaflo) and, while moving it around for a few seconds, examine it for any faults which might cause the print to be discarded. When the inspection is completed, place the print emulsion side down in the fixing bath for 10 to 20 minutes.

Some papers may have a tendency to float in the fixing bath. If they float, they should be pushed into the solution and watched carefully. Be sure, also, that no air bubbles have formed on the underside of an immersed print. If a print is exposed to the air during fixing it may become stained.

11. When the print has been thoroughly fixed, the residual chemicals that remain in the emulsion and base of the photographic paper must be washed away.

Wash the print in a quantity of circulating fresh water (60° to 75°F) for 30 to 45 minutes (one hour for double weight paper). A certain amount of soaking is necessary in the wash; the water must not circulate too quickly. Prints must not be washed too long. Extended washing will cause softening of emulsion, dimensional changes in the paper, and loss of water resistance in RC papers.

12. When washing is complete the print may be dried by any convenient means. Because proof sheets will not be used for presentation, it is not necessary to take elaborate steps in drying — placing the print in a blotter roll will suffice.

When the proof sheet is dry, the results of camera work may be inspected and negatives selected for enlarging. Negative quality should be noted. You may decide from the evidence on the proof sheet that corrections are needed for a given negative. The needed corrections can be remembered, jotted on a tablet of paper, or written on the proof sheet itself.

Enlarging differs from contact printing only in the way the exposure is made, the type of paper to be used, and developing time. All other processes are similar.

THE ENLARGER

The enlarger is essentially a camera in reverse; it projects rather than receives an image. Every enlarger has: a lamp house with a light source and a reflector; piece of diffusing glass or set of lenses for obtaining even illumination over the negative; a negative carrier or holder; a lens with diaphragm; and a device for focusing the lens. All these components are suspended above a printing easel in such a way that the planes of the negative, the lens, and the easel are parallel and the distances between these planes may be changed.

The distances between these planes determines image size; the greater distance between the planes, the larger the image. Changes in negative to-lens distance are smaller but proportionate to changes in lens-to-easel distance.

The light source for an enlarger is usually an opal incandescent lamp which is located within a lamp house which is constructed with a reflector that directs light down toward the negative carrier. The light-tight lamp house is ventilated to prevent ex-

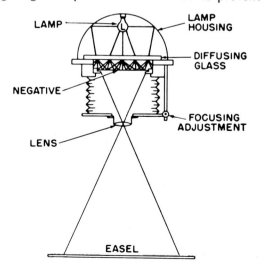

Figure 3 — Diffusing Enlarger

cessive heat from the light source which can ruin both negative and lens.

Enlargers are divided into two classes according to the methods by which they distribute light over the negative. The first of these, the *diffusion enlarger*, has a set of diffusing glasses (usually ground or optical glass) between the lamp and the negative carrier to spread the light evenly over the entire surface of the negative. The lamp housing is generally parabolic and the interior is a matte surface — either white or silver. The light source is an inside-frosted or opal incandescent lamp (some diffusion type enlargers use fluorescent tubes) which is located so that the light is reflected diffusely down toward the negative and lens. This gives soft, even illumination and tends to minimize negative flaws (such as abrasion marks and surface scratches) and grain.

The diffusion enlarger does not render an image as contrasty as a condenser enlarger because the

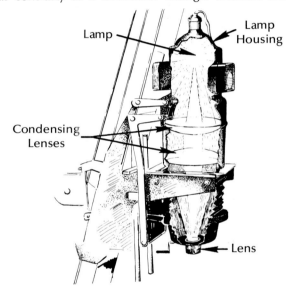

Figure 4 — Condenser enlarger

diffused light is softer than the direct rays formed by the condensing lenses. The difference in contrast between the diffusion enlarger and the condenser type is approximately one grade; *i.e.*, prints made on No. 3 contrast paper with a diffusion enlarger are approximately the same as prints made from the same negative on No. 2 contrast paper with a condenser enlarger. Exposure times for the diffusion enlarger are generally longer than those for the condenser type enlargers, *due to the considerable loss of light caused by diffusion*. The diffusion enlarger is especially suitable for portraiture and other printing involving negatives 4 × 5 inches and larger.

The second class of enlarger, the *condenser enlarger*, has a set of condensing lenses to project the

light rays evenly from an opal incandescent lamp through the negative. The condenser is a pair of plano-convex condensing lenses mounted as a unit with their convex surfaces opposed. The common condenser types of enlargers used are Simmons

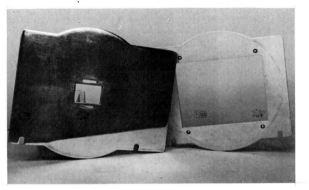

Figure 5 — Dustless negative carriers

Bros. Omega D-2, and Simmons Bros. Model Automega D-3. The enlarger is supplied with an f/4.5, 2-inch focal length lens; and f/4.5, 3½ inch focal length lens; and f/4.5, 5¼ inch focal length lens; and the necessary condenser lenses set for use with each lens. The condenser lenses are mounted in a housing with a separator between them. The condenser housing has three bayonet type notches to permit assembly to the lamp house, where it is secured with knurled locking screws. The condenser type enlarger produces a sharp brilliant image with more contrast than can be obtained with the same negative in a diffusion enlarger.

Where accurate reproduction of detail is important, as it is in police work, the condenser enlarger is preferable to the diffusion enlarger.

The negative carrier may be of two types — dustless or glass sandwich. The dustless carrier consists of two shaped and metal sheets, or plates, with die-

Figure 6 — Easel

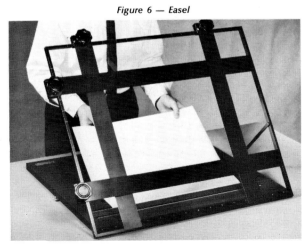

cut openings in the center. The negative is placed between these plates and positioned in the opening. When the hinged plates are closed, they clamp the edges of the negative and hold it in position. If properly designed, they function excellently for negatives 4 × 5 inches and smaller. The glass sandwich carrier is simply two sheets of glass in a wood or metal frame, between which the negative is placed. They are necessary for negatives larger than 4 × 5 inches, because large negatives have a tendency to sag in the center of dustless carriers. One disadvantage of glass sandwich carriers is that any dust or lint on them becomes part of the projected image.

Lenses for projection printing should be anastigmats with an angle of field large enough to cover the negative. No shutter is necessary because the exposures are usually measured in seconds. On enlargers using tungsten lamps, the exposure is made by turning the light on and off. With fluorescent tubes, however, the light should remain on and the exposure be made by uncovering and covering the lens. Practically all enlargers are equipped with a mounted ruby safety filter which can be swung under the lens for this purpose.

There are many types of easels, each serving the same basic purpose — holding the printing paper in a flat plane. Most easels have adjustable masking strips to regulate the borders of the prints. Those equipped with masks usually have an adjustable guide for placing the paper evenly under the masking strips. The adjustable guides and masks will enclose almost any size rectangle from 3 to 24 inches.

In order to obtain changes in the scale of the projected image, it is necessary to alter the conjugate distances in a manner similar to that in cameras. To enlarge a negative to a greater degree, the lens-to-easel distance must be increased and the negative-to-lens distance must be decreased. Some enlargers, called autofocus, and so designed and constructed that when the lens-to-easel distance is altered the negative-to-lens distance is automatically adjusted and the image is always in focus. These printers operate conveniently for enlargements, but an auxiliary optical system must be attached to reduce the image size. An attachment of this type is not as convenient to use as the manual-variable-focus models, which can produce both reduced and enlarged images with the same optical system. The majority of projection printing requires enlargement, and for this work autofocus models are satisfactory.

Although it is theoretically possible to make reduction to any desired size, the bellows on most enlargers cannot be extended far enough to make reduced projections smaller than 1:1. Smaller reduction may be accomplished by substituting a lens of shorter focal length, but a more satisfactory method is to use a reducing attachment. This attachment, available as auxiliary equipment on some enlargers, consists of a section of bellows to which is attached a short focal length lens. The regular enlarger lens is not used in conjunction with a reducing attachment.

MAKING AN ENLARGEMENT

To make an enlargement:
1. Select a negative. If you have made a proof sheet, you can check negative quality from the print, note any flaws, and choose the negative by the number which appears in the frame of the film.
2. Insert the negative in the appropriate size negative carrier so the emulsion side is down. With some negative carriers it will be necessary to cut the negatives apart. Avoid this if possible. Place the negative carrier in the enlarger so that the emulsion side faces the lens; the shiny side faces the lamp house. Be sure that the carrier is seated properly.
3. Set the paper corner guide and the masking device on the easel to form the border width and length for the print size needed. Place a sheet of white paper in the printing position to aid in composing and focusing the image.
4. Check that the darkroom is fully prepared. Solutions should be in their trays, the desired paper should be ready beside the easel, and the safelight (O or OA) should be turned on. Turn off the general illumination.
5. Turn the enlarger lamp on, open the lens to its maximum aperture, and move the easel around until the desired portion of the image is on the mashed opening. Raise or lower the enlarger unit on the standard so that the image is enlarged or reduced according to the desired result. When enlarging small negatives, check to see that the grain will not yield an unpleasant image. With each change of lens-to-easel distance it will be necessary to re-focus.

The image will be easier to compose if it is right side up from your point of view. If it is upside down, either rotate the negative carrier in its housing or remove it and reposition the *negative*.

Most printing papers are rectangular; determine whether to use a vertical or horizontal format. In many cases, the manner in which the scene is composed on the negative will determine this; however, when the choice of vertical or horizontal images seems to be arbitrary, use a horizontal format.

You are not bound to the overall composition of the negative image. Prints of excellent composition have been produced from badly composed negatives. Try to correct any errors of image composition in the negative. Straighten the horizon; if possible, try to prevent it from cutting the image on the print into two equal sections. If the horizon is not visible, make sure that vertical objects are parallel with the side of the masked area on the easel. If the space around the subject is not pleasing, try to remedy the error. Distortion of perspective can be reduced by making corrections while arranging the easel and focusing.

the strip should be close to normal in appearance.

Ten to twenty seconds of exposure will yield an adequate print — more than twenty seconds may cause damage to the negative from the heat of the lamp; less than ten seconds will allow less margin of time for printing errors. Thus, if the best exposure on the test strip is 2–8 seconds, the lens aperture on the enlarger must be stopped down. If 32 seconds of exposure yielded a good print, the aperture should be stopped up.

8. Turn off the general illumination, select a sheet of paper of desired size, and expose it for 12–15 seconds. Develop, rinse, and fix as

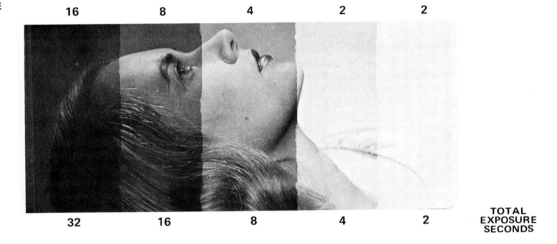

| EXPOSURE SECONDS | 16 | 8 | 4 | 2 | 2 |

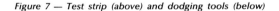

| 32 | 16 | 8 | 4 | 2 | TOTAL EXPOSURE SECONDS |

Figure 7 — Test strip (above) and dodging tools (below)

6. Close the aperture of the lens to f/8 for a dense negative or f/11 for a thin negative and be sure that the lens is clean. Switch off the enlarger lamp.

7. Select a sheet of paper for printing, cut it lengthwise into several strips about one inch wide, and place one of these strips, emulsion side up, in the easel. This is the *test strip*.
Cover four-fifths of the strip with a sheet of opaque paper and expose the uncovered fifth for 16 seconds. Uncover another fifth and expose for one half the time (in this case 8 seconds) and continue to uncover portions of the strip and half the exposure until the entire strip is exposed. This produces a series of exposures in which each succeeding section of the strip has received *half* the exposure of the preceding section — in this case 32, 16, 8, 4, and 2 seconds. Develop and rinse the strip as for a contact print. Fix the strip for two minutes, rinse it, and inspect it under general illumination. At least one of the exposures on

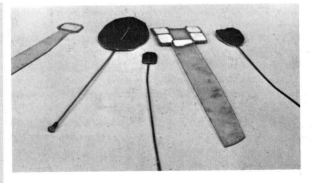

Shaded areas indicate that the procedure is to be done under safelight.

before. Inspect the print under general illumination. The exposure should be approximately correct. Check for contrast; a good print usually has a white somewhere in a highlight area, a black in the deepest shadow, and a well-modulated scale of grays between these two tonal extremes. If in doubt about proper contrast, make additional prints on two other grades of paper. Inspect the group and decide which print has the most pleasing or realistic contrast. This method also reveals how easy it is for a mediocre print to appear acceptable until a direct comparison is made with the same image correctly exposed on the proper contrast paper grade. If there are distracting areas which are too light or dark they can be darkened or lightened by additional exposure control in successive prints.

It is usually necessary to lighten or darken some parts of most prints to produce a correctly exposed image.

9. Areas which appear too dark in the print may be lightened by creating a shadow, thus exposing the too-dark areas for less time than the overall exposure. This is called *dodging* and is accomplished by placing an opaque card or dodging tool between the lens and the dark area of the image for short durations during the exposure.

Accurate dodging can be done with the hands or variously shaped cards cut from black paper and used when needed. A favorite tool for dodging small areas is a card of suitable size and shape pinned to one end of a stiff wire handle.

The size of the area being dodged is controlled by the size of the card or dodging tool and its distance from the image. Dodging should be done for only part of the exposure. The card or tool must be moved up and down slowly and constantly to prevent a sharp line between the dodged area and other parts of the image.

10. Areas which appear too light in the print may be darkened by exposing them for a longer period than the overall exposure. Called *burning-in*, this process is basically the opposite of dodging. After the normal overall printing exposure has been made, switch off

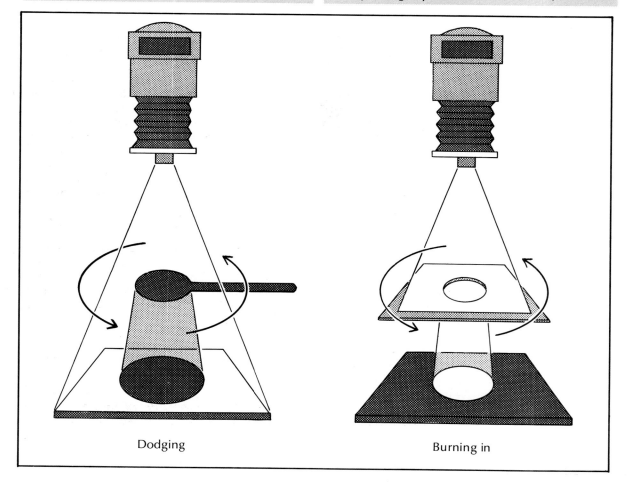

Dodging   Burning in

the enlarger. Place between the lens and the easel a piece of opaque paper with a hole in the center that is smaller than but approximately the same shape as the area to be burned-in, switch the enlarger back on and expose the too-light area through the hole for an additional five seconds, moving the paper slowly but constantly to prevent a sharp outline of the hole.

When dodging and burning-in, time the amounts of exposure for every step of the printing procedure. This is the only manner in which the procedure can be controlled well enough to be duplicated for additional prints, or changes made in any portion of the image as needed. For example, the entire print may be exposed for 5 seconds, while the spot to be lightened is dodged, and the image exposed for another 5 seconds. Then the portion needing additional exposure may be burned-in through the hole in a card for 5 seconds. This requires a total exposure time of 15 seconds, which is as long as should be tolerated without changing the lens stop.

Experience shows that exposures of much less than 10 seconds are not easily made because of the difficulty in making the dodging or burning-in begin properly. If the test proves correct, duplicates can be made with no trouble. If not, any desired changes can be made in the corrective steps taken, and good results may be expected after a few test prints.

11. After all the printing data has been obtained, make all prints needed from the negative.

12. Develop each final print as for a contact print. The developing range for enlarging papers is generally from 60 to 180 seconds with 90 seconds recommended. For some papers when using Dektol, a dilution of 1:3 is sometimes advisable. The directions packaged with the paper may indicate a 1:3 dilution; if so, a development time of 1½ to 3 minutes is necessary. One-half ounce (15 cc.) of potassium bromide, diluted 10 percent, should be added for each 32 ounces of stock Dektol to increase the restraining action of a diluted developer. This may cause a greenish tone, but the tone will improve with a longer developing time.

13. Rinse as with a contact print. *Kodak Indicator Stop Bath* is an excellent acid stop for papers. If the excess developer is drained off prints before they are placed in the stop bath, 32 ounces of Indicator Stop Bath will properly stop development and give adequate protection for approximately twenty-five 8 × 10 prints. When Indicator Stop Bath is exhausted it becomes purple and must be discarded.

14. Fix as for contact prints with Kodak Fixer or Kodak Ektaflo Fixer. A gallon of either fixes one hundred or more 8 × 10 prints when an acid stop rinse bath is used. Fix for no longer than 20 minutes and no shorter than 10 minutes. Overfixation tends to cause thinning or bleaching of the photographic image; inadequate fixing leaves prints vulnerable to stains and early deterioration.

The use of twin fixing baths is recommended for thorough fixation when many prints are processed daily. Begin the twin fixing cycle with two fresh trays of fixer. After fixing 200 prints, discard the first bath and prepare a new bath, rotating the baths. Only 3–5 minutes of fixing is required in each of the twin baths, thus reducing total fixing time from 10–20 minutes to 6–10 minutes. Also, a 30 to 60 percent savings in chemicals is possible because overall contamination of the bath is retarded by splitting the bath. At the end of five cycles, discard all used fixing solution, wash both trays, and begin a new cycle.

15. Wash the print. Although most prints are washed in mechanical washers, small groups may be washed by successive changes of water in a tray. Two trays having deep sides should be used. The size of the trays is determined by the size and number of prints to be washed. Both trays should be filled almost completely with water and all the prints placed emulsion side up in one tray. The prints should be separated, agitated, and then transferred one at a time to the other tray. The first tray is then emptied, refilled with fresh water, and the procedure repeated until the wash is completed. When using the tray method, the prints should be agitated 2 or 3 times in each change of water and the water changed at 5 minute intervals until about 6 changes have been given for single-weight prints. Double-weight prints in a tray involves the use of a tray siphon. The siphon directs fresh water into the top of the tray and at the same time it removes the chemically contaminated water from the bottom of the tray. The tray-siphon method of washing prints is quite effective.

16. When washing is complete, the prints may be

Shaded areas indicate that the procedure is to be done under safelight.

dried by any convenient means, depending upon the type of paper and the available means for drying. Prints may be dried in blotter rolls, on ferrotype plates, and on mechanical apron or conveyor belt dryers. When using glossy surface papers, the photographs do not have a pleasing appearance unless they are dried in close contact with a high polished surface. The equipment for drying glossy prints is usually a metal plate or drum with a chromium-plated surface.

Ferrotyping is a process for producing high gloss on prints. Only prints on paper having a glossy surface can be ferrotyped. The principle of ferrotyping involves placing the emulsion side of a wet print (under pressure) into close contact with a smooth surface; the gelatin of the emulsion is compressed in drying, causing an increase in the gloss of the print. A ferrotype plate, sometimes called a ferrotype tin, is made of metal and has a highly polished chromium-plated surface. These plates should be handled with extreme care to avoid scratches. Whenever ferrotype plates appear dirty, they should be washed in warm water with a mild soap. If the plates are neglected, the dried prints stick firmly, and prolonged soaking in water is necessary to remove them.

Lay the prints emulsion side down on the polished surface. Lay a blotter over the print and use a print roller to secure complete contact between the print and the plate. The emulsion must be in perfect contact to produce a uniform glossy surface. The plate is then placed on a small drying unit, one plate on each side, the canvas pulled over the plates and secured by notches, and dried by electrical heat.

17. As soon as the prints are dried, examine them closely for defects or other unsatisfactory qualities. If any of the prints need trimming to even the borders or remove frayed edges, it should be done at this time. Prints are trimmed to obtain clean cut edges and to make width of borders uniform and reduce prints to desired size. Small prints are trimmed to make the width of the white margins equal on all sides. The margins may vary in width from ⅛ to ¼ inch, according to the size of the print. For example, a ½ inch border of an 8 × 10 inch print may be trimmed to ¼ inch. In the case of large prints, the borders may be uneven for artistic effect.

18. The appearance of photographic print is enhanced when the print is properly spaced on a mount of proper color, texture, and size. Mounting makes the photograph more permanent only when the material used for the mount is chemically pure and the adhesive is one which does not, in time, stain the mount or print. Cardboard is the material most often used for mounts. The mount should be large enough to balance and to appear as amply supporting the photograph. If the mount is too small, the impression of skimpiness is given, if too large, it belittles the print and makes it appear lost.

While no definite rules can be given, a 5 × 7 inch print may be placed on a mount 8 × 10 inches in size. This gives a 1½ inch border. An 8 × 10 print should have not less than a 1½ inch border, and usually appears better if mounted with a 2-inch border.

The adhesive generally used for mounting is dry mounting tissue, which is in the form of sheets. It is manufactured to have a heat-sensitive adhesive. When heat is applied to the tissue, it becomes tacky and, when cooled, it is an excellent and permanent adhesive. A sheet of tissue is tacked to the back of the print by means of a regular laundry iron. The print and tissue are then trimmed and tacked in position on the mount and placed in a heated dry mounting press — or a regular laundry iron may be used. The iron should be set for the "silk" temperature and then two fingerprint cards, or the equivalent thickness of cardboard, placed over the photograph, before ironing.

The dampness of mounts or prints is frequently responsible for failures in dry mounting. If the prints are damp, the gelatin melts from the heat of the press and the emulsion becomes sticky. If the mount is damp, the heat of the press causes it to warp.

PRINTING DEFECTS AND CORRECTION

Abrasions or streaks

● *Appearance*: The surface of the paper is abraded or scratched and results in fine dark lines on the surface of the print, especially with glossy paper.

● *Cause*: The cause is friction or rubbing on the surface of the paper.

● *Prevention*: Store paper boxes on their edges. Handle with care. Make sure that processing solutions are free from grit or undissolved particles.

● *Appearance*: Parts of the print that are poorly defined have been blurred, as if out of focus, though the negative is sharp.

● *Cause*: Buckling of the paper in the contact printer.

● *Prevention*: Check the contact pad in the printer.

Bad definition in parts of print

● *Appearance*: The appearance is a completely blurred print from a sharp negative.

● *Cause*: This may be due in contact prints to printing from the wrong side of the negative. This defect in enlargements may be due to careless focusing or, more often, to vibration of the enlarger.

● *Prevention*: Emulsion side of paper must always be in contact with the emulsion side of the negative in contact printing. The enlarger should be firmly braced against vibration.

Bad definition over entire print

● *Appearance*: A contrasty print is one in which all the tones are too harsh. The print has excessive contrast, and is lacking in detail in the highlights and shadows.

● *Cause*: This is caused by using the improper grade of printing paper for the range of densities in the negative.

● *Remedy*: The remedy is to use a softer or less contrasty paper.

Contrasty prints

● *Appearance*: A flat print is one in which all the tones are as one. The print lacks contrast, the dark areas are too light and the light areas are too dark.

● *Cause*: This is caused by using the improper grade of printing paper for the range of densities in the negative.

● *Remedy*: The remedy is to use a higher or greater contrast paper.

Flat prints

● *Appearance:* A muddy print is one in which the tones have a gray mottled appearance.

● *Cause:* Prints which are overexposed and underdeveloped usually have this muddy appearance. The developer does not have a chance to complete its work, so the result is a flat, muddy print.

● *Remedy:* To remedy this appearance, expose the paper for the proper time and develop it for the proper time, according to the time recommended for the paper and developer being used.

Muddy prints

● *Cause*: Round dark spots on prints are due to air bells in the fixing bath. Development has proceeded in those spots after being stopped on other parts of the print.

● *Prevention*: Use shortstop between development and fixing. Agitate thoroughly in fixing bath.

Round dark spots

● *Cause*: These spots are caused by air bells in washing that prevent the removal of hypo from these spots.

● *Prevention*: Thorough washing with constant agitation.

Round discolored spots

● *Cause*: Round white spots are due to air bells which prevented the developer from acting on parts of the paper.

● *Prevention*: Proper agitation while in the developer will prevent this.

Round white spots

● *Cause*: Brown spots are caused by particles of rust from the wash water, iron washing tanks or ferrotype tins or particles of chemical dust.

Small, well defined brown spots

● *Prevention*: A water filter should be used where much rust is present. Rusty tanks should be discarded or painted.

Stained prints

● *Appearance*: Stains that appear on a print usually have a brownish smudged look.

● *Cause*: Those stains that are due to printing or developing are usually caused by old, brown, or oxidized developer. Holding a print up out of the developer too long for inspection causes a yellowish or brownish stain, due to the oxidation of the developer clinging to the print while it is held in the air.

● *Remedy*: The remedy for this is to use fresh developer at all times, do not hold the print up for inspection in the air any longer than absolutely necessary, and be sure that the print is quickly and completely immersed in the developer at all times.

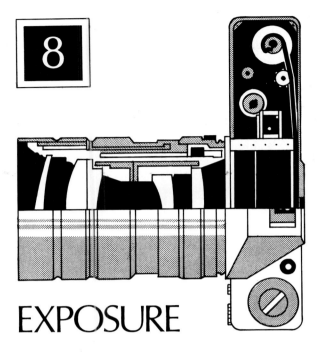

EXPOSURE

tions. For basic exposure, he need concern himself with only two settings: aperture and shutter speed. Aperture controls the *intensity* of light that is let inside the camera and shutter speed controls the *time* which it spends inside the camera. A formula for setting the adjustable camera might look like this: INTENSITY × TIME = EXPOSURE.

EXPOSURE

Exposure is the amount of light that you allow to reach the film by controlling the variables of aperture and shutter speed. Light meters quickly, accurately, and conveniently measure light in almost any photographic situation and help you to determine the appropriate aperture and shutter speed combination. The development of light meters and faster, more sensitive films makes it possible for contemporary police photographers to use illumination from any direction — back, side, diffused through the atmosphere, or front. Light can also be used to produce many different aesthetic effects.

Most black-and-white films have some exposure latitude built into them, but other films, such as color slide film, have practically none, making careful exposure more critical. Even the best film can register only some of the many different tones your eyes can see. Some tones, and therefore some detail, are lost in the photographs. Thus in every situation you have to choose between tones to emphasize and tones to neglect.

Accurate measurement of light with a light meter tells you how to set the aperture and shutter to get both the best detail the film can register and the aesthetic effect you want.

Many modern cameras, especially the 35mm cameras, have built-in light meters, but the police officer will find out that he has to use a larger format than the 35mm camera, and anything larger than a 35mm format does not have the automatic built-in light meters. The police officer, if he is to become a professional, must act like a professional photographer and learn how to use a light meter so he can get photographs which will be a credit to him when he appears in a court room. The police officer will see it is to his advantage to use a handheld meter because of its greater accuracy and versatility.

There is an old photographer's maxim: "Expose for the shadows and develop for the highlights." That is, if you must choose between over and under exposure, it is better to overexpose to bring out the detail of the shadow areas than to underexpose, especially since most film has higher tolerance for overexposure than for underexposure. It may be possible to correct for some degree of overexposure in printing the negative.

As was shown in Chapter 2, passable photographs can be made with a simple box camera. But the rigors of police photography demand that the photographer make pictures in all conditions of light. He must make photographs of subjects which are far away or objects that are no more than a few inches from the camera lens. In order to do so, he must control the light which enters his camera.

The adjustable camera was designed so that the photographer could control the light which he records on film. The focusable lens allows him to focus sharply on objects three feet away or at infinity if he wishes. The adjustable shutter permits him to let light in for as little as 1/1000 of a second or for many minutes.

In addition to adjusting the focus and the shutter, the photographer can control the amount of light that enters the camera at any given moment. He can, by changing the *aperture*, or diameter of the opening, let in as little light as a pinhole or as much as the diameter of the lens will allow. The mechanical device which allows the photographer to adjust the aperture is called a *diaphragm*. Usually, the diaphragm is an integral part of the lens system. On cameras which have detachable lenses, the diaphragms are a part of each lens and not a part of the camera itself.

Letting just enough light into the camera to expose the film is called *exposure*. With the simple camera, the photographer decides whether there is enough light for an exposure. If there is not, he does not take a picture or he takes a picture with flash. But the adjustable camera allows the photographer to photograph under many different condi-

THE "F" SYSTEM

There have been at least a half dozen systems to mark the opening of the diaphragm, but most cameras use the "f" system. The diaphragm opening, which is called a stop, is usually marked in numbers on the exterior of the lens.

The "f" system is a relationship between the diameter of the lens opening, or aperture, and the focal length of the lens. The "f" indicates the speed of the lens or, in other words, the amount of light the lens lets through in proportion to its focal length. Some years ago the photographer more or less guessed at the size of the lens opening and then guessed at the exposure that would be required. In 1881, some members of the Royal Photographic Society of Great Britain worked out a system of apertures based on a sequence of ratios

Inexpensive box cameras were usually equipped with a single metal plate which is attached to a spring. When a lever is pushed the spring rotates the plate allowing the light to enter for about 1/50 of a second. These mechanical devices, which are used to control the amount of time the light is allowed to pass, are called *shutters*.

Many of the better cameras have a very complicated device which allows exposure times of from one second to 1/4000 second. This is indeed a wide range. In addition, they have provision for time and strobe exposures. Some of the modern 35mm cameras have still another feature which delays the opening of the shutter for several seconds, and enables the person to take his own picture. This type of shutter which is usually in the lens is called a compur shutter or a leaf shutter.

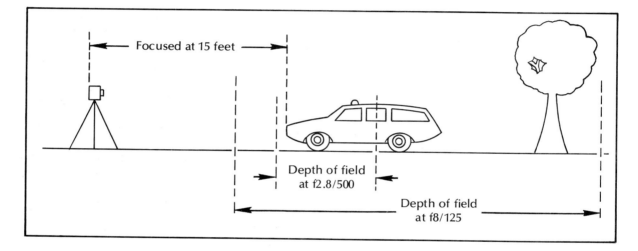

so that aperture and exposure time could be controlled scientifically. They began with a unit of *one* as an aperture of f/4. The ratio worked out gave each succeeding stop an area of just one-half (½) of the previous one. Each numerical stop, as the stops become smaller, lets in just half as much light as the preceding one.

The "f" system is used in most of the world today. The following table shows the common f/stops in use today, the fraction of the focal length which each represents, and the ratio of exposures.

f-	1.4	2.8	4	5.6	8	11	16	22	32	45	64
Fraction of Focal Length	$\frac{1}{1.4}$	$\frac{1}{2.8}$	$\frac{1}{4}$	$\frac{1}{5.6}$	$\frac{1}{8}$	$\frac{1}{11}$	$\frac{1}{16}$	$\frac{1}{22}$	$\frac{1}{32}$	$\frac{1}{45}$	$\frac{1}{64}$
Exposure Ratio	$\frac{1}{4}$	$\frac{1}{2}$	1	2	4	8	16	32	64	128	256

METHODS OF REGULATING TIME

The oldest method of controlling the amount of time was to have a light-tight cap on the lens which was removed by hand, and replaced when sufficient time had elapsed.

CONTROLLING INTENSITY

The diaphragm of a camera or camera lens is graduated into measurements of the intensity of the light which it will let pass through the lens. The measurements, called *f-stops*, are standardized and are usually printed or engraved on the lens barrel as follows: 1.2, 2, 2.8, 4, 5.6, 8, 11, 16, 22, 32. Confusingly, an f-stop with a larger number, such as f/16, lets in less light than one of a smaller number, such as f/5.6.

Each f/number indicates that the diaphragm is allowing twice the light that the next higher number would let pass through the lens into the camera and half the light that the next smaller number would let pass. That is, f/11 is twice as bright as f/16, but only half as bright as f/8. While he is learning about aperture, the photographer would do well to think of f/numbers as fractions; just as ¼ is smaller than ½, but larger than ⅛, so is f/4 larger than f/5.6 but smaller than f/2.8. F/1, then, lets in 1,024 times as much light as f/32!

CONTROLLING TIME

The shutter on an adjustable camera can be set so that, once it is released, it will stay open indefinitely or for as little as 1/1000th of a second. In between these extremes are various fractions of a second, for example: 1/15th of a second, 1/30th, 1/60th, 1/125th, and 1/250th of a second.

On the camera setting, these fractions are engraved or printed as whole numbers: 15, 30, 60, 125, and 250, respectively. The fractions of a second may vary from camera to camera; some cameras are marked 25, 50, 100, 200, indicating that shutter speeds of 1/25th, 1/50th, 1/100th and 1/200th are available to the photographer. Also, short shutter speeds of 1/500th and 1/1000th of a second are not available on all cameras. The letter B on a shutter setting means *bulb exposure*; with this setting the photographer may open the shutter and hold it open indefinitely. The letter T means *time exposure*; the photographer can open the shutter on a time setting and walk away from the camera. When he returns and trips the shutter again, it will close.

COMBINING CONTROL OF INTENSITY AND TIME

The aperture and shutter speed work together to provide the film with an accurate amount of light. Which shutter speed and aperture the photographer chooses depends upon (1) the amount of available light and (2) the depth of field required by the subject matter of the photograph. Depth of field will be discussed in a section below.

Films respond to light quickly or slowly, depending upon their ASA (see Chapter 4). A film that reacts quickly to light, such as Tri-X, will require far less light for a good exposure than will a relatively slow film, such as Panatomic-X. Therefore, the photographer will keep his aperture smaller and his exposure shorter for Tri-X than he will for Panatomic-X in the same light. He must know the speed of the film he is using and become familiar with the properties of the film in relation to various light sources.

When shooting outdoors in daylight, the photographer can divide the intensity of light into five categories: bright sunlight, hazy sunlight, cloudy bright, cloudy dull, and cloudy dark. If he sets his aperture at f/11, a different shutter speed will be required for each category of light. Cloudy dark will require the longest exposure, and bright sunlight will require a short exposure. Conversely, if he shoots only at 1/125th of a second, he must adjust the aperture for variations of light intensity.

In practice, however, the photographer must choose the best possible combination of aperture and shutter speed for the light conditions and the subject matter. A photograph of a moving object always requires a fast shutter speed in order to capture the object. The photographer who wishes to photograph a moving car will shoot at 1/250th or 1/500th of a second and adjust the aperture according to the light available. When photographing still objects, though, depth of field becomes the most important consideration in choosing exposure.

DEPTH OF FIELD

The art photographer often takes pictures in which one object, a model or a flower for instance, is in sharp focus while the foreground and background are a blur. The effect is pleasant and suggests a painting. But the police photographer is not concerned with art; he must present facts and to do so, details must be clearly represented. The distance from the closest clear object in a photograph to the farthest clear object is called the *depth of field* and the police photographer must always strive to obtain the greatest depth of field possible in each of his photographs.

Fortunately, depth of field increases as the lens aperture decreases; to get greater depth of field, the photographer *stops down*, or uses a smaller f-stop. Thus, for most police photography, the photographer will use the smallest possible aperture and adjust his shutter speed accordingly. It is no exaggeration to say that the smaller the aperture is, the better the picture will be.

The trick of using small apertures for greater depth of field does have its limitations. When the photographer focuses on an object close to the camera, his depth of field will be less than for objects farther away so he must focus more accurately on nearby objects than for distant objects. Also, as was the case of the speeding car in the preceding section, or for any fast moving object, a fast shutter speed will be required and a small aperture may therefore be impossible. The photographer must then be extremely careful to focus accurately on the moving object.

MORE ABOUT FOCUS

Incorrect exposure, resulting in imperfect negatives, can be corrected in the darkroom. Faulty focusing cannot. Improperly focused photographs seldom appear in the courtroom — they end up in File G — the garbage can.

The most important thing a photographer can do is to focus correctly on his subject before snapping the shutter. Single or twin lens reflex cameras (see Chapter 3) are easily focused, but cameras with separate viewfinders require more attention. Usually the photographer must estimate the distance between the camera and his subject and set his lens accordingly.

When focusing, it is well to remember that *the closer a subject is to the camera, the farther the lens must be from the film*. This is more easily seen with a bellows type camera which becomes elongated when the lens is focused on a nearby object, but compact if focused on an object far away. Most 35mm cameras have screw-type lenses which are focused by turning the lens as one would a screw. The lens moves closer to or farther from the film when it is turned, but the change of distance is not as obvious as it is with a bellows camera.

Many police photographs are taken at night, making focusing difficult. Whenever the photographer cannot focus on his subject accurately, he should set the focus at infinity and use the smallest possible aperture (thus insuring depth of field), and hope for the best.

PHOTOGRAPHY OF MOVING OBJECTS

When a subject is in motion during exposure, its image on the film moves. Even when the duration of exposure is only 1/1000 of a second, the image moves a small fraction of an inch during this time. However, the movement at 1/1000 is only 1/10 as far as it is at 1/100 of a second.

The photographer must determine just how much image movement can be tolerated before it becomes objectionable; then he must regulate the shutter speed accordingly. It is necessary to visualize the use to which the negative is to be put in order to determine what constitutes an "objectionable" blurring of the image. A negative which is to be contact printed will permit considerably more blurring than one which is to be enlarged many times. Also, if a print is likely to be examined through a magnifying glass, the image must be sharper than would be necessary when the print is viewed from a distance.

Unusual circumstances may make it impossible to obtain great degrees of sharpness of a moving object. In such cases, it will be necessary to decide whether it is more important to make a picture even though the subject is somewhat blurred than to leave it unphotographed. When it is imperative that a sharp image be obtained of a fast moving object it is possible to use the "follow through" method of keeping the camera constantly trained on the object and following it until after the exposure is made, rather like shooting a duck. Of course, this method will completely blur the background, but will provide a sharp image of the object itself, even at relatively slow shutter speeds.

Although it is not always possible to do so, the photographer will get better results if he can pick the direction of movement. An object moving toward or away from the camera will not be as blurred as an object crossing the camera.

A SIMPLE EXPOSURE METHOD FOR POLICE

The following system, called the F-16 System, has been used with astonishingly good results by Shaker Heights Police Department since 1956. Here is how it works:

1. Set the aperture at f/16. This will insure good depth of field.
2. Set the shutter at a speed closest to that of the ASA rating of the film being used; for example, the shutter speed when shooting with Tri-X will be 250 or 500 because Tri-X is rated at 400.
3. *Focus the lens.*
4. Corrections for under-exposure or over-exposure are made in the darkroom. No exposure meters or estimating is needed.

CORRECT EXPOSURE

The F-16 system works, but the professional police photographer should set his exposure accurately every time he shoots. This is best done with an exposure meter (see Chapter 9) which measures the amount of available light and indicates several combinations of aperture and shutter speed which could be used in that light. The photographer should learn to judge available light so he can set his exposure at combinations which he knows have worked well in the past.

AUTOMATIC CAMERAS

Automatic cameras are of two basic types: shutter priority and aperture priority. Cameras with *shutter priority* automatically set the aperture, but the photographer must select a shutter speed first. A photocell is activated on shutter priority cameras when the photographer pulls up slightly on the wind-up lever. A needle mechanism in the viewfinder will indicate whether or not there is enough light for the pre-selected shutter speed. If there is not, the photographer selects another speed and tries again.

Aperture priority models automatically set the shutter speed after the photographer has selected an aperture. Although this system gives the photographer far more control over depth of field, the mechanism is also far more complicated than the shutter priority mechanism and, if not maintained in optimum repair, may throw the camera off by one complete f/stop without any indication to the photographer.

BUILT-IN METERS

Many of the better 35mm cameras being made today come with built-in exposure metering which, simply and accurately, tell the photographer whether or not there is enough light for a good exposure with the combination of aperture and shutter speed which he has selected. A needle inside the viewfinder window indicates whether the shot will be underexposed, overexposed, or correct.

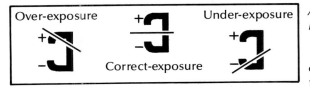

Figure 1 — Built-in meter

SUBJECT REFLECTANCE AND NEGATIVE DENSITY

Instead of one single density, nearly all negatives have a great many different densities, ranging from almost clear film to a very dense deposit of silver. Each different degree of density in the negative represents a different degree of reflectance from some part of the subject. The average scene is composed of many shades of gray from black and colors ranging from the faintest suggestion of a color to colors of great brilliance.

When a negative is made of any scene, it theoretically records all the tones or brightnesses as varying degrees of density. A print made from such a negative should represent the subject as seen by the eye, reproducing each shade or tone from the lightest to the darkest in the same relative degree of brightness.

While the eye observes a scene in its true colors, the photographic process usually records colors in various shades of gray from black to white. The portion of the scene which appears brightest to the eye should be reproduced as the lightest part of the print and the dullest part of the scene should appear darkest on the print. Whether or not the subject is faithfully reproduced depends on the recording of various subject brightnesses as varying densities in the negative in the same relative degree.

For the average outdoor scene (which consists of many degrees of brightness) we are not concerned with the exposure necessary to produce a particular density in any one part of the scene, but in the exposure for the scene as a whole to produce a general negative density. Those parts of the scene which appear brightest to the eye produce the greatest density in the negative and the darkest parts produce the least density.

If the scene appears average (having an equal distribution of light and dark reflecting surfaces), use the *basic exposure*. When there is an abundance of bright reflections in the scene (such as from a sandy beach), close the diaphragm at least one full f/stop. However, if a scene has a generally dark appearance because of numerous large areas of low reflectance, open the diaphragm one full f/stop.

A FORMULA FOR EXPOSURE WITH BELLOWS EXTENSION

The f/numbers engraved on a lens can be relied on to be sufficiently accurate to produce a satisfactory exposure as long as the lens is focused at or near infinity. It is only necessary to calculate the new effective lens speed when photographing nearby objects which are within a distance of eight focal lengths from the camera. Considering that in closeup photography this may mean as much as two whole f/stops and may reduce the image brightness by one-fourth, the film can be excessively underexposed.

On a 35mm camera, when using a bellows extension adapter or when the bellows is extended beyond one focal length, the new effective f/number can be determined by the following formula:

$$\text{Effective f/No.} = \frac{\text{Indicated f/No.} \times \text{Lens-to-film distance}}{\text{Focal length}}$$

For example, an 8-inch focal length lens is focused on a close object so that the lens-to-film distance is 16 inches. If the indicated stop is f/16, what is the effective f/number?

$$\text{Effective f/No.} = \frac{16 \times 16}{8} = \frac{16 \times \overset{2}{\cancel{16}}}{\cancel{8}}$$
$$= 16 \times 2 = 32 \text{ or } f/32$$

FILM LATITUDE

The human eye is extremely inaccurate in the process of determining exposure. It is such a remarkable mechanism, in automatically compensating for extremes in brightness range, that it has difficulty in recognizing the problems which are inherent to the film. The pupil of the eye opens or closes as necessary to compensate for extreme differences in brightness values. We can read a newspaper in bright sunlight or moonlight, even though there may be a measured difference in illumination of almost a million to one. Extensive training and experience enables the human eye to estimate roughly both the intensity of light and the range of brightness of a scene. This is inadequate, however, to achieve the accuracy necessary to consistently expose film correctly. An exposure meter is far more accurate than the human eye for the purpose

proximate. Each policeman may have his own personal concept of how the subject can best be reproduced and this may vary somewhat from the opinion of another.

Exposure meters may vary slightly in their calibration, lenses may vary considerably in the percent-

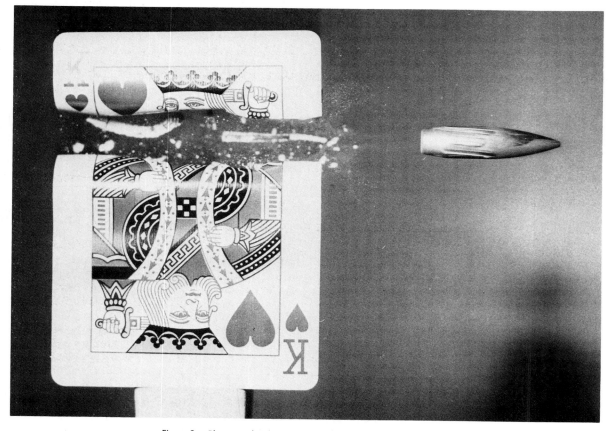

Figure 2 — Photographer using a single strobe at a high shutter speed.

of determining exposure. The "eye" of the meter stays open all the time (remains at a constant setting) to tell the exact intensity of light.

The exposure latitude of modern negative-making materials usually takes care of a considerable error in exposure, but does not tolerate carelessness. To use any film to the best advantage, it is necessary to know the correct exposure required. It is also necessary to develop the film according to the recommendations of the manufacturer. Film speed values (and consequently exposure) are dependent on the film being processed according to instructions. Developing in other than the recommended solution may result in an apparent gain or loss in film speed. By developing in a solution of unknown potential, the results are unpredictable.

It is impossible to formulate a set of specific rules or tabulate the exact exposure required for a certain subject under each possible lighting condition. The best that can be done is to generalize and ap-

age of light transmitted, and the actual speed of operation of the shutter may not be the same as the speed indicated on the shutter housing. For these reasons it is not unusual to obtain negatives varying considerably in density when exposed in different cameras, even though the same indicated shutter speed and f/number is used with each one. It is necessary for the serious photographer to make a series of practical tests with his equipment and determine or account for these possible variations. In this manner "normals" can be established by which the most desirable density can be consistently obtained in negatives.

ARTIFICIAL LIGHT

In Chapter 2 it was said that photography involves controlling, recording, and creating light.

Much of the police photographer's job requires that he create artificial light; most auto accidents occur between 4 P.M. and midnight, most house jobs happen between 8 P.M. and 3 A.M. During these hours of peak activity, there is seldom enough daylight to photograph without the use of flash.

Two types of flash are used by photographers: strobe and photoflash. Photoflash refers to any kind of flash which is created by an instantaneous ignition of a flashbulb which, once used, is discarded and replaced by a fresh bulb for the next shot. Strobe refers to a recharging unit with a flash tube which flashes thousands of times before requiring replacement. Strobe and photoflash units are discussed in greater depth in Chapter 9.

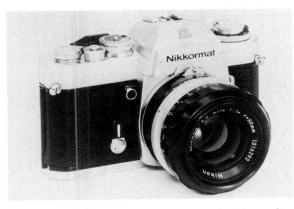

Figure 3 — This camera is equipped with a "hot shoe" for attaching flash. The conscientious photographer will never use the shoe

SINGLE FLASH

Most cameras come equipped with a shoe or bracket to which a flash or strobe is attached when needed. They are also built with an electric input which, when connected to the flash, synchronizes the flash to the shutter. Because of the convenience of attaching a single flash directly to the camera and shooting, most amateur photographs are made with a single flash at the camera. Such pictures are characterized by flat lighting on the subjects and harsh black shadows in the backgrounds. When the flash originates very close to the lens, the eyes of any persons in the photograph will appear red; this is called the "red-eye" effect and can be most disconcerting.

The objectionable effects of single flash lighting can be minimized or overcome by several methods, the simplest of which is to detach the flash from the camera. If the flash must remain on the camera, it should be covered with some kind of diffusion material, such as a white handkerchief, cheesecloth, or frosted cellulose acetate. Diffusion, however, reduces the intensity of the light; the exposure must be increased accordingly.

OFF-CAMERA TECHNIQUE

One of the best methods for using single flash is to detach the flash from the camera and direct it at a surface other than the object being photographed. The light will bounce off of the surface (a wall or ceiling) and provide the subject with a soft, even illumination. This technique is called *bounce flash* and works best in a low-ceiling, white or off-white room. It is totally ineffective outdoors where there are no surfaces to reflect the light.

Bounce flash is so effective that some strobe and photoflash units are made to tilt and can remain attached to the camera. The photographer should, however, learn to hold his camera in one hand and direct the flash with the other.

Adjustments in exposure must be made for bounce flash because the light must travel farther; this will be discussed in another section.

MULTIPLE FLASH

If the flash needed for a photograph comes from more than one source, the light will be more even and will create fewer harsh shadows. Multiple flash can be accomplished by stringing together a number of flashes or by purchasing slave units which flash automatically when the main flash goes off.

Multiple flash is particularly helpful for shooting outdoors at night where bounce flash is impossible. Ten units can be used to illuminate an entire parking lot.

When setting up multiple flash, the photographer should take his time and work slowly and carefully so that he omits nothing. Once, at the Eastman Kodak Company in Rochester, a group of photographers (the author among them) was assembled for a group photograph. One hundred large flash bulbs were scattered throughout the large auditorium to insure soft, adequate light. After the camera was triggered and the flashes went off, it was discovered that the photographer had neglected to pull the slide out of the film holder. From all the preparation, they had no photograph at all!

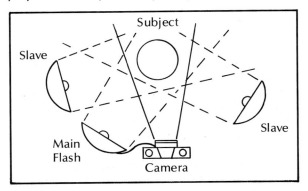

Figure 4 — Use of multiple flash

PAINTING WITH LIGHT

Painting with light is a technique which simulates multiple flash, but requires only one flash unit. It can be used only with subjects which are absolutely stationary. Here is how it works:

1. Two people are required for painting with light; one walks around with a strobe unit while the other remains at the camera.
2. With the shutter of the camera open (a T setting), the photographer at the camera holds his hand over the lens to keep out stray light.
3. The photographer with strobe in hand walks to the first position from which a flash would be fired, instructs the photographer at the camera to remove his hand from the lens, and then fires the flash. The photographer then re-places his hand over the lens.
4. The photographer with the strobe walks to a new position and repeats the process again and again until the entire area to be photographed has been illuminated.

When painting with light, the photographer who carries the strobe must be careful to remain outside the field of view of the camera, or he may appear as a ghost not once but several times in the finished picture. Also, the photographer must take care that nothing moves while the process is taking place, or the evidentiary value of the photograph will be lost. A photographer could, using the painting with light technique, fill an entire parking lot with the same automobile photographed over and over again.

Figure 5 — Photo showing use of fill-in flash for good contrast

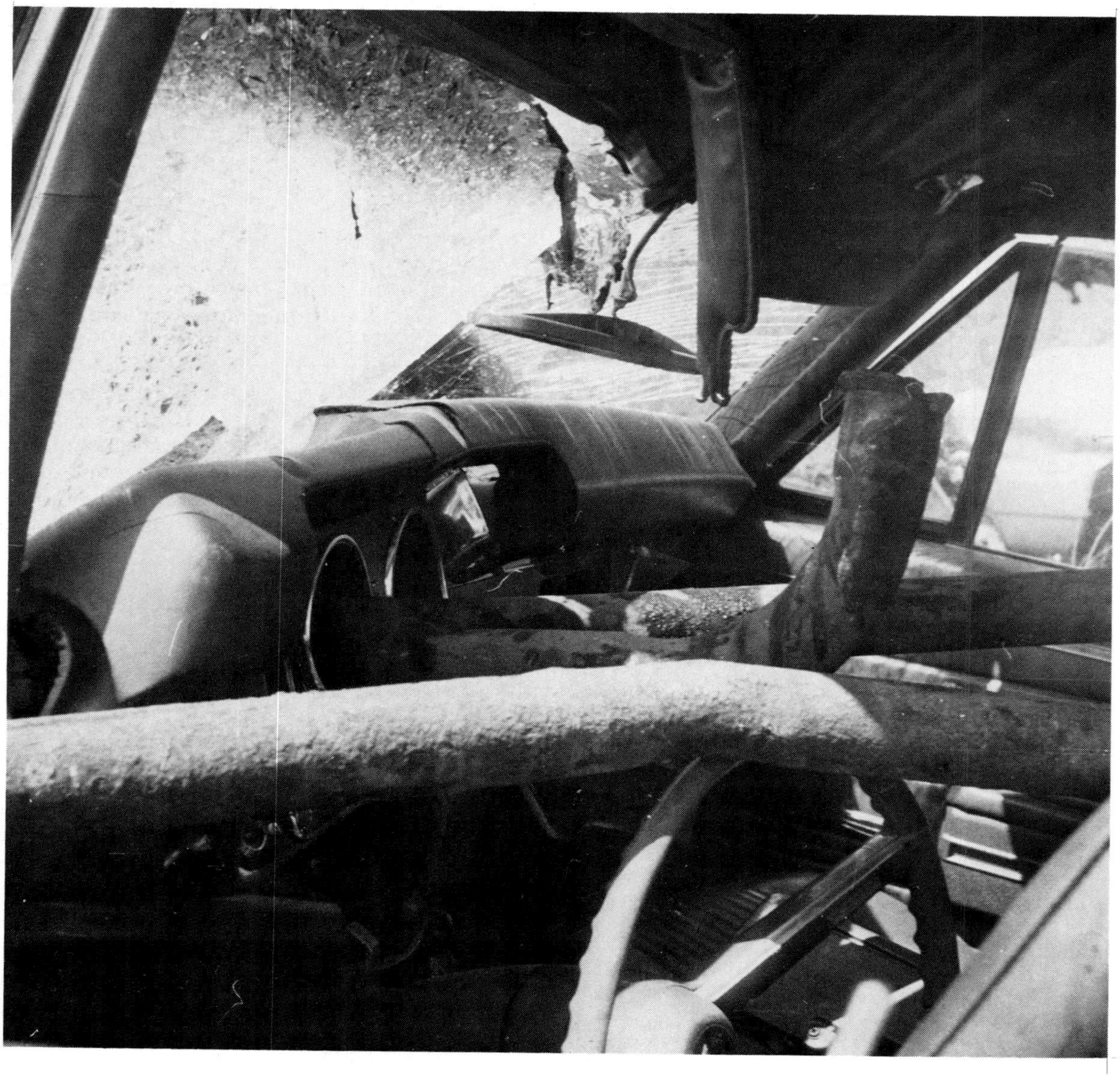

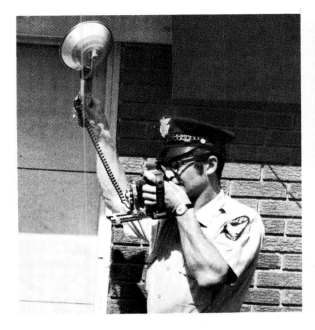

Figure 6 — Bounce flash technique

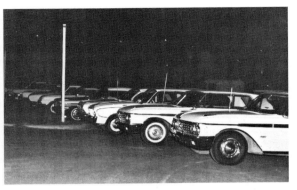

Figure 7 — Difference between photos taken at night with (above) a single flash and (below) painting with light technique.

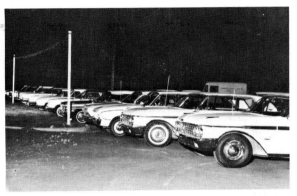

FILL-IN FLASH

Many photographs taken in daylight would be improved by using flash as fill-in. Many areas in daylight are in dark shadows (for instance: the underside of a car or the area under the hood) and need fill-in flash in order that they appear on the finished photograph.

It may appear utterly ridiculous at first glance to observe a photographer using a flash when taking a picture in bright sunlight. Actually, it is just as sensible as using two or more lights when taking any interior view or a portrait; one is the key light and the other the fill-in. Working in bright sunlight, the sun is the key light and flash is the fill-in. It is often desirable to reduce or otherwise change the lighting contrast of a subject in bright sunlight. When the sun casts deep shadows on the subject, it is quite difficult to obtain both highlight and shadow detail in the negative. By filling in the shadow areas with a flash, the contrast is reduced to obtain good detail in all parts of the subject and make a much more pleasing picture. Synchro-sunlight is a method of using supplementary illumination synchronized with sunlight for the purpose of obtaining better shadow detail in all types of outdoor photography.

The outdoor flash can do an excellent job of lighting a difficult shot if properly handled. It can also produce the crude overilluminated effect of having been shot at night with a single flash. The basic problem is to balance two extremes of exposure on a single negative, each in itself providing the correct exposure to the film. These two extremes are the normal daylight exposure for the highlights and the normal flash exposure to light the shadows. Thus, a flash exposure and a sunlight exposure must be harmoniously balanced during the instant the shutter is open in order to achieve a pleasant result. Naturally, the ratio between flash and sunlight varies according to subject matter and the particular effect desired. Whether the shadows are to be eliminated or merely subdued must be determined by the photographer and the flash and sunlight balanced accordingly.

EXPOSURE FOR FLASH

Determining exposure for flash is very different from deciding upon a correct daylight exposure because the light from a flash cannot be metered — it is too short. Also, the primary consideration when figuring exposure for flash is the distance of the subject from the flash. In daylight photography, the distance between the subject and the camera makes little difference to the exposure; with flash photography, the distance from flash to subject is crucial.

THE INVERSE SQUARE LAW

As the light created by a flash moves away from

the bulb or strobe, it seems to dissipate — to disappear. The light from a single flash will illuminate a subject twenty feet away only slightly, but at ten feet the single flash is quite adequate and at five feet it is too bright. Why?

As the flash is moved away from a subject, the light must not only travel farther; it must spread out more. A single flash one foot from a subject will provide a square foot of light but a flash two feet from the same subject will provide four square feet of light. If the subject being photographed has a surface area of one foot, it is plain that it will be illuminated by four times as much light at one foot than at two.

This is called the *inverse square law*. Inverse means fraction and square means a number multiplied by itself. An object illuminated at twenty feet is five times as far from the flash as one illuminated four feet from a flash. Five squared is twenty five; the inverse is 1/25. Therefore, an object twenty feet from the flash receives only 1/25 the light that it would at four feet — the photographer must adjust his camera accordingly.

GUIDE NUMBERS

Correct exposure for flash is determined with the use of mathematical formulas which have been greatly simplified by the manufacturers of flashbulbs and strobes who have worked out guide numbers and tables for figuring exposure. For every combination of shutter speed and film speed (ASA), there is a *guide number* which represents the product of the flash-to-subject distance multiplied by the f/stop.

For instance, when using Plus-X film with an ASA of 125, the guide number for a shutter speed of 1/250 of a second is 180. If the photographer places his flash fifteen feet from the subject, he divides this distance into the guide number to get the f/stop. In this case, 180 ÷ 15 = 12; the photographer would use an aperture of slightly less than f/11 for this exposure. If he moved his flash closer, to within eleven feet of the subject, his f/stop would then be f/16.

If the photographer wishes to use a particular f/stop, he then divides the f/stop into the guide number; the answer will then be the number of feet he will have to place the flash from the subject. If he is shooting Plus-X film at 1/250, and wishes to stop his aperture down to f/32, then he must place his flash five and one-half feet from the subject.

The key word in understanding guide numbers is *guide*; a guide number cannot compensate for the many variables which make up exposure. In general, exposures made on the basis of guide numbers produce satisfactory negatives. But if results obtained by following guide numbers consis-tently show under or over-exposure of negatives, more or less exposure should accordingly be given in making future pictures.

Some of the variables which may account for incorrect exposure when following the guide numbers are reflector, lens, shutter, synchronizer, power supply, subject matter and method of operation. It is seldom the fault of the flashlamps. Some reflectors are far more efficient than others in that they throw more light on a scene, all other factors being equal. One type of lens may transmit more light than another at the same diaphragm setting. Two lenses of identical design may vary in their ability to transmit light if one has its glass surfaces coated. Shutters are made to operate within a limited range of efficiency and seldom remain open the exact amount of time indicated by the speed setting. Synchronizers, although quite dependable as a general rule, may get out of adjustment and fail to open the shutter at the proper time to fully utilize the flash. The power supply is a common cause of poor synchronization, due to the fact that weak batteries (or loose or dirty electrical connections) cause the lamp to be delayed more than normal in reaching its peak intensity as explained earlier.

Guide numbers are based on the use of a lamp in a good metal reflector, indoors in an average-size room with medium-colored walls and ceiling, and with the reflector and camera in a straight line with an average subject. Smaller rooms require 1 f/stop less exposure (smaller aperture). Taking pictures outdoors at night or in a large dark-colored interior with side lighting, requires 1 f/stop more exposure (larger aperture.)

If more light is needed on the subject, one of the following methods is suggested:

1. Move the lamp 25% closer to the subject. This increases the light on the subject by 1 f/stop.
2. Move the lamp 50% closer to the subject. This increases the light on the subject by 2 f/stops.
3. Use a more powerful lamp.
4. Use more lamps.

If less light is needed on the subject the following methods are suggested for use with flashbulbs only:

1. Drape one layer of clean white handkerchief in front of, but not touching, the bulb. This reduces the light about 1 f/stop.
2. Drape two layers of handkerchief in the same manner, thus reducing the light about 2 f/stops.

If less light is needed on the subject the following methods are suggested for use with any lamp including flashbulbs:

1. Move the lamp 50% farther from the subject, thus reducing the light 1 f/stop.
2. Move the lamp 100% farther from the subject, reducing the light by 2 f/stops.
3. From the camera position, aim the lamp at a light colored ceiling or wall, instead of directly at the subject. This reduces the light about 2 f/stops. This bounce light technique requires some practice.

Another important factor which may make it desirable to alter guide numbers is the method of processing the negative. Some people prefer a vigorous-working developer to obtain the maximum effective speed of the film; others a slow-working developer to obtain a relatively thin negative with fine grain and good shadow detail for fast projection printing.

GUIDE NUMBERS FOR STROBE

Although the guide numbers for various flash bulbs are usually very accurate and need only minor revision for varying conditions, the guide numbers for strobe units are often greatly inflated by the makers of these units and must be carefully tested by the photographer and, in many cases, completely reassigned. Frequently, strobes are not working at peak power and will not produce as much light as they should. Here is how to arrive at a guide number for strobe:

1. Load your camera with Kodachrome II film, ASA 25.
2. Set up a subject exactly 10 feet away from your flash. It is suggested that large f/stop numbers on a gray card be used. (8 × 10).
3. Place the camera on a tripod.
4. Attach the strobe unit to the camera in the position normally used.
5. Make a series of exposures at half stop intervals (f/5.6, 6.7, 8, 9.5, 11, etc.).
6. Print the f/stop used on a gray card and include it in the picture as a reminder when the roll is returned.
7. Have the roll processed by a reliable camera dealer.
8. When the slides come back, pick the slide with the best exposure.
9. Multiply the f/stop by 10 (the distance used in the test) and this will be the guide number for the strobe unit. If the picture with f/8 was the best photograph, then 8 × 10 = 80, so 80 would be the appropriate *Guide Number*.

TIPS ON EXPOSURE FOR FLASH PHOTOGRAPHY

Remember the word "GAD". . . . It is the key to flash exposure problems.

G — **G**uide number
A — **A**perture or f/stop
D — **D**istance in feet. . .flashbulb to subject

GAD may be written:

$G = AD$ Guide Number = Aperture × Distance

$A = \dfrac{G}{D}$ Aperture = Guide Number ÷ Distance

$D = \dfrac{G}{A}$ Distance = Guide Number ÷ Aperture

This simple formula has many uses in flash photography. Published flash guide numbers are only guides to correct flash exposure. They give good results with most flash cameras, but they can't be exact for every camera because of differences between individual flash reflectors, shutters and synchronizers.

For the best possible flash pictures, it is recommended that the photographer make guide numbers which are tailored to his own equipment. Making guide numbers is easy:

1. Load the camera with any color film and attach the flash-gun to the camera, or as near the camera as possible.
2. Place the camera on a tripod (or other solid support), exactly 10 feet from a model.
3. Set the f/stop according to the published GE guide number for the film, shutter speed, distance, flashbulb and reflector type used.

$$\frac{A \ (f/stop \ to \ use) \times G \ (GE \ Guide \ Number)}{D \ (Distance, \ bulb \ to \ subject)}$$

4. Shoot one picture at this setting.
5. Now, using this basic exposure, make additional exposures at ½ f/stop larger, 1 full f/stop larger, ½ f/stop smaller, 1 full f/stop smaller.

For example, if the GE guide number was 80 for step 3, the exposures would be at f/8, f/6.3, f/5.6, f/9.5, f/11. Record the sequence of exposure for later reference. Transparency type color film is preferable for this test because of its limited latitude. If the photographer wishes to use negative type film, make the five exposures in full f/stop steps.

One of the processed pictures will be better than the others. Let's say it's the one taken at f/6.3 . . . then using the formula AD = G we find that:

$$f/6.3 \text{ (A)} \times 10' \text{ (D)} = 63 \text{ (G)}$$

the exact guide number for your equipment.

This works fine if this particular film is used with just this shutter speed, but what happens if the photographer wants to use other films or shutter speeds with this camera-flash equipment and the same type of flashbulbs?

First a ratio must be established between the GE guide numbers and the guide numbers that the photographer has been using. Merely divide the guide number obtained in the test by the GE guide number used in step 3. A multiplying factor is now available which will convert any GE guide number to an "exact guide number for the photographer's equipment" with any film or shutter speed he wishes to use, providing he use the same size flashbulb as the one used in the test.

In the example, above, the new guide number is 63, the GE Guide Number is 80.

$$63 \div 80 = .78.$$

Now, if the photographer wishes to use the same film at a faster shutter speed or any other black and white or color film, he must look up the correct GE guide number and multiply it by this factor (.78 in this example) for an exact guide number for his equipment.

EXPOSURE FOR BOUNCE FLASH

Whenever the photographer bounces his flash to provide even light, he is causing the flash to travel farther than the flash-to-subject distance; he must adjust his exposure accordingly. The exposure is determined by adding the flash-to-ceiling distance to the ceiling-to-subject distance, dividing the total into the guide number, and then increasing the exposure indicated by approximately two f/stops. Although this is a very useful method, it does require some experience to estimate the distances and reflective ability of the surfaces of the room. Obviously, dark-colored surfaces reflect less light than those painted white and require additional exposure.

EXPOSURE FOR MULTIPLE FLASH

When calculating exposure for multiple flash, the photographer should consider one flash as his main flash and all others as fill-in. He then makes a standard computation with the guide number for the main flash.

MAGIC CUBE, FLASH CUBE, ETC.

The rules for using these types of flash are also the number one argument for *not* using them. Because they provide very little light, and because the cameras which use them are not usually adjustable, the subject-to-flash distance must never be more than ten feet for proper exposure. These types of flash can seldom be bounced or held away from the camera and, although some outfits come with a flash extender which eliminates "red-eye," pictures taken with these types of flash will always be flat and harsh.

If they must be used, the camera should be mounted on a tripod because the shutter speed of a camera with cube in its socket is usually 1/40 of a second.

FILTERS

Filters are colored disks of glass or gelatin which, when placed in front of a camera lens, stop one or another color of light from passing through and striking the film. Usually they are used only for black and white photography and even then should not be used for most police photography.

There are, however, certain instances when a filter is used to highlight a subject, such as blood, which would not normally contrast readily with its surroundings.

FILTERS FOR POLICE PHOTOGRAPHY

Blue filters. A blue filter can be used effectively when photographing blood in black and white. When used outdoors, a blue filter will make the sky, or any blue object, appear white in the photograph.

Green filters. Green filters are now used in place of blue filters for photographing blood. Often, they work better than blue.

Yellow filters. Yellow filters can be used to photograph white cars; the detail of the car will stand out. Yellow filters also cut through haze to a certain extent and can be used with good results to photograph an accident on a hazy day.

Ultraviolet filters. An ultraviolet filter is *not* a filter for ultraviolet photography (the correct filter for ultraviolet photography is a special 18 A deep purple filter); rather, it is a filter which screens out the violet end of the spectrum. Placed in front of a lens and left there, it will not only improve most of the police photographer's work — it will also prevent his lens from being scratched.

UV filters are often used in photomicrography; its short wavelength gives better definition of fine detail.

EXPOSURE WITH FILTERS

Filters cut down on the amount of light which reaches the film, so exposure must be adjusted accordingly. With automatic cameras, this is not a problem because the through-the-lens metering will compensate.

For all other cameras, the photographer must know the *filter factor* of the filter he is using. The filter factor is a figure which tells the photographer how much more light he will need for correct exposure. A filter factor of 2, for instance, means that the exposure should be doubled. For an exposure that would be 125 at f/16, the photographer would double his exposure and shoot with the filter at 125 at f/11, or 60 at f/16.

Some filters are marked with figures like this: 1X, 2X, etc. These are not filter factors; they mean that for a filter marked 2X, the aperture should be opened up two stops.

Before using any filter, the photographer should read carefully any directions which come with the filter.

POLARIZING FILTERS AND NEUTRAL DENSITY FILTER

Some filters can be used for black-and-white and color photography, among them, neutral density filters and polarizing filters. Neutral density filters are used to cut down light transmission. They do not otherwise affect the color or tonal quality of the scene. They are very handy when using a high speed film under bright light conditions, or where the use of a slow shutter-speed or wide aperture is desired for a creative effect. Neutral density filters are available in strengths designed to cut down specific amounts of light by f/stop units.

Polarizing filters, like neutral density filters, are a neutral gray and do not affect the transmitted color in a way that will change its color temperature. When light is reflected by a nonmetallic surface such as water, it is polarized. With a polarizing filter (in a rotating mount) the photographer can intercept this polarizing light and dramatically reduce reflections in the photograph. These filters also increase the saturation of a blue sky in a color photograph (or darken the tone of the sky in black-and-white photography) as long as the lens/filter combination is not pointing directly at the sun. This is the only filter that can increase the blue saturation in the sky in a color photograph without altering the remaining colors in the scene. The polarizing filter is a very handy filter for photographing many different vehicles in auto accidents.

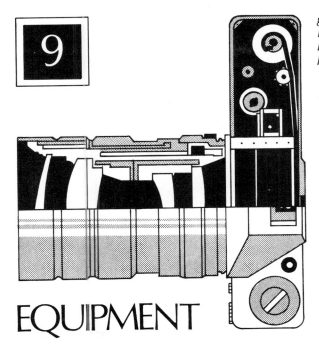

9

EQUIPMENT

LENSES

The police photographer frequently needs a change of lens in order to accomplish a given task. The need for special lenses which can be readily purchased and easily interchanged is often a primary factor in the photographer's choice of a camera.

Lenses for special purposes add greatly to his system of photography and allow him to take photo-

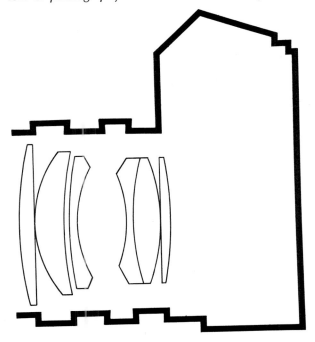

Figure 1 - Lens elements

graphs which would have been incomplete, misleading or even prejudicial had the photographer been restricted to using only the "normal" lens for his camera.

A lens is an optical device which gathers light from a subject and focuses onto a screen or film. Lenses used for photography are plastic or glass bounded either by two curved surfaces, or one curved surface and one plane. The lens is, or should be, the most expensive component of any camera system.

A simple lens (a single piece of glass or plastic) is known as a *lens element*. Two or more elements, cemented together, comprise a lens *component*. Free standing single elements may also be considered components; thus, an optical system which includes two free-standing lenses and two lenses cemented together is said to have three components.

There are three basic categories of lenses for use in photography: normal lenses, wide angle lenses, and telephoto lenses.

NORMAL LENS

Lenses are generally referred to by the measure of their focal length. A lens with a focal length of four inches is a four inch lens though it may only be a half-inch in diameter. In photography, a normal lens is one with a focal length equal to the diagonal measure of the image area. The image area of a 35mm camera is 24 × 36mm; thus, a normal lens for any 35mm camera is 50mm. By international standards the acceptable measured focal length of a lens may be with four percent of its marked nominal value; a 50mm lens may then have an actual focal length of 48mm to 52mm. The lens maker generally does not mark such deviations.

The normal lens is usually standard equipment on a camera, and is intermediate between wide angle and telephoto lenses. The picture angle of a normal lens is 45° which corresponds to the viewing angle of the human eye.

For the average police photographer who will be photographing accidents, crime scenes, and other general scenes, the normal lens is adequate. However, it is not an all-purpose lens. *There is no all purpose lens*; the advanced or professional police photographer must look to specialized lenses for particular purposes.

WIDE ANGLE LENSES

Selection of a lens is governed by the distance from a subject at which the photographer must work and by the field which must be encompassed within the picture area. The wide angle lens has a

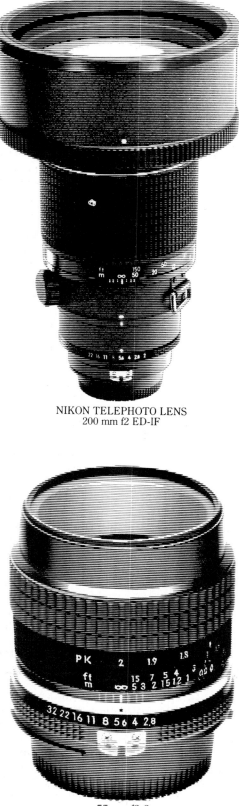

NIKON TELEPHOTO LENS
200 mm f2 ED-IF

Figure 2 — Various lenses

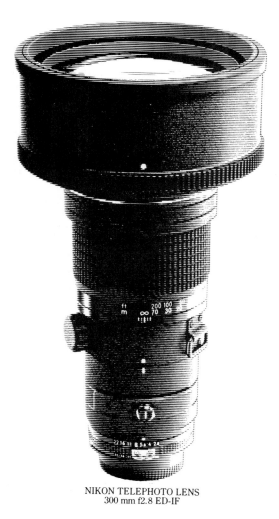

55mm f2.8
MICRO NIKKOR LENS

NIKON TELEPHOTO LENS
300 mm f2.8 ED-IF

shorter focal length than the normal lens and, as a result, it covers a picture angle wider than 60°. It enables photographing a widely extended scene from a close proximity or within a confined area. In police work, wide angle lenses should be used under restricted conditions when the policeman is unable to cover the desired picture area with a lens of longer focal length.

Typical uses for the wide angle lens are for photographing buildings, street scenes, and interiors of homes where a crime has been committed. Crimes committed in bathrooms, for instance, are not easily photographed without a wide angle lens.

The wide angle lens is also convenient for the photographer who is doing candid work where exact focusing is not always possible. The large depth of field resulting from the short focal length of a wide angle lens compensates, to a degree, for inexact focusing.

A remarkable effect that can be achieved by the wide angle lens is exaggeration of perspective. A close subject will appear larger than usual in the ultimate picture. Such exaggeration may sometimes result in a distorted impression, depending on the subject and viewing angle, and it gives a peculiar, interesting effect which cannot be attained otherwise.

The range of wide angle lenses for 35mm cameras includes 8mm, 20mm, 21mm, 24mm, 28mm, and 35mm. The 28mm and 35mm are the most important for general wide angle police work. Nikon put out a 35mm PC lens which can correct for parallax. The 20mm lens has the shortest focal length usable with viewfinder focusing; a certain amount of edge distortion will be noted. This is a problem of all wide angle lenses regardless of the manufacturer. The peripheral light rays are recorded with some degree of elongation, which is due to the angle with which they are received. Apparent perspective distortions are magnified by wide angle lenses. When shooting with a wide angle lens, the photographer should use a tripod and a small level to aid in maintaining normal perspective effects.

Wide angle lenses for reflex cameras are also subject to design limitations caused by the need for an adequate back focus to clear the reflex mirror. This calls for inverted type construction.

Hasselblad has a very good super wide angle camera which can be held in the palm of a hand. Used by many professionals for close-up candid work, it will only accept a 40mm lens.

TELEPHOTO LENSES

A telephoto, or long-focus lens has a longer focal length and provides a close-up image of a distant subject. In contrast to the wide angle lens, the tele-photo covers a smaller field of view and a shallower depth of field. Owing to this shallowness, the ultimate picture assumes a relief-like quality resulting from the lack of sharpness of the out-of-focus areas. Another characteristic of the telephoto lens is production of a flat composition; far objects appear enlarged while near objects do not appear proportionately large.

Normally, lenses beyond 58mm come within the telephoto group. A technical distinction should be made between telephoto and long-focus lenses: a true telephoto has a shorter physical length while achieving the same angle of view as the long-focus lens. The shortening and physical convenience of the true telephoto is accomplished through use of negative rear elements for image dispersion. The front elements converge; the rear elements diverge. Optical aberrations are more easily corrected in regular long focus lenses (whose physical size approximates focal length) than in telephoto lenses. Optical designers have overcome telephoto lens aberrations but the effort in doing so is reflected in the cost of an advanced lens. In actual practice, all long lenses are usually called telephotos or tele-lenses.

Telephoto lenses are used to bring inaccessible objects into the image area in greater size than would be the case with a normal lens. Image magnification is proportional to focal length. A lens of about 100mm shows twice as much detail as a 50mm lens would. The area covered is much less; the 100mm lens covers ¼ the image area of a 50mm lens. *When using a telephoto lens, always shoot with the shortest telephoto lens which adequately encompasses the desired picture area.*

Two other operational uses of telephoto lenses are: (1) to achieve better perspective control by being able to work at a distance and (2) to maintain the relative size of objects placed at varying distances from the camera. These purposes are served mostly by lenses up to about 200mm.

For identification shots in police work, lenses of 85 to 135mm focal length are frequently used. Many departments photograph their arrested persons in 35mm color; the medium telephotos effectively avoid lending undue prominence to the nose, lips, and chin of a subject. Also, they crop out extraneous matter while best utilizing the film area with reproducible matter of importance.

Long *tele-lenses* are those beyond 200mm. Their angle of view and areas of image coverage are progressively narrowed as focal length becomes greater, but they show details in greater size and clarity than would be possible with an enlarged section of a picture made with a shorter focal length lens. The particular hazard of the long tele-photo lenses is camera movement. Lenses up through 200mm represent a safe limit for hand-held camera use, but the slightest movement during exposure of a camera with a long lens will show up as image displacement and blurring on the film. This becomes increasingly apparent as lenses with narrow angles of view are used.

The longest hand-held exposure should be the reciprocal of the focal length to the nearest shutter setting. For a 50mm lens this would be 1/60 sec.; for a 135mm lens, 1/125 sec. To minimize camera movement, the photographer should use a tripod, cable release, the highest feasible shutter speeds, and self timer for shutter triggering. Sometimes supports can be improvised from the back of a chair, a fence top, a table top, top of a car, a tree or any other object. The photographer may use bean bags on top of his tripod to stop the vibration of his camera. The bean bag idea is good and can be used for many shots in police work.

CARE OF LENSES

A dirty lens cannot yield sharp pictures; the lens must be kept clean.

Cleaning must be done carefully or scratches in the lens will result.

All outside optical surfaces should be protected as much as possible from dust, dirt, and finger marks. Carrying cases should be closed over lenses when not in use, and lens covers should be placed over the lens. Many professionals keep a UV filter on their lens at all times for protection and also to improve the quality of their pictures. A folding camera should, of course, be folded and latched when not in use.

To clean a lens safely:

1. Blow on it gently, either with your breath or with a rubber bulb syringe.
2. If the lens is still dirty, dust it with a soft camel's-hair brush, and blow again. Do not use this brush for any other purpose. Keep the brush covered and protected from dust and grit.
3. A smear or finger print can be removed by breathing on the surface (which leaves a film of moisture) then wiping the surface with a *clean* piece of *lens tissue*. Use a circular motion. Do not wipe with a rag or handkerchief. If the lens is still dirty, a drop of cleaning fluid may substitute for breath vapor.
4. Brush and blow again to remove any lint left by the tissue.

Lenses should be protected from jars and jolts and from extreme and sudden temperature changes. They should not be stored in hot or moist places.

Do not attempt to take a lens apart. If the lens or mounting requires adjustment, bring it to the attention of an experienced camera repairman.

EXPOSURE METERS

It is almost impossible to make a good print from a bad negative but making a good print from a good negative is a simple process, requiring little effort and only a reasonable amount of skill and care. It is important, therefore, that the negative be uniformly exposed and processed. A good exposure meter, properly used, is the best insurance a photographer can carry to be sure of uniform exposure.

The photoelectric type is the most accurate exposure meter available. With this instrument the intensity of light is measured, and the light value of a scene is indicated on a scale. Calculator dials attached to the meter are designed to compute the correct exposure rapidly by considering the light value in relation to the film speed. The problem of transcribing light values into terms of exposures is simplified, and direct readings in numerous combinations of f/stop and shutter speeds suitable for photographing the scene are shown on the calculator dials.

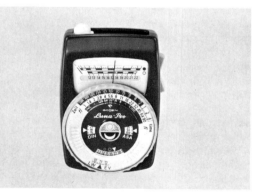

Figure 3 — Luna PRO exposure meter

From experience, it is recommended that the Luna PRO exposure meter be used for police work. The Luna PRO is exceptional in that it is the first *system exposure meter*. By means of instant-lock-on attachments, it makes possible refinement of measuring techniques not only in camera work on location and in the laboratory, but in enlarging or in photomicrography. Figure 3 shows the Luna PRO meter and the various attachments. There is an enlarging attachment which can be attached easily to the front of the meter and used to read correct exposures under the enlarger. This feature alone in a few months can save enough on the expense for paper to pay for the meter, and also saves a great deal of time. For police departments this is a valuable asset. The Luna PRO is so easy to use that, within a short time, its operation will become almost automatic.

CHOOSING A METER

The most important part of the exposure meter is the *photocell*. It is basically a simple device that takes in a certain amount of light and emits a current in proportion to the amount of light falling on it.

The first practical exposure meter came about as a result of the invention of the selenium barrier-layer photocell, which was incorporated in the earliest Weston meters and in all others until very recently.

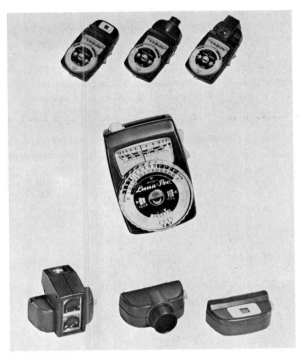

Figure 4 — Luna PRO meter and accessories

The barrier-layer cell is self generating — that is, it emits current in proportion to the light falling on it and does not require batteries or other outside sources of current. Some meters today have two cells — a normal one for average illumination and an attachable "booster" cell for making readings in dim light. With the introduction of the cadmium sulfide photoconductive cell came a great breakthrough for the exposure meters. This cadmium sulfide cell does not generate any current at all; it merely changes its resistance according to the light falling upon it. The more light it receives, the

more current will pass through it. But the current must be provided from an outside battery, a new type which is very small, has a long life under small loads, and whose voltage is quite constant until it is finally exhausted. Some meters (such as Luna-PRO) incorporate a cadmium sulfide cell and a small mercury battery as their basic elements. Generally a push-button switch is provided so that current is drawn from the battery only when a reading is being taken. Under these circumstances a single battery will last up to a year and, in some cases, longer.

Although the Luna-PRO has been highly recommended for police work, the photographer may wish to experiment with several of the many meters on the market. The Luna-PRO, with its system attachments (note the availability of an enlarging attachment) is a most versatile meter, however, and should not be overlooked when making a choice between meters.

USING A METER

The principle of operation of most exposure meters is basically the same. The film speed number and the light value reading are set on the calculator dials. Numerous combinations of exposure are then shown opposite each other as pairings of f/stop and shutter speed.

To use the meter:

1. Set the calculator dial on the ASA rating of the film. Once this setting is made, it need not be changed as long as film of that rating is used.
2. Direct the meter at the scene to be photographed and obtain a light value reading. Usually this reading is taken from or near the camera position. The reading should be taken from a position which includes only the area to be covered in the photograph. Hold the meter near eye level with the photoelectric cell directed at or near the center of the scene. Do not hold the meter so that light from the sun, auxiliary lights, or large highly reflective surfaces can reach the cell directly. Avoid including more sky than necessary by directing the meter slightly downward. Be particularly careful not to obstruct or interfere with light which should reach the cell.
3. Set the light value reading on the calculator dial. Then all that remains is to select the desired combination of f/stop and shutter speed from those indicated on the dials. On Luna PRO set light value reading on yellow triangle at bottom of meter.

PROPER EXPOSURE

There are many more shutter speeds and aperture numbers on the meter calculator dials than are found on any one make of camera. These calculators were designed to make the meter convenient for use with every standard type of domestic and foreign camera by including practically every f/stop and shutter speed found on them. Select and use only those combinations which are marked on your camera and disregard the others. Remember that intermediate shutter speeds cannot be obtained by setting the index between two marked speeds on the shutter housing. However, should the meter indicate a diaphragm setting which is not marked on the lens, the index may be set between two marked f/stops for an intermediate setting, or it may be set to the nearest f/number.

Figure 3 shows the face of a light meter set for Tri-X film. The ASA is 400. The meter was sketched while pointed at a subject which gave a reading of f/8 at 1/60 of a second. A camera shooting the same subject would give a good, even exposure if set at f/8 and 60. Other combinations of exposure are available with this reading: f/11 at 30, f/32 at 1/4, etc.

Any combination of exposure settings can be used for a given reading, depending upon the effect desired by the photographer. For instance, an action photograph of a speeding car may be shot at f/2 at 1000; an unmoving subject may be photographed at f/32 at 1/4 sec. for a sharp image (a tripod would be a necessity for a shot this long.) Considerations concerning the best combination for a shot are discussed in Chapter 8.

INCIDENT AND REFLECTED LIGHT

Light values may be measured in either of two ways: as incident light or as reflected light. An incident light reading is taken by holding the light meter in front of the subject and pointing it back at the camera. With the Luna-PRO and other meters, an opal white bulb must be placed over the light cell before taking an incident light reading. Reflected light is read by pointing the light meter toward the subject, holding it slightly downward, and taking the reading.

There is considerable controversy regarding the subject of determining light values as to whether the reflected or incident method is superior. Each method has certain advantages and disadvantages. The incident method is especially useful when the intensity of illumination is very low. It is extremely accurate in measuring the intensity of light falling on the subject. On the other hand, the photographer is more interested in the amount of light which is reflected from the subject. Black velvet absorbs a very high percentage of incident light while a sheet of white paper reflects perhaps as much as 85 percent. Obviously, the light reflecting quality of the subject must be carefully considered when determining exposure by incident light readings. Some meters are manufactured specifically for reading incident light values. Certainly these meters are just as capable of accurate readings as those reading reflected light. Either type is quite reliable, but both must be used with intelligence.

CAUTIONS AND TECHNIQUES FOR METER USE

The ASA setting of most meters is connected to the aperture dial. A change in the ASA reading will change the aperture reading, while the reading for speed will remain the same.

Because a light meter averages light values, it cannot guarantee 100% accuracy, particularly in situations where there is a bright sky, snow, or at the beach. On a bright day the meter should be aimed downward to measure the light reflected from the ground and not the light in the sky. When the ground is highly reflective, as when it is snow covered or when the photographer is over water, readings should be taken of lighted areas and also of areas in shadow. The aperture set midway between these readings.

An 18% gray card, available at any camera supply store, is often useful for taking readings of reflected light. The palm of the hand may substitute for a gray card in many situations.

FLASH

Whenever the photographer goes inside to shoot photographs or must work outdoors at night, he must concern himself with making use of available light or creating light to suit his purposes. Although the available light may be sufficient to shoot with a wide aperture, the photographer may wish to stop down for a clearer image. In this case, the available light may not be enough. No matter what his desires or limitations may be, the police photographer will eventually, and may more often than not, need to create light.

To do so, he merely adds a piece of equipment — electronic flash or photoflash — which will give him, on cue, a satisfactory amount of light for the short period of time during which his shutter is open.

The principle of flash (synchroflash) photography is essentially nothing more than igniting a flashlamp at the proper time so that it burns at peak brilliance while the shutter is open for exposure. Where there is no movement in the scene being photo-graphed, the shutter may be opened before the lamp is ignited and closed again after the light has completely expired. In such cases, it is a very sim-ple matter to synchronize the action of the shutter with the firing of the lamp. However, when a fast shutter speed is necessary, an extremely sensitive and accurate synchronizing mechanism must be employed. This mechanism is usually an electrically or mechanically operated device which trips the shutter after the lamp, and tripping the shutter must be accurate to approximately the thousandth part of a second (millisecond) to insure correct synchronization at faster shutter speeds. If the shutter opens too early or too late, only a small portion of the flash is used, resulting in underexpo-sure of the film.

ELECTRONIC FLASH

Electronic ("strobe") flash has been around for more than 100 years. Electronic flash units have come a long way, and today there is an electronic flash unit for everyone's taste.

A typical flash unit consists of a power source (AC or battery), one or more energy-storing capaci-tators or condensers, a triggering circuit, a flash tube through which the stored energy is released as a brief flash of light, and a reflector that directs the light toward the subject. The duration of the flash from a strobe unit is intense and very short, making it excellent for stopping action and minimizing the effect of camera movement.

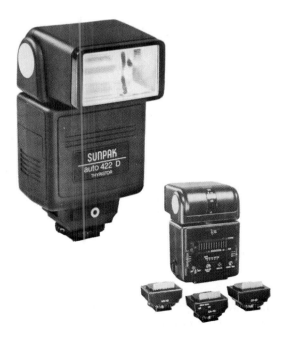

Figure 5 — Sunpak 422D

The quantity of light produced by a strobe unit is determined by the watt/second rating of the power supply, the size of the flash tube, and the size of the reflector. A large energy charge in the power supply will produce a brighter light than will a smaller charge; a large flash tube will produce a brighter light than a small tube. The size, shape, and surface texture of the reflector greatly affect the light output; a large reflector yields more light than a small one, a bowl-shaped reflector yields more light than a flatter one, and a polished reflec-tor yields more than one with a matte (dull) finish. An average reflector increases the light output of a flash tube by ten times — about three f/stops — by directing the light forward.

Power source. Strobe units use one or more of the following power sources: penlight batteries, nickel-cadmium batteries, high-voltage batteries, and AC (house) current. Penlight batteries are cheap and provide up to 300 flashes per set. These penlight batteries are not rechargeable, but they are not very expensive, either. Nickel-cadmium units are more expensive than penlight-powered units, and they must be used at least once a month or their capaci-tators will deform, causing very long recycle times and possibly prevent the unit from recharging at all.

Many two piece units operate off high-voltage batteries, which are heavy and expensive, but give very short recycling times and provide around 1000–1500 flashes before having to be replaced. High voltage batteries cannot be recharged, and they wear down even when not in use. These units are usually more powerful than others, and more expensive.

Some penlight-powered units, most ni-cad (nickel-cadmium), and high-voltage battery units can be operated with AC house current power. This provides an almost infinite number of flashes with-out recharging/replacing batteries. Recycling times are usually slightly longer when using AC power.

Most strobe units have ready lights that indicate that they have recycled and are ready to flash again, but on many units this ready light comes on at less than full charge. Since the output of a unit is con-trolled in part by the amount of energy stored in the capacitators the light output of a partially charged unit will be less than the full-charge out-put. If the unit's ready light comes on when it is 70% charged, the unit will put out half as much light as when fully recycled. Therefore, the expo-sure will be one full stop underexposed. This can be corrected in the darkroom, or, if foreseen by the photographer, the aperture may be stopped up one full stop to compensate.

Flash tubes. Flash tubes used in most strobe units are generally good for 10,000 flashes. For persons that do a lot of flash shooting, this can be most eco-nomical.

Synchronization of a strobe unit. For flash photography with a strobe unit, the camera should be set on "X" synchronization. Cameras with focal-plane shutters may have a maximum shutter speed which will function with strobe (usually 1/60th second.) The maximum allowable shutter speed should be noted and not exceeded.

Automatic strobe units save time and trouble. Instead of determining the flash-to-subject distance, and then using the guide number to figure out which f/stop to use, the photographer just sets a predetermined f/stop on the lens and proceeds (See the instructions with the automatic unit to determine the right f/stop to use). Automatic units have a sensor which reads the light reflected from the subject and alters the flash duration to produce the right exposure. Flash durations as short as 1/50,000 second are possible with some automatic units.

Some of the newer units have *thyristor circuits* which save power, recycle in a very short time, and permit up to 400 flashes between chargings with nicad units. The principle involved is that it takes a certain amount of power to produce a 1/1000-second flash. It takes much less power to produce a 1/50,000-second flash. When a subject is at the maximum distance of an auto unit's range, the flash duration will be the same as the flash duration with the unit on manual (non-automatic) setting. If the subject is closer, the sensor in the unit cuts the flash short, to produce the correct exposure. If the flash duration is less than the unit's maximum (usually 1/1000-second), the thyristor circuit saves the excess power which would otherwise have been wasted.

PHOTOFLASH LAMPS

A flashlamp is a sealed glass bulb containing a highly combustible material and sufficient oxygen to insure complete and extremely rapid combustion. It is clean, safe, and silent to use and requires a very small amount of electrical current for ignition. Each bulb is used for one flash only, then it is discarded. The glass bulb is coated on the inside and outside with a thin film of cellulose acetate to prevent the bulb from shattering due to the intense heat and explosive force generated by the flash. Often, this coating is tinted blue for use in color photography.

Many flash units are available for flashlamp photography, as are a variety of flashlamps. The police photographer should use numbers 22, 11, and 5 flashbulbs, although the photographer who uses instamatic-type cameras will be restricted to flash cubes or flash bars.

STROBE OR PHOTOFLASH?

The decision of whether to use strobe or photoflash may be simply answered: when in doubt, use photoflash.

Large strobe units are excellent for all around work, but are heavy (the power source is often a separate unit, requiring the photographer to juggle camera, flashtube, and power unit all at once.) They do, however, produce a flash of high intensity and short duration which is excellent for stopping action and minimizing camera movement.

Smaller strobes are frequently unsuitable for use in police photography. The flash from a small unit may be totally inadequate for use outdoors and the

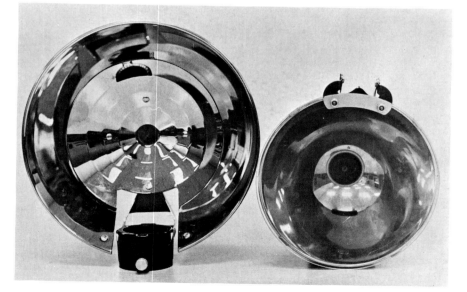

Figure 6 — 7 inch and 5 inch reflectors

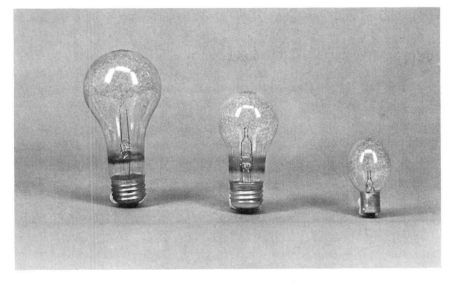

Figure 7 — (Left to Right) No. 22, No. 11, and No. 5 flashbulbs

power sources for small strobes are seldom sufficient for most police work.

Strobes are, to some degree, more delicate than cameras and should not be passed from photographer to photographer. In departments where equipments must change hands frequently, the use of strobe may be a false economy and the more durable photoflash may be preferred.

FILTERS

As the photographer becomes more proficient in the use of basic pieces of equipment, he may wish to improve the quality of his work by modifying the light which reaches his film. This can be done by employing filters.

Filters are used to change the composition of available light before allowing it to strike the film. These changes may be desired for artistic effect, to increase or decrease contrast, or for photographing certain colors at the exclusion of other colors. The intelligent use of filters improves a large percentage of photographs.

When the term filter is used in a photographic discussion, it usually refers to a transparent colored medium employed to regulate either the color or the intensity of the light used to expose the film. The color of the filter determines the color of the light which reaches the film, but in the case of a neutral density or colorless filter, only the intensity of the light is regulated. Filters for these purposes vary considerably since they are composed of transparent materials which may be colored to greater or lesser degrees. Some are so nearly colorless that they escape casual notice, whereas others are so deeply colored that they appear almost opaque. In

all cases, however, the filter is used to modify the light which passes through the camera lens to the film. This discussion of colored filters is primarily concerned with photographing all colors as different shades of gray and should not be confused with the subject of color photography.

FILTERS FOR POLICE WORK

A good photographer can make a good picture without a filter but a professional photographer can make a better picture with the use of the proper filter. For most police work, the use of filters should be considered optional if not unnecessary; for the police photographer with a 110 or 126 camera, filters are superfluous and often impossible to use.

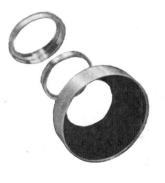

Figure 8 — Filter and holder

A filter of poor construction may cause distortion in a photograph; thus, filters should be carefully chosen if used. Never use a filter which is merely held over the lens. This type of filter is extremely unpredictable.

An adequate filter is constructed of filter material sandwiched between pieces of glass. When buying a filter for a threaded lens, it is necessary to know the correct size of the lens and the type (e.g. fine or medium) of thread.

The photographer with more than one camera may purchase filters to fit the larger of his cameras and an adaptor-reducer for fitting the filter to his smaller camera.

FILTERS FOR SPECIAL PROBLEMS

Accident photography. A dark yellow filter will accent the tire marks in a shot of an automobile accident. A blue filter or, if grass is unimportant, a green filter will bring out a red stop sign. See Chapter 10.

Document work. Filters are used extensively in document work, particularly in ultraviolet and infrared photography. More discussion of these uses can be found in Chapters 15 and 16.

Polarizing filters. Often, the police photographer must photograph subjects from which a great deal of light is reflected. Unfiltered, this light will appear as glare in a finished photograph. A polarizing filter will eliminate most of this glare.

A polarizing device at the camera gives the photographer control over the brightness or glare of polarized light. That is, the intensity of polarized light from the sky or objects in the subject can be reduced much more than the unpolarized light from the scene. The polarizing screen acts selectively on the scene and the excessively brilliant portions of the subject can be controlled without affecting the diffusively reflected light from other parts of the subject. Since this control does not affect the color or light, the polarizer can be used effectively for color photographs.

A polarizing filter looks like a neutral density filter, but its action is concerned only with the direction of light wave motion. The glare of oblique reflections is produced by plane polarized light, which can be subdued by rotating the polarizing device over the camera lens.

Any synthetic material that polarizes light may be called a polarizer or polarizing device. A polarizing screen is a polarizer in sheet form. The term Polaroid is a trade name which refers to polarizing materials and processes developed by the Polaroid Corporation. Polaroid is used in making polarizing screens and filters. The polarizing filter is composed of Polaroid sheets cemented between glass which is then suitably mounted. Polaroid is used for many devices, whereas polarizing screens and filters are used only for photographic purposes.

There are a number of different polarizing filters produced by manufacturers. Basically, there are only two main types; (1) the type used over the camera lens, and (2) the type designed to be used over studio lights. Polarizing screens and filters may be used for both black-and-white and color photography. Polarizing devices used over the lenses have small posts known as indicator handles projecting from the rims of the metal cells for aligning the axis of the polarizing grid.

The polarizing filter may be thought of as a screen with an optical grid or slots which stops all light that is not vibrating in a plane parallel to the axis of the grid. This film or sheet of plastic may be used by itself, or may be cemented between thin sheets of glass and mounted in metal cells. The mounted filters are attached to a lens by means of a filter holder and lens shade.

CARE OF FILTERS

The simplest form of filter is a sheet of dyed gelatin, which requires considerable care in handling. Scratches, discolored spots, and fingermarks render them useless. They are supplied in various sized sheets that are individually wrapped in tissue paper and supported by lightweight cardboard. These filters may be used between the lens cells, behind the lens, or in suitable holders, which usually means that individual filters must be cut to the desired size. When cutting the filter sheet to fit a lens or holder, remove the cardboard. Do the cutting with the tissue coverings in place. These papers should be removed only after the filter is placed approximately as desired. Only the edges of the filter should be touched with fingers.

Colored glass filters and filters cemented between glass should be treated as carefully as the lens. If dirty or injured they detract from the quality of the final picture. Filters of this type should be cleaned by polishing them with lens cleaning tissue. Any lint or dust on them, however, should first be removed with a camel's-hair brush. A lens tissue slightly moistened in lens cleaner or pure alcohol may be used if necessary, but care must be taken to keep the liquid away from any exposed edges of cemented filters.

When not in use, filters should be stored in their cases. All filters must be protected from moisture, excessive heat and unnecessary exposure to strong light.

MISCELLANEOUS EQUIPMENT

Certain pieces of equipment are available which do not so much expand the photographer's system as give him more control over his system. Foremost of these is the tripod.

TRIPODS

For exposures of long duration and for added accuracy with an exposure of any length, a tripod is a necessity. This is particularly true in the case of cameras which have a ground glass focusing screen, such as 4 × 5's or most 2¼ cameras. Tripods provide a degree of stability which is not possible when a camera is hand-held.

Many tripods are available from camera supply shops; the photographer must be careful, when choosing a tripod, to purchase one which is stable and does not prove a hindrance.

The legs should be given special attention. Most tripods are built with telescoping legs. The legs lock at full extension; or, in the case of some tripods, they can be tightened at any length desired by the photographer. The more sections a leg uses to extend, the more "rickety" the tripod will be; thus, the most stable tripod will be one with the fewest sections to be extended.

The locking mechanisms of tripods' legs are usually of two types: those that snap, and those which must be screwed. The latter is preferable because the tightening of the lock tends to strengthen the leg, but the photographer must be sure that the locks are in good working order and do not allow the leg sections to "creep."

Most tripods include a cranking rack and pinion type elevator which allows the photographer to further adjust the height of his camera once the legs are adjusted and locked. The elevator must be of sturdy construction and must not have any "play" which may transmit vibrations to the camera even though the legs are stable.

The head of the tripod on which the camera is mounted should be large and balanced enough to support the weight of the camera without vibration. It should allow the camera, when mounted, to move freely both vertically and horizontally until locked.

Any time a camera is mounted on a tripod, the danger of accidental damage to the camera is increased. For this reason, it is strongly recommended that a camera never be left unattended while on a tripod. To lessen the danger of breakage, set the tripod on firm footing with its legs spread well apart. On a hard surface where a tripod leg may slip and allow the camera to fall, use a tripod brace or a triangle to prevent the legs from spreading. A triangle is an adjustable, folding device made of lightweight metal especially for use with tripods. If this device is not available, a triangular-shaped frame can be constructed of wood to serve the same purpose. If possible, the tripod should always be set up with one leg pointing forward. This places the legs in such a position that more freedom of movement about the camera is allowed, with less danger of tripping over one of the legs and upsetting the camera.

TRIPOD SUBSTITUTES

Where storage space is limited, or when the photographer needs more versatility in camera placement, there are substitutes which, although not wholly replacing a tripod, can help to steady a camera. The monopod is simply one leg, usually collapsible, of a tripod. The monopod steadies the camera to a degree but will not, of course, permit the photographer to stand free of the camera.

There are also numerous mounts to which a camera may be attached and steadied. Some rest on the shoulder of the photographer. Some merely have a large handgrip which transmits less vibration from the hand to the camera. Some are even constructed like a gun butt. These mounts can be more of a hindrance than a help, but are available should the photographer want or need them.

CABLE RELEASE

As is a tripod, a cable release is essential for lessening vibration when using long exposures. A good rule is this: use a tripod and a cable release as an inseparable pair. Together, they can eliminate all but the slightest vibration.

Cable releases come in various lengths and are made flexible with cloth or wound metal cover which permit the photographer to stand close to or away from the camera as he pleases. Some cable releases have locks for time exposures.

LENS BRUSH

Lens brushes are usually made of camel's hair, and some are attached to a rubber bulb which, when squeezed, creates a stream of air to blow dust off of a lens. Brushes should be covered (there are retractable brushes which, when capped, resemble a tube of lipstick) when not in use to prevent them from collecting loose dust.

PAPER AND PENCIL

Although a picture can tell a thousand words, two pictures may become hopelessly confused in the photographer's mind and may need a word or two to distinguish them. He should always carry note writing materials in order to annotate his shots or his work may become as worthless as it would be had he left his lens cap on.

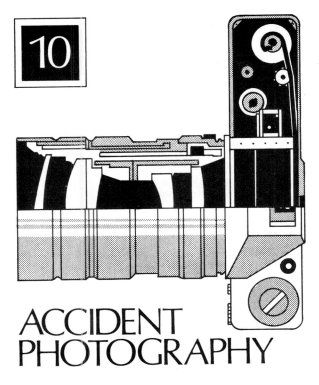

ACCIDENT PHOTOGRAPHY

Traffic accidents take very little time to happen. For the drivers and passengers of the car or cars involved in an accident, the short time in which the collision takes place can be traumatic and influence the perceptions of all involved. Descriptions of the accident are not always dependable. Therefore, the patrolman who arrives at an accident scene must determine and record whatever evidence is available. He will note the descriptions of the accident as told by driver or drivers, passengers, and witnesses. He will take measurements and note weather conditions. And, if he is equipped with camera and film, he will photograph the accident scene.

With traffic accidents on the increase and because of rising insurance costs, the importance of permanent, accurate, and unbiased records of an accident scene cannot be over-stressed. Photographs, carefully taken, can provide a good part of the record of an accident. Measurements and other descriptions are also very important. But for the many minor details of an accident, a good photograph can capture many aspects of an accident scene which may go overlooked in the turmoil of the moment.

WHO SHOULD PHOTOGRAPH VEHICLE ACCIDENTS?

The question I hear over and over again is,"Who should photograph the auto accidents?" Many police think that the insurance company should photograph the auto accident. How absurd a thought like this is. The police are on duty 24 hours a day, and 365 days a year. They are professionally trained to investigate accidents; they are usually the first person to arrive at the scene of the accident. I strongly feel that the police, with their training, should not only take the accident reports, but, should also take all the photographs that are necessary, for they alone know that the accident case will not come before the court within six months to one year. Because of police officers' attitude that it is not their job to take accident reports, the state of Connecticut is now in the process of filling such jobs with civilian personnel. They will be trained to take the accident reports completely, gathering all necessary data and photographs. With the cost of automobiles being so astronomical today, it is the duty of the police to help citizens, who are regularly being asked to pay higher taxes, for they deserve a thorough police investigation.

Necessary photographs should be taken. They may be a great aid to the prosecution as they present physical circumstances of a case in a manner that is easily understood. Most people are visually oriented. A photograph of large or perishable evidence is accepted in place of the original. Include such items as skid marks, footprints, or a body to show the location and type of injury. But before the shutter is snapped, the investigator should ask, "What will this tend to prove?" If the answer is "nothing," the photo should not be taken.

The police photographer must be qualified. He must know what he is doing and why, for the more important the picture, the stronger will be the attempt to discredit or disprove it. A commercial photographer is usually not satisfactory for several reasons. In addition to being expensive, he may not know what is required, is often reluctant to appear in court, and may not keep proper data to insure that the photograph will be admitted as evidence. If a commercial photographer is used, the officer should direct the photographer to take the type of picture the officer needs and to record exposure and other related data. It should be remembered that these photographs are not for publicity but are for evidence, as is the sketch of the crime scene. Valuable as they may be, the investigator should not depend on photographs alone. They may be an important part of the case, but photographs alone do not constitute a complete investigation.

Pictures of the following subjects are often needed as evidence or to complete the records of a case: general scene from driver's viewpoint; point of impact; traffic control devices; skid marks showing length and direction; condition of roadway at location, showing defects, position of cars, victims, and parts of vehicles after impact, indicating points of collision; view obstructions or lack of them; blood, flesh, hair, fabrics, scrape marks, and the like which are frequently useful in hit-and-run cases; tire prints; footprints; defects in vehicles involved, such as missing headlight; trucks lacking turn signal indicators; the roadside showing the kind of district; sagging springs of an overloaded vehicle, and the license number of the vehicle for identification.

Photographs, however, do not show measurements or dimensions. The photo may be incorrectly exposed, blurred, or otherwise worthless. The accident sketch, therefore, is important as the record of the investigator's intricate, personal examination of the scene.

In photographing the scene of an accident, the usual limitations of color, lighting and contrast effect the choice of film, lenses, filters and developer conditions. It is essential to obtain extreme definition and clarity in photographs for presentation in court; so that points of importance such as position of vehicles, point of impact, parts of damaged vehicles, etc. are clearly defined. Combined with these desirable properties, the police photographer strives to obtain the absolute minimum of perspective distortion possible.

When photographing the scene of an accident, the object is to include all possible details that have a bearing upon the cause of, or reason for, the accident. The experienced police photographer can get a reasonable estimate of the exposure required. With today's wide range of automatic 35mm cameras, it is almost impossible for a person to get a bad exposure. Even with the modern cheaper cameras, after a policeman learns how to use the camera, it is a simple matter to get a well exposed photo.

The viewpoint from which the photograph is taken is important. By directing the camera in a slightly different direction, obstruction to vision at a cross-roads, for example, or the visibility of a sign may be magnified or minimized, thus giving a false impression.

When photographing the approach to the scene of an accident for the purpose of showing obstructions to the view of the driver, the camera is held at eye level of the driver of the approaching car. This gives a true picture of what he could see when approaching a crossroad or a rise, such as a humped back bridge. In the latter case, the camera held down or at normal eye level or higher would give a false impression of the amount of obstruction offered by the bridge, being excessive in the first case and minimizing in the second. The photographs should also be taken in line with the travel of the driver's body relative to the road if a photograph representing the driver's view is to be produced. In the case of a pedestrian witness, the camera should be at the eye level of a pedestrian

to give an effect of what the witness saw. Markings of the first impact are carefully recorded to assist in establishing responsibility for the accident.

This is a rather important point about the type of lens used to take the photograph. A normal angle lens is the best for the purpose as, when the scene is completely and pleasingly located in the viewfinder, the photograph will show normal perspective. A too distant viewpoint, minimizing distances in depth, or a viewpoint too near, exaggerating these distances, will not be obtained by the above method. Such photographs would be otained by the use, for example, of a long focus or telephoto lens and a short focus or wide-angle lens, respectively.

Panchromatic or color film should, of course, be used to take the photograph. Especially when multi-colored road signs may be involved in the case, or if a wrong filter is used, the clarity of the signs may be falsified to give the impression of clarity where none exists or of obscurity where the sign is perfectly clear. The best practice when filming an accident scene is to use a normal angle lens, a panchromatic or color film with a correction filter, to focus on the main object and then to stop down the diaphragm to the smallest possible aperture. This last phase will be determined by the presence or absence of motion at the scene. If persons or objects are moving about the scene, then the aperture must be such that the exposure is sufficient to record these moving objects reasonably free from blurr. For car interiors, the photographers expose for the shadows. For general views of cars, any medium speed emulsion can be used with the exception of slow "process" types since these are designed for low contrast subjects.

BASIC CONSIDERATIONS

The police officer has control of the accident scene. He must assure that no one moves the vehicles involved in the accident until all the needed photographs and measurements have been taken. Many weeks may pass before the case comes to court so he must be prepared with careful records covering any detail of the accident which might be needed by the attorneys in court.

The entire scene of the accident should be photographed with all the vehicles in the position of collision and later with the vehicles removed. An overall view should be taken, along with *four* different angles — one each from the north, south, east, and west. While photographing an accident, the photographer should ask himself, "Will this view, angle, or position be of any value to me later when I am called to testify in court?"

In addition to taking all the necessary photographs, the photographer should draw a diagram showing all the distances from the camera to the object photographed. All material objects should be measured. Everything should be written down.

PERMISSION TO PHOTOGRAPH

Although some people object to being photographed at the scene of an accident, the police photographer has the right to photograph any evidence available at the scene of an accident on public property.

Private property (such as a shopping center parking lot) poses a problem to the police photographer. Technically, the security officer who is employed by the owner of the property is responsible for investigations concerning accidents on the property. Permission to photograph may, however, be obtained in writing from the owner who is often willing to cooperate.

If necessary, a search warrant may be obtained which will take the place of the owner's signed permission.

VIEWPOINTS WHEN PHOTOGRAPHING ACCIDENTS

The viewpoint from which each photograph is taken can make a great deal of difference in the story the picture can tell. A shift of only a few inches can, for instance, hide a stop sign behind a bush although it may have been visible from the road. Obstructions to vision at a crossroads are relative to the positions of a driver; the nature of such obstructions may be maximized or minimized in a photograph merely by moving the camera a few feet. Thus, it is very easy for the photographer to give a false impression which will not be helpful in conducting an investigation.

When photographing the approach to the scene of an accident, the photographer may wish to show any objects which obstruct the view of the driver. The camera should be held at a distance above the ground which approximates eye level of the seated driver. The distance above the ground will vary from vehicle to vehicle and with the physical height of the driver. (The photographer may have to squat to photograph the view from a sports car, or stand on top of a ladder in the case of a large truck.) Any appreciable variance from this position will create a false impression of the driver's view. The camera should, of course, be pointed in the driver's direction of travel. When photographing what a pedestrian saw, the camera should be held at the eye level of the pedestrian.

WORKING UNDER BAD CONDITIONS

Accident photography is nearly always done outside and (because foul weather, darkness, and glare are often the causes of accidents) the photographer must often work under poor conditions.

1. *At night:* Making pictures in the dark is a very difficult job. Even with the largest flash, most of the flash will not be reflected. Foreground areas will be overexposed and the background will be underexposed.

   The photographer will get good results at night with a multiple flash method such as painting with light or strobe and slave (see Chapter 8).

   Focusing in the dark, though difficult, can be accomplished by shining a flashlight or spotlight at an object to be focused. The camera should be on a tripod to aid this process. If this is not possible, the lens should be focused at infinity; most objects will then be in focus.

   Photographing license plates at night can be very tricky. The flash unit must be held at a distance from the camera so that glare from the highly reflective plates is directed away from the lens. Three shots of a plate with the flash unit five, seven, and thirteen feet from the camera will yield a good result.

   Kodak Tri-X and Kodak Royal Pan are good films for outside work at night. For color slides, Kodak high speed Ektachrome is recommended.

2. *At dusk:* Shooting at dusk should be done with a combination of available light and flash.

3. *Foul weather:* The Rochester, New York Police Department has a novel approach to the problem of protecting photographic equipment, and preventing flash units from shorting out during rain or heavy snow. Before leaving his car, the police photographer tightly covers his camera with a clear plastic bag from which he has sucked out the air. In Shaker Heights, Ohio, policemen use a large golf umbrella, which they carry with their photographic equipment. One officer holds the umbrella over the head of the officer holding the camera. (Figure 1.)

4. *Daylight flash:* Unlike most outdoor photography, the subjects of accident photography cannot be posed nor can the photographer manipulate his camera to get only the most well-lighted angles or wait for the sun to move for better lighting.

   When shooting the shaded side of a car, the underside, or taking interior shots, flash should be used to bring out details that would otherwise be hidden in shadow. The photographer should cover his flash with a double thickness of handkerchief when shooting inside a vehicle or his shots will be terribly overexposed.

Automatic strobes must be used carefully because the daylight will throw the flash off.

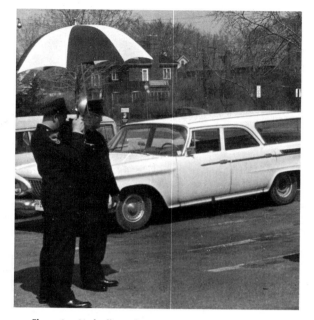

Figure 1 — Umbrella used to protect camera in foul weather

BASIC RULES FOR ACCIDENT PHOTOGRAPHY

Photographing an auto accident is similar to photographing a wedding. The act cannot be repeated for the photographer; he must get all the photographs in a few minutes and omit nothing. The accident photographer must be doubly careful to record everything important because the omission of a key photograph may prejudice the case.

Upon arriving at the scene, the photographer should reconstruct the accident in his mind; then, using the proper equipment (35mm cameras are particularly suited to this task) he must photograph the scene following these basic rules:

1. *Quickness counts.* If any of the drivers, passengers, or by-standers at the accident are injured, they should receive the police officer's first attention. Then he should take all the necessary photographs so that the vehicles may be moved if they are obstructing traffic.

2. *Avoid unnecessary surroundings.* Objects which are not pertinent to the case should not be included in photographs of the accident. If only a small portion of a photograph is of interest in this case, you should be careful in in-

troducing it. It is similar to a witness who rambles on with minor details which are of no importance to the case. Whenever possible, a series of photographs of a traffic accident scene should be taken from several different camera viewpoints that will afford an effective presentation of the complete scene without showing too much of the surrounding area.

People and animals should be avoided in the photographs unless they are involved in the case or serve some useful purpose such as showing the size or location of objects. Living creatures always attract the attention of the observer of a photograph and if they have no purpose in the picture, their presence will weaken the effectiveness of the photographic evidence, as shown in Figure 3.

3. *"See" through the driver's eyes.* Photographs should be taken from the eye level of each driver. If there are witnesses, photographs should be taken at their eye levels from the spots where they were standing.

4. *Angles to take.* Shots should be taken from the four points of the compass and twenty-five feet from the vehicle. Additional shots, from one hundred feet, will show the approach and terrain. If only a few shots can be taken, they should be at forty-five degrees from the front and rear of each vehicle. This allows two sides of a vehicle to appear in one photograph.

5. *Close up shots.* From a distance of eight to ten feet, shots should be taken of the damaged parts of each vehicle. Different perspectives of the damage may be obtained by photographing each damaged area from two angles.

6. *Tie the shots together.* Some order of photographs must be established from the photographer's notes so that their order will aid him in telling a story. He must be prepared, with the aid of the photographs, to tell a court of an investigation exactly how the accident occurred.

7. *Practice makes perfect.* The photographer must practice his craft so that he need worry only about how to tell his story in pictures and not about how to operate his camera.

8. *Remember the chalk.* Before any bodies are removed from the ground, they should be outlined with white chalk. If a vehicle must be removed, its four wheels should be outlined with chalk. It is a good idea to chalk a white arrow indicating which direction is north for inclusion in each photo.

9. *Be sure.* If there is any doubt about whether or not to take a shot, it should be taken. Film is the most inexpensive part of the photographic process; a saving of film may be a false economy in the case of an accident where a person is injured or killed. It is a good idea to take

twenty to thirty pictures — more evidence is better than not enough.

USE OF SPEEDLIGHTS

Most of today's 35mm cameras are automatic, and some of them have a built-in flash system. It is suggested that policemen use some kind of a camera, even if it is a cheap "Sure Shot" or a "Talker." I have used these cheaper cameras at the college, and my students have produced some good work with them. I have seen some of the photographs taken with these cheaper cameras after they were blown up to 11" x 14", and they were good enough to be accepted in a court room.

There are many good "strobe units" available, and any maker of a good 35mm camera puts out a good speedlight for their camera; namely, such well known manufacturers as Nikon, Pentax, Minolta, etc.

SPEEDLIGHT SB 14

Designed to meet the needs of police officers when it comes to professional police photography, the speedlight for the police to look at is the compact and light Nikon SB 14. Covering the picture angle of a 28mm wide angle lens without using an adapter or accessory, the SB 14 provides even illumination throughout the picture. It has a guide number of 105 (ASA/ISO 100 in feet) for ample light output. The SB 14 uses a silicon controlled rectifier and thyristor circuitry to provide automatic flash output control. This eliminates discrepancies in light measurements, thus assuring exposure accuracy. Also, the SB 14's flexible flash head can be tilted and rotated to bounce flash photography which is used often by police. Of importance is the use of TTL remote cord. This is a 3.3-foot long cord enabling the police officer to take the flash off the camera and point the light where he needs it. Police should be aware that there are slave units that can be placed anywhere they wish, to give them more light for use in accident shots at night. Many slave units can be placed at different positions of the accident scenes at night. You can buy slave units that do not need any wiring to the camera. When you shoot the flash at your camera, it will shoot off the slaves at any other position. There are many advantages to having an SB 14 Nikon unit. I like having the flash on the side of the camera. For police work this is very important. Most units are put above the center of the camera which makes the reflection of the strobe come into the center of the photograph, and when photographing a person, it gives them what they call in photography "a pink eye."

TTL (THROUGH-THE-LENS) MULTI-FLASH SYSTEM

Nikon has developed a professional quality TTL multiple flash system that any police officer can master easily. You can choose any combination of TTL units to benefit you. There are TTL remote or multi-flash sync cords available for TTL off-camera or multi-flash photography, making possible good police photography—without the strong shadows. The Nikon's camera body's built-in sensor automatically measures and controls the light from all the units.

WHAT TO PHOTOGRAPH:

1. All vehicles in their original positions. The officer has the authority to disallow any movement of vehicles until photographs are taken.
2. Victims which have been thrown from vehicles.
3. Debris is the best indication that the photographer can show of where the first impact occurred.
4. License plates of vehicles. These should be clear on at least one photograph of each vehicle.
5. All skidmarks and tiremarks. Patches of oil or water, if present, should be included in these photographs. The tiremark will be straight and is caused by braking. Skidmarks deviate from the general line of travel and are usually made by the front tires.
6. If a vehicle has gone off the road and has made any marks in soil or soft berm, these should be photographed. They may give an indication of the speed of the car.
7. A close-up of marks made in macadam roadways should be taken to indicate the texture of the road.
8. Photographs of the vicinity of the accident should be taken which do not include the accident scene itself. These should be carefully noted for reference points.
9. Special care should be taken when photographing a hit-and-run case. The investigator of a hit-and-run has only a part of the evidence and must make a case from the best photographs the photographer can take.

HOW TO PHOTOGRAPH AN AUTO ACCIDENT

There is a five-step procedure that provides adequate photographic coverage of most automobile accidents. The following deals with an accident at an intersection, but it applies equally well to any vehicular accident.

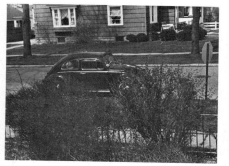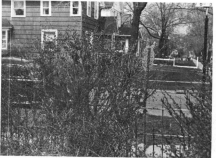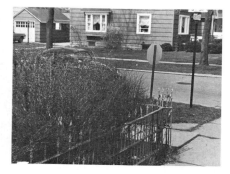

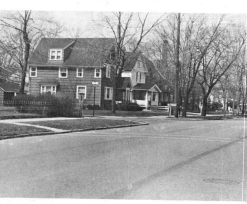

Figure 2 — Three shots from 25 ft. and two shots from 100 ft. show how the camera position can create false impressions

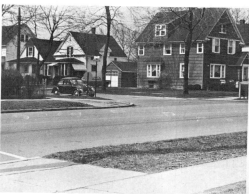

Figure 3 — Distraction caused by people obscuring vehicles involved in an accident

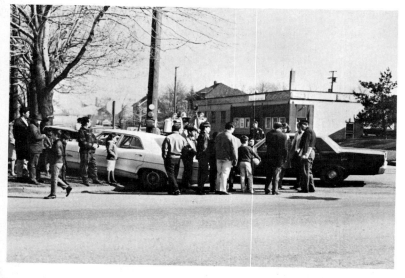

1. From about 100 feet the photographer shoots toward the intersection to show how it appeared to the driver. Then from the same spot, he turns and shoots toward the direction from which the second car was coming. This will establish if any obstruction could have prevented the first driver from seeing the second driver. (See Figure 4.)
2. The photographer then moves up to about 25 feet from the probable point of impact and shoots again. This will establish what traffic controls were present and show skid marks or lack of skid marks.

3. Next, he takes these same basic three shots from the viewpoint of the second driver. He simply reverses the order. First, he shoots from the direction the second driver was coming, at 25 feet from the probable point of impact, then moves back and shoots the other two basic shots from 100 feet.
4. These six basic shots, three from each driver's viewpoint, should be taken quickly, in from three to five minutes. The overall scene, the probable point of impact, the final locations of the vehicles and pedestrians have all been well covered. As soon as the photographic activity that interferes with the flow of traffic is over, the photographer begins photographing each vehicle to illustrate damage. In the close-up views, the cars should be photographed from north, south, east and west. Close-up views of the car's damaged areas can give a good idea of the force of the collision. (Figure 6.) Color photographs will show where one car's paint has been transferred to another, and also make it easy to distinguish the damage under investigation from rusted areas of old damage.

License plates should be photographed. (Figure 7.) Photographing shoe soles of a car's occupants can settle a possible dispute over just who was driving if an imprint from the brake or accelerator pedal shows up on the sole of one of the occupants.

5. Any skidmarks or tire tracks should be photographed head-on, to show the direction the

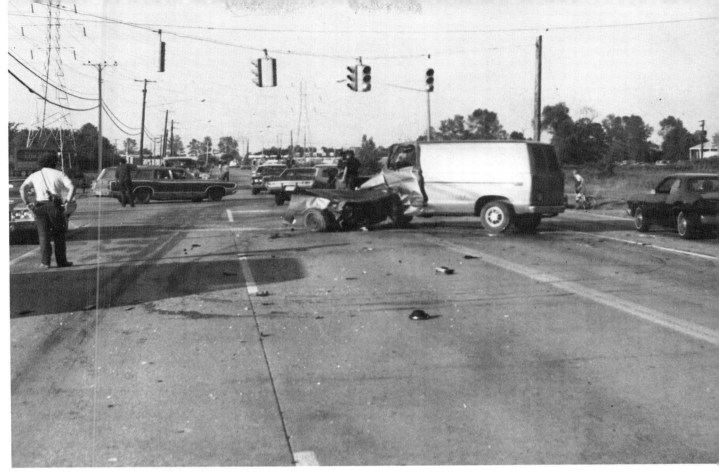

Figure 4 — Two shots from 100 ft. showing intersection

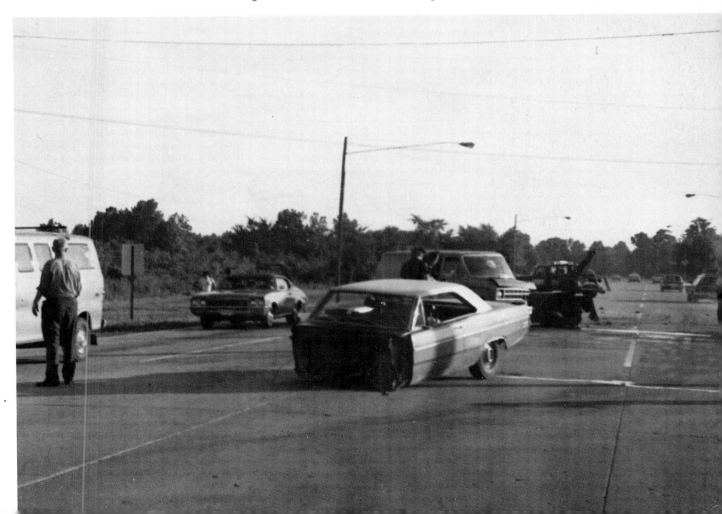

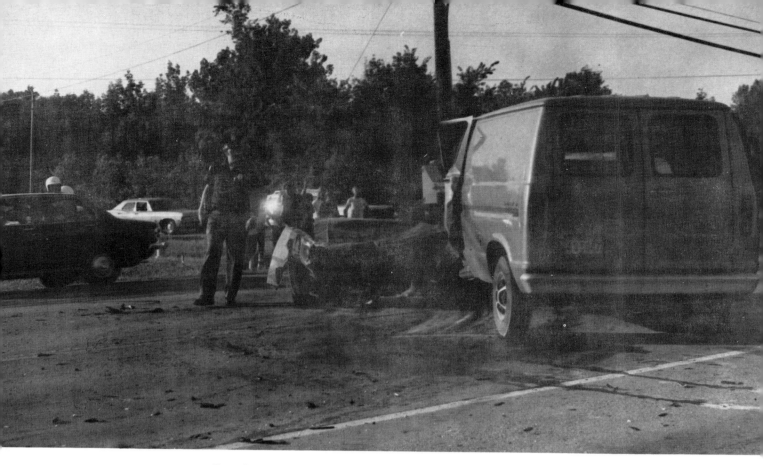

Figure 5 — Four shots of the accident from 25 ft., south (below), west (above)

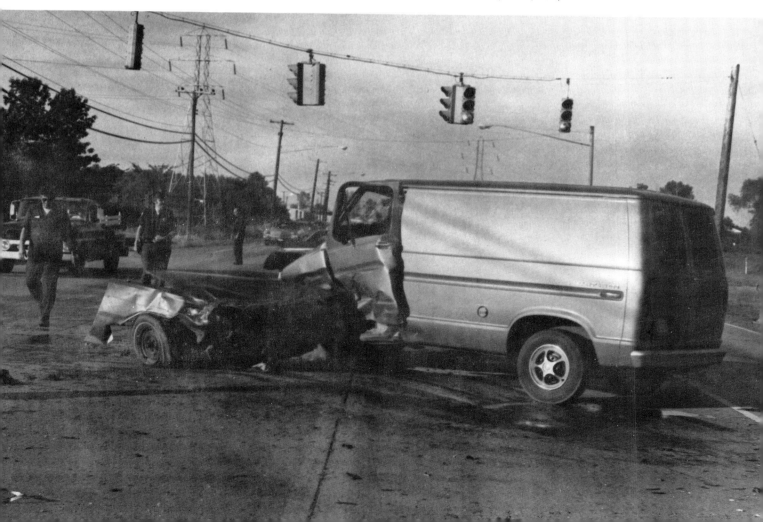

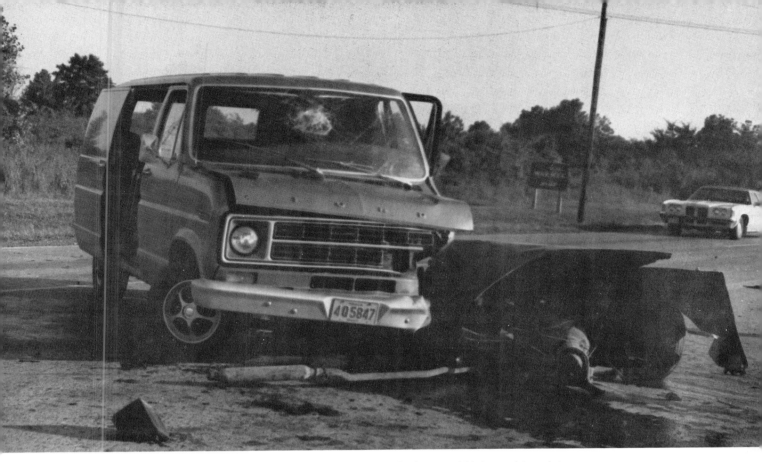

— North (above) and east (below). Note that rear of sedan is not visible in any of these photos

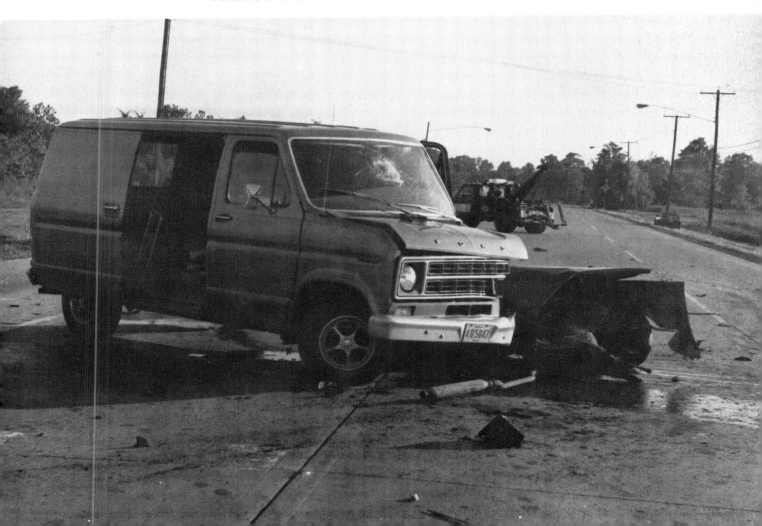

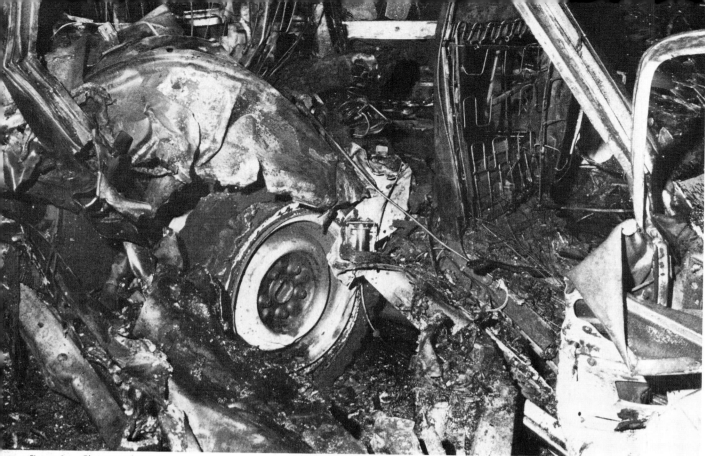

Figure 6 — Close-up of interior

Figure 7 — License plates

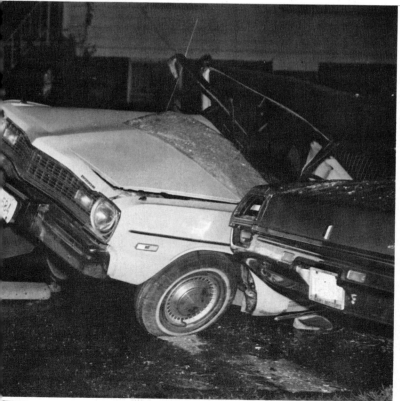

vehicle was traveling; and side-on to show their length. (Figure 8). These photographs will help determine the speed the vehicle was traveling and just when the driver perceived danger. To get the best views of the marks, it's usually best to place the camera as high as possible (Figure 9). The Wyoming, Michigan Police Department has devised a unique system for taking pictures from a high vantage point. Their photographic car is equipped with a wooden board mounted about 4 inches above the roof of the car. (See Figure 9). The tripod can be mounted there and photographs taken from this spot produce a good view of the tire marks. When photographing tire marks, great depth of field is desirable to insure that the entire length of the mark is in sharp focus. In order to accomplish this, it is best to set the aperture at f/32. This is the diaphragm opening which allows the greatest depth of field. Using this exposure will naturally depend on the available amount of light.

HIT-AND-RUN

Identifying the missing vehicle is, of course, the biggest problem in a hit-and-run accident. Photography can make the task much easier.

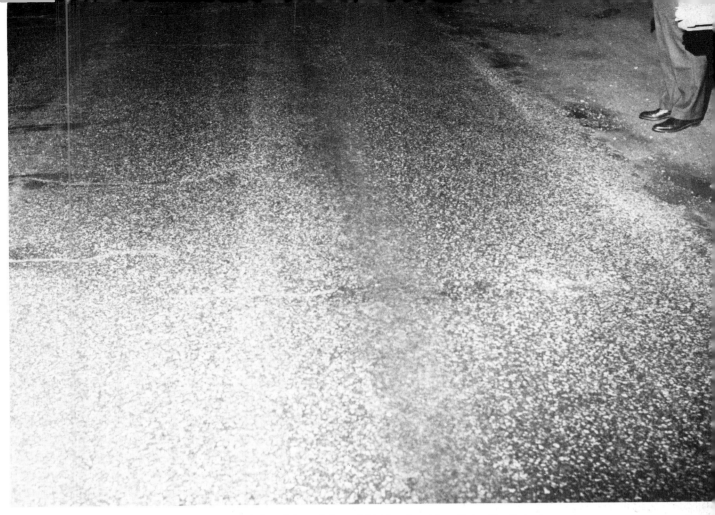

Figure 8 — Skid mark in asphalt, at right (above) and in soft shoulder (below)

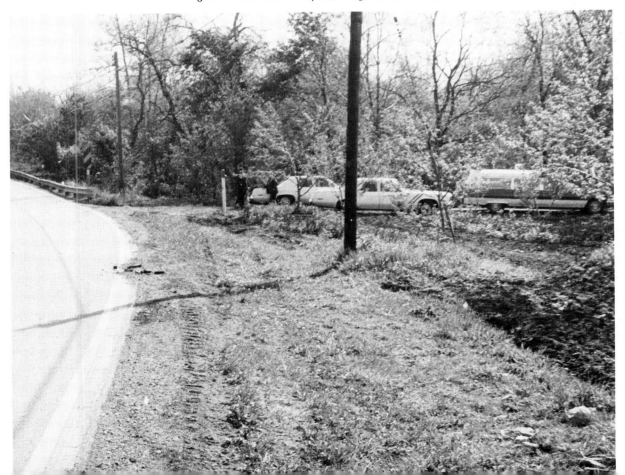

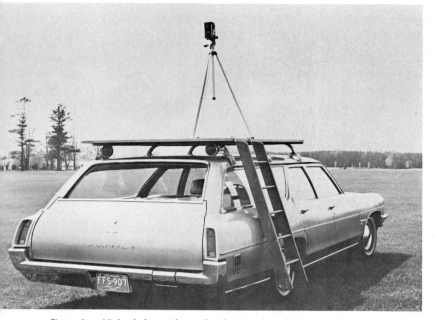

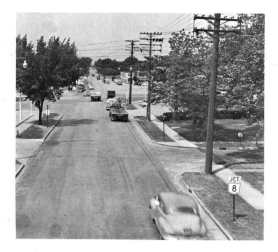

Figure 9 — High platform (above) for shooting from high angle (right)

1. *Debris:* Any debris possibly connected with the hit-and-run accident should be photographed at close range. One photo showing, for example, a paint fragment from the hit-and-run vehicle on another vehicle or on a pedestrian's clothing can spell the difference between a criminal's acquittal or his conviction. All the debris in the immediate surroundings should be photographed to show the point of impact. Defense lawyers will be very interested in seeing the point of impact in the auto accident.

2. *Tire impressions:* Even if tire impressions will be reproduced by plastic castings, it is a good idea to photograph them first. The camera should be placed on a tripod, with the back of the camera parallel to the ground. The photographer should select, when possible, a length of track that reveals any defects, such as cuts, that could help identify an individual tire. He should always photograph, in sections, enough length of tire track to equal the circumference of each tire.

3. *Blood:* To capture as much contrast as possible between a bloodstain and its surroundings, color film should be used. But if black and white film is used, the photographer can make the blood show up lighter than its surroundings by using a Kodak Wratten Filter No. 25 (Red) with Kodak Tri-X Pan film. He can make it show up darker by using a Kodak Wratten Filter No. 47 (blue) with Kodak Tri-X Pan film. And he can make fresh blood, and

sometimes even oxidized blood, fluoresce by illuminating it with ultraviolet light and shooting in the dark, using a Kodak Wratten No. 2A on the camera. Because only the area that fluoresces will record, another photo should be taken from exactly the same camera position. The exact location of the blood spot in relation to its surroundings can be illustrated by superimposing a positive transparency of ultraviolet negative over the other print. A photo of the trial of the pedestrian's blood can establish the direction the hit-and-run vehicle was traveling; the small points of the blood drippings point in that direction.

POSSIBLE MURDER OR SUICIDE

There is nothing accidental about some fatal "accidents." So, it is always a good idea to photograph anything that is suspicious. If, for example, a dead person is found behind the steering wheel of a car that has been in a serious collision and he shows few bruises and little bleeding, a photo could help show that he was dead, possibly murdered, before the accident occurred. Often, especially when dealing with head-on collisions, it is wise to photograph the brake and accelerator pedals, the floormats, and the soles of the driver's shoes. If the accelerator pedal imprint shows on his right shoe and the floormat impression on his left shoe, there is good reason to suspect suicide. In any fatal accident, the interior of each car involved should be well photographed (Figure 10). Areas of deformation should be emphasized, particularly where there is any indication of occupant contact. Anything in the car's interior that indicates body contact, the steering wheel, the instrument panel, the interior of the door, bent knobs, broken windshields should be photographed.

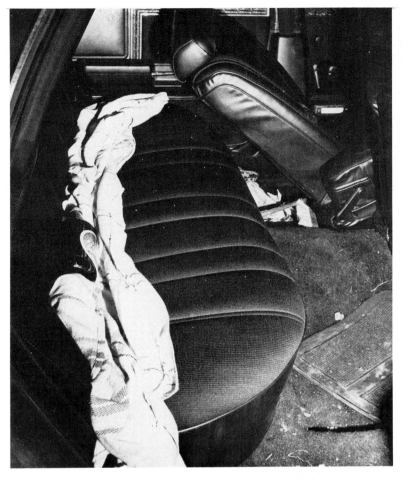

Figure 10 — Interior shot. Was the driver drinking?

WARNING

It immediately seems evident just who the guilty party is in the accident. Nevertheless, the police photographer must keep his mind open and not let any quickly formed opinions influence his approach to his job. If he does his work well, he'll soon have plenty of solid evidence on which to base a sound conclusion.

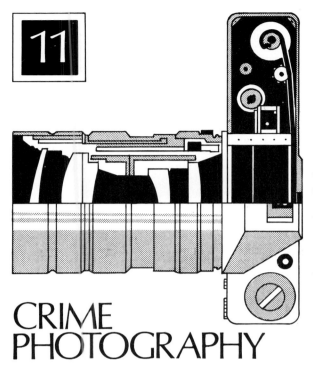

CRIME PHOTOGRAPHY

Photographing the scene of a crime is very important, whether the case eventually comes to court or not. In fact, very few photographs wind up in the courtroom. Photographs are not taken for courtroom presentation alone; they help the police department in many ways which benefit the taxpaying citizens. When a suspect is being questioned, a photograph of the crime scene may be used to refresh his memory. The guilty party will sometimes be induced to confess when confronted with relevant photographs. Often, detectives must take a suspect around the city to show him, for instance, the homes which he is suspected of having burglarized. By showing the suspect or suspects different photographs of these scenes, the investigators can be saved many precious hours — and the municipality, many dollars. If the case should come to court, the photographs can give both the judge and the jury the best possible idea of the crime scene as it was at the actual time of the crime.

It is, or should be, a general practice for the police photographer to take photographs of the crime scene immediately after a crime has occurred and before anything has been disturbed or removed. _No one should be permitted to touch anything at the scene of a crime before it is photographed_, be that person the first policeman to arrive at the scene, or a civilian, or a priest. A priest is mentioned because of a particular case in which a girl was brutally murdered in her home. One of the first persons to arrive at the scene was a priest. He immediately lifted the girl off the floor and put her on a bed. No one could ever reconstruct the scene of the crime accurately — an important matter later in the case. It may be an unfortunate rule; but in police work, facts must sometimes take priority over compassion.

HOMICIDE

One of the most difficult jobs that a police photographer may have to do is photographing a homicide. Most police photographers spend many hours learning how to photograph a homicide, yet have the fortune throughout their careers of never having to put their learning to use. Others have to do this job but once or twice — and though they have had little practice, they must carry out their task to the fullest of their training, talent and intelligence.

A homicide is a one-time thing. The material below discusses the major points that should be stressed when covering a homicide; each angle mentioned should be taken carefully. But the photographer may use his discretion in taking any additional shots which he feels may help to solve a case. Film is cheap when one considers that these photographs cannot be taken again.

In all cases of murder it is essential that the photographer arrives at the scene as soon as possible. Nothing should be moved or any search made at the scene of a homicide until all photographs are taken which accurately record the scene. On occasion, it is necessary for the doctor to examine the body to ascertain if life is extinct, but usually it is not necessary to move the body for this purpose.

Full coverage of the scene of the crime must be made, showing the body in relation to the other objects at the scene. If outdoors, several shots from different angles and a shot from overhead of the body and the weapon or instrument is usually sufficient, but if there are any footprints, tire marks or other marks which would assist in tracing the person responsible, they must be taken. As has often been stated, it is better to take too many photographs than too few; this is especially the case in a murder enquiry when the photographer will not have another opportunity to return to the scene and take further pictures.

Sometimes it is necessary to photograph injuries on the accused person as well as on the victim; these injuries as a rule amount to scratches or other signs that the victim attempted to defend himself. As the accused may be in custody charged with the offense, the photographer can make his own arrangements to obtain the necessary pictures.

If the crime occurs indoors the same photographs will be required, but there the photographer can be handicapped by the size of the room and furniture or other objects which cannot be moved. These disadvantages can be overcome by the use of a camera arranged to take photographs from directly overhead. A fairly small camera, either a special wide-angle camera or a 35mm camera with a wide-angle lens, can be adapted for use in this way. A long boom attached to the camera tripod, with the camera fixed on the end, is steadied against the ceiling, and the exposure made either by means of a long cable release or by the use of a solenoid and a battery. Some professional photographers use rubber suckers to attach the camera to the ceiling, and others have obtained the same results with a cramp and a suitable attachment to the lamp fitting in the center of the room.

Whatever method is used to obtain overhead photographs, the lighting which gives the best results without harsh shadows or "hot spots" is a flashbulb fired, without a reflector near the camera, against the ceiling which acts as a large diffusing reflector.

These overhead cameras are the only satisfactory means of photographing bodies in such places as lift shafts, small bathrooms, lavatories and other small rooms where corpses are sometimes found.

Having covered the scene, it is necessary to photograph anything which has any bearing whatsoever on the crime, such as blood splashes, signs of struggle or indications of drinks or drugs. Any mark of any kind should be recorded: a man was once identified by teeth marks on an apple he had bitten at the scene of the crime. All outstanding

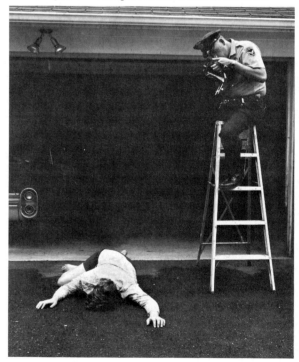

Figure 1 — Taking an overhead shot of the victim

peculiarities should be recorded as in the case of the man who took off his shoes and socks so that he could use his feet to trigger off a shotgun, the barrel of which he placed in his mouth.

Any signs of entry or exit must be recorded, and also any fingerprints left at the scene. As all of these photographs have to be taken before the investigating officers can search the scene or move the body, it is obvious that the photographer will have to work fast. This can be done only if he has suitable equipment maintained in top condition and an adequate strobe unit for flash photography.

Having taken the photographs at the scene, the police photographer has not finished by any means because he now has to attend the post-mortem examination and take photographs as directed by the pathologist.

It is useful at this time to take photographs of the body fully clothed before it is stripped for the autopsy. Small format cameras capable of close-up work — and if necessary, having correction for parallax — can with a small electronic flash unit, deal with this kind of work. Should the pathologist require color pictures, the electronic flash will deliver light at a consistent color temperature.

Prints from all the photographs will be required without delay by the investigating officers, especially any fingerprints which may have been found. A number of copies of these will be required so that a search may be made, and copies will also be wanted to send to other police departments. Other prints will be required for the purpose of house-to-house enquiries or for showing on television. All these requirements must be met by the police photographer with as little delay as possible, and he should therefore standardize his processing procedure and have ample assistance available to enable him to do this.

The police photographer has to take photographs at post-mortem examinations in cases of death other than that brought about by murder. Street accidents, accidents in the home, industrial accidents, suicides, drownings, etc. and most cases where an inquest has to be held, are instances where photographs are taken at a post-mortem examination. The photographs are usually required by the coroner at the inquest, though in some instances where there are proceedings either in civil or criminal courts, the photographer can be called upon to give evidence.

Lighting can be by electronic flash. If you have an electronic flash that can be held away from the camera, you can direct the light to go wherever you want it to go.

Where cases of serious assault occur, there usually follows a charge of robbery, wounding, or causing grievous bodily harm. Photographs in these cases will be required to show the extent of the victim's injuries in order that the court may

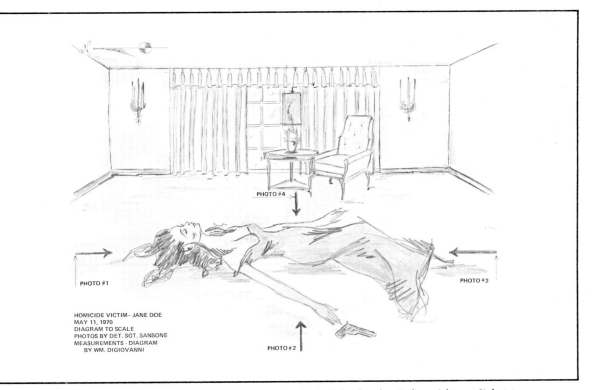

Figure 2 — Sketch demonstrating shots to take circling body 1) head to feet 2) from right arm 3) feet to head 4) from left arm

Figure 3 — Close-ups of gun shot and stab wounds

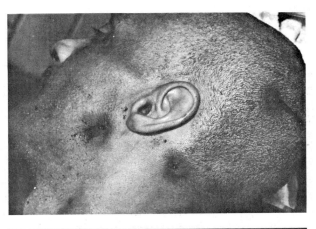

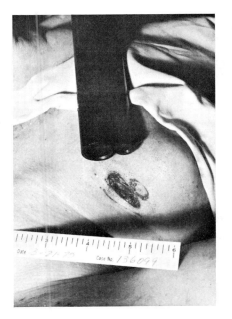

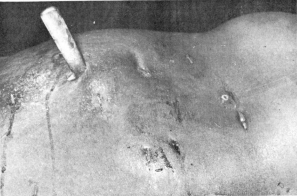

Within the sketch:

PHOTO #4

PHOTO #1

PHOTO #3

PHOTO #2

HOMICIDE VICTIM-- JANE DOE
MAY 11, 1970
DIAGRAM TO SCALE
PHOTOS BY DET. SGT. SANSONE
MEASUREMENTS - DIAGRAM
    BY WM. DIGIOVANNI

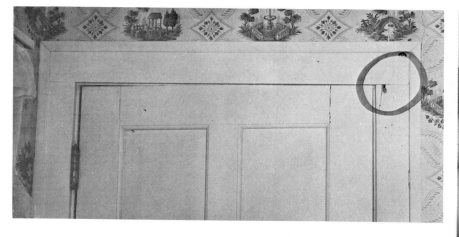

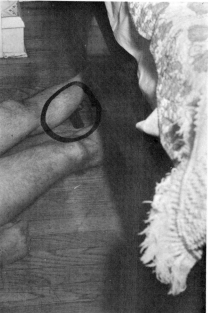

Figure 4 — Homicide details (clockwise). Bullet hole in door, unmoved weapon, the place from which it was taken and a close-up of weapons

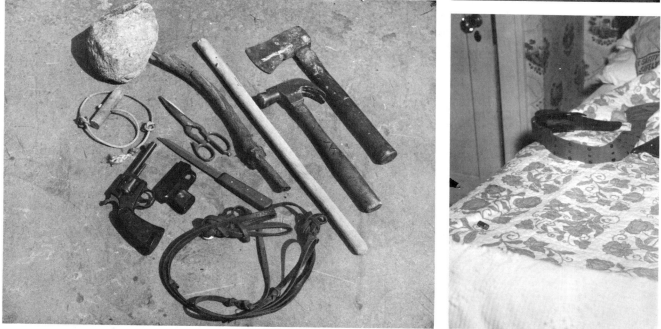

assess the violence of the assault. The hearing of the case may occur weeks or even months after the assault, and during that time the victim has usually recovered from the attack and, if he is fortunate, the marks of his injuries have healed. Without photographs it would indeed be difficult for any court to realize, from a medical description, the extent of the injuries. For this reason certain arrangements have to be made by the photographer to obtain photographs of personal injury. If the injured person is able to travel, is only bruised or has no wound covered with dressings, then perhaps the best way of obtaining the photograph is to get him

to a laboratory for the picture to be taken.

In the case of bruising, always remember that the effect is more severe at about twenty-four hours after the assault, and it is better to wait awhile to allow the bruising to develop than to take the photographs too soon after the occurrence of the assault. Besides this, the victim is always in a state of shock, and a delay will usually produce a more cooperative sitter.

Regarding wounds, these have to be treated by a doctor as soon as possible and so, of course, are covered with dressings. There is no point whatsoever in photographing any person covered with bandages because however incapacitated the person may appear, there may be very little or even nothing under the bandages.

The photographer should not on any account remove any dressings in order to obtain a photograph. If it is necessary to obtain photographs of wounds this must be done by arrangement with, and in the presence of, the doctor. A telephone call will reveal when the doctor has directed that the dressing should be changed. There is normally no objection to the photographer being present when this is done, so that he may obtain the necessary photographs. Doctors are helpful in instances such as this because the photographs are very useful to them when they attend court to give medical evidence with respect to the wounding.

In cases of wounding, most victims are kept in the hospital, and the photographer is requested to work speedily in order to cause the patient as little discomfort as possible and to avoid the risk of infecting the wound. The same equipment as that suggested for use at post-mortem examinations would be ideal for this kind of photography. Flash of course is essential, as lamps with trailing wires would not only be a nuisance in the hospital, but, because they are not sterile, there would be a danger of introducing infection to the patient's wounds. In these cases it is generally only necessary to show the extent of the wounding, and that being so, it is doubtful whether a color photograph would do a better job than one in monochrome. The photographer should be guided by the doctor in this, and should he consider that a color photograph is required, then the same equipment will produce the result.

The first man to arrive at the scene of a homicide has the responsibility of making sure that the victim is dead. This is the only exception to the rule that nothing be touched. In order to ascertain that the victim is actually dead, the officer should observe carefully whether or not the victim is breathing and then feel for a pulse beat at either the neck or wrist. While doing this he should touch the body as little as possible and try not to move it out of the position in which it was found. The first duty of the policeman is to protect life and property. If there are any signs of life, first aid should be administered or the person should be taken to the nearest hospital.

If there is no sign of life in the victim, the police photographer should ask himself, "What will I have to photograph now so that I can convince a jury that this is the way the scene actually appeared?" All the officers at the scene should be instructed not to touch *anything* until the series of pictures is complete. This series of pictures should be taken with the idea in mind that other investigators or persons will have to understand, *pictorially*, how and where this crime was committed.

Not all homicide cases will wind up in court, but those that do will require good negatives from which courtroom presentation photos can be made. A Chicago detective, giving a talk on homicide photography at a convention, said, "On arriving at the scene of a homicide, always keep your hands in your pockets and survey the situation for at least ten or fifteen minutes. Figure out all the possible angles you would need and then begin taking your photographs." The photographer may not be given so much time to compose his work, but the basic idea of patience and thought before photographing should be kept in mind.

HOW TO PHOTOGRAPH A HOMICIDE

The police photographer is always under a great deal of pressure from the coroner or someone else at a homicide scene. They may wish to rush the body to the morgue. The police photographer must not allow these pressures to interfere with his work. Later on these same people will want to have photographs that were accurately taken. Views should be taken of the entire scene showing the location of the body and its position in relation to its surroundings.

To photograph a homicide:

1. Start by taking a picture from as close as you can get to an overhead shot of the subject. Try to get as high as you possibly can for this shot. You may have to improvise. If you can get a stepladder, this will suffice. Get as high as you can on it. Then shoot straight down on the subject and try to avoid shooting from any angle other than vertical. (Figure 1) A shot from an angle or a long shot of the subject will show distortion.

2. If the body is in such a position that you can circle it, your first shot is from the head to the feet, then you go clockwise to the subject's right arm and take another shot. Then move down below the subject's feet and take a shot from the feet to head position, and for your last clockwise shot, move over to the subject's left arm and take a picture from that angle. (Figure 2) If this scene were outdoors you would have no problem taking these shots because you would easily have enough room to operate. But you will find that most of the homicides are committed indoors where you will have a much more limited amount of space in which to work.

3. After you have taken the general scene and shown the location of the body in relation to its surroundings, then begin to take close-up views of the body and its immediate surroundings. In step two you took the general

views and the full length shots of the body. Now you move in closer and closer, taking pictures of the head, body, arms, hands, legs and feet. Be sure to take specific photographs of the wound marks, whether they were made with a weapon or any other instrument. (Figure 3) These can be very important photographs for the police officer later on in the courtroom.

4. If a gun was used in this homicide be sure to take photographs of any bullet holes in the furniture, walls, floors, or any other place where the bullet might have landed. (Figure 4) Always take close-ups of a bullet hole itself.

5. Next look around the vicinity of the crime and if you find any weapons, objects or instruments which were used to perpetrate this crime, be sure to take close-up views of all these objects. (Figure 4.)

6. If it is at all possible, use a tripod to take all of the above shots. This is a good example of shooting to get fine detail in your negative, so try to shoot these shots at f/16 or at least f/22. The speed can then be obtained from your light meter reading. If you are using a tripod you can use any speed all the way from time to 400 depending on what your light meter calls for.

7. After you have taken the above shots and before the body is removed, you should chalk the outline of the body and also chalk any other objects which are related to the crime. Now they may remove the body. After the body is gone, you begin taking all the shots over again which you took before the body was removed. One of the major reasons for this is that once the body is gone there is less confusion at the actual scene. Secondly, repeating the same shots with the chalk image insures having one good negative out of two shots of the same scene. Show the chalk marks in relation to the furniture if indoors, or to other objects if outdoors.

8. Be sure to photograph the entire inside of a home. If the murder happened upstairs in a bedroom, photograph all other rooms upstairs, especially those adjacent to the crime room. Be sure to photograph every ingress and egress room to the homicide room.

9. If the crime happened in a bathroom which is rather small, you should put a wide-angle lens on your camera and shoot with it. This is a good example of a time when you will probably have to shoot at f/22 or f/32. Remember also that if you have to use flash in the bathroom scene, you may have to put a handkerchief or two over your flashlamp because tile reflects a great amount of light.

10. The next step is to photograph anything which you consider might have fingerprints on it. This can best be done by using a 4 × 5 camera with the Faurot Foto Focuser attachment on the front of the lens. If the objects are removable and you can take them into the laboratory, it is much better for the fingerprint specialist to photograph the object in his own lab because he can do a better job there than on the scene. But, if it is impossible to bring the object into the laboratory, then you will have to photograph the fingerprints or any other evidence at the scene of the crime.

11. Now begin, in a clockwise fashion, to photograph the exterior of the house, usually from distances of about 75 to 100 feet away from the house. Start with a shot of the driveway side of the house, showing the driveway and front of the house, and move in the clockwise fashion taking views from each side of the house. Include a view of the backyard and garage. Be sure to show all possible entrances and exits which the perpetrator may have taken.

12. Take photographs showing the landscaping, shrubbery, fences, next door buildings, and all surrounding homes to show what kind of a neighborhood this is.

13. Later on, if this develops into a very important case, the city may feel it is worthwhile for them to rent a helicopter and have several shots of the house taken from this height to show the house where the homicide occurred and all its surroundings.

14. Take some shots from in front of the home looking down the streets from both sides of the home. Of course, you should include the driveway and all other access to the home.

15. Go to the rear of the home and take some shots from the rear showing any possible way the intruder may have come to the home from the rear, and go out to the next street.

16. The best shots that you can take of a room will usually be those taken from the corners of the rooms. Shoot a shot from all four corners of the room. Be sure to place a yardstick or some other type of measuring device in the scene so that you will have an approximate size of distances in the photograph.

The homicide may have been committed in a small room. Always treat the small room as you would a bathroom scene and use your wide-angle lens. The courts usually admit wide-angle pictures of room interiors because they often furnish pictures which cannot be had in any other way. Be sure to draw sketches as you work to show exactly where you were when each of the above photographs were taken.

LIGHTING FOR A HOMICIDE SCENE

Proper lighting is the biggest problem of the police photographer. Unlike the professional studio photographer who has a relatively fixed lighting arrangement, the police photographer must frequently work outdoors at night where his flash is not enough. Indoor photography, day or night, is simple by comparison.

There are several ways of attacking the problem of lighting for outdoor photography at night. The photographer can:

1. "Paint with light"
2. Use a large strobe unit, fully charged.
3. Use three or more strobe units as slave units. The strobes may be connected with cords to the main strobe, or they can be rigged to last independently.
4. Use photoflood where house current is available. Light bars of the type that movie cameras use can be set on tripods or improvised stands and aimed at the subject.

When using color film to shoot a homicide scene (see Chapter 17) it is best to use strobe for all lighting. Photofloods must be checked to see that the color temperature is correct for the color film that is being used.

The photographer should practice shooting outdoors at night and keep a record of everything he does so that when his practice film is developed he will have a record of what he did right or wrong.

PHOTOGRAPHING A HOMICIDE IN COLOR

Years ago, the use of color for photographing homicide scenes was unthinkable not only because color film was imperfect and expensive to use but also because the courts were, to some extent, visually opposed to the added realism of color photographs. Although the courts are no less squeamish about color in homicide pictures, color has become more or less acceptable. Also, the cost of color photography is now well within reason. The obvious advantage of being able to show blood as red and not as a shade of grey must not be overlooked by the police photographer.

For more information on color photography, see Chapter 17.

SUMMARY

When photographing the scene of a homicide, the photographer should reproduce what his eyes are seeing and relate this scene to other people. He will have to show the manner in which the homicide occurred, views of the room with the body in it, all the rooms surrounding the room with all ingress and egress to the room. He must show whether there is any evidence of a struggle, and try to show what was happening in this room prior to the crime. Obvious evidence such as drinking glasses, bottles, or any trace evidence such as cigarette butts, bloodstains, or broken glass should not be overlooked.

The circumstances of death can be illustrated by various views of the body, including close-up shots of the wounds and bruise marks. Without saying, the photographer must photograph the weapon (Figure 4) and the place from which it may have been taken. (Figure 4.)

SUICIDE

Of the many investigations to be performed by the police, one of the most difficult is a suicide. The investigator often determines whether the act is suicide, homicide or an accident.

Suicides are prone to wound themselves with a knife in the throat, wrist, or heart regions or with a gunshot through the temple, forehead, the center of the back of the head, mouth, chest or abdomen.

Although some wounds, such as a knife wound in the back or cuts on the palm of the hand, tend to suggest a crime other than suicide, neither the position and depth of the wound nor the seeming difficulty of self infliction should exclude suicide as an explanation.

HOW TO PHOTOGRAPH A SUICIDE

If there is any doubt as to whether a death may possibly be a case of suicide, the scene should be photographed in the same manner as a homicide. It may not be determined until several days, weeks, or months later whether or not it was a positive suicide; if the case should turn out to be a homicide, you will have photographs.

Suicide by shooting. Photograph both the entrance and exit wounds. Place identification alongside each wound as well as a ruler for measuring. The entrance wound is always larger than the diameter of the bullet. Usually, the hairs surrounding the entrance wound will be singed and the skin will be burned to a reddish- or a grayish-brown color. Also, if the shot was fired from a range of less than eight inches, a smeary black coat of powder residue may be evident. If possible, photograph close-ups of the wound in color to show these various discolorations.

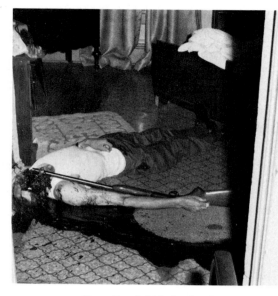

Figure 5 — Suicide by shooting

Figure 6 — Simulated suicide by hanging

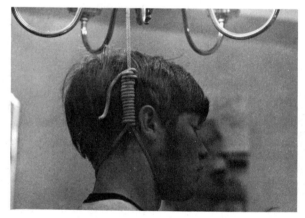

If the victim has been shot through his clothing, infra-red photography (see Chapter 16) will record a better pattern image.

Suicide by hanging. Strangulation by hanging is the most common form of suicide. But the investigator must not assume that a victim found hanging is a suicide.

Photograph the subject at a distance from four views, showing the full body. Then move in close and show the knot, bruise marks and, if shooting in color, the discoloration of the body.

SUMMARY

A suicide case should be photographed as though it were a homicide, but the photographer should not assume that it is one or the other. Care-ful work is important because, should the case be determined a suicide, the victim's insurance company may need photographs of the deceased before settling a claim.

SEX OFFENSES

The crime of rape may be taken as typical of this class of offense. The purpose of the photographic subjects listed below is to offer useful information on signs of any struggle; indications of the victim's efforts to resist, such as bruises or black-and-blue marks; and evidence of the presence of either or both parties at the scene.

SCENE OF THE CRIME

A photo of the locale itself may be important to show that the outcries of the victim could not be heard or to illustrate the fact that the nature of the place would make it an unlikely meeting ground for ordinary social purposes. Photographs to show the remoteness of the scene from general traffic or from the nearest dwelling house may be useful. Four views diagonal to the purported scene of the crime should be taken. One shot in a case like this may be very misleading. For example, a view of the scene may show it as a desolate and uncivilized area, while a slight change in the position of the camera may show that the spot is very near a dwelling house.

The positioning of the camera at an improper height above the ground also may create misleading photographs. For example, suppose the scene of an alleged sexual offense is a deep hollow in a park; if the camera is placed close to the ground near the brink of the hollow, the resulting photograph will create the impression that no hollow exists. This is because the farther bank blends with the nearer bank, creating the impression of level ground. The proper way to take such a picture is to raise the camera sufficiently to include both the hollow and its nearer and farther banks. From this level, a correct view of the surroundings will be obtained.

Photographs of stains or marks should also be taken at the scene of the crime. When photographing blood stains it is permissible to use contrast filters. Selection of the proper filter often will enable the photographer to bring out marks that are practically invisible to the naked eye. After the stains have been photographed, specimens should be carefully preserved for submission to the medical doctor or other specialist whose duty it will be to identify them and prepare photomicrographs for use as evidence.

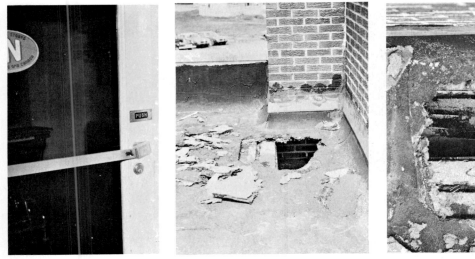

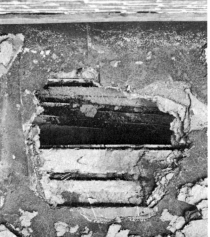

Figure 7 — Points of entry (clockwise from above left) doorway; hole in flooring; close-up of hole; basement window; close-up of tools used to pry window; broken window; and another doorway.

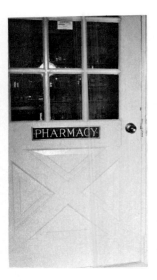

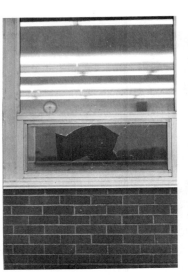

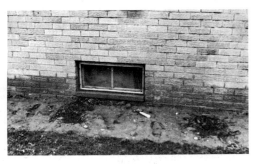

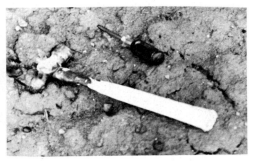

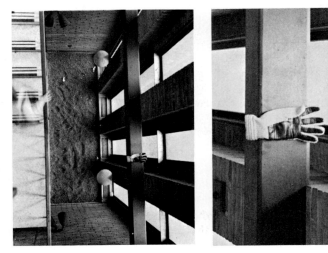

Figure 8 — A glove left behind by surprised burglar (left) and close-up (right)

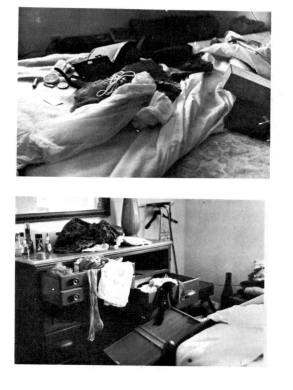

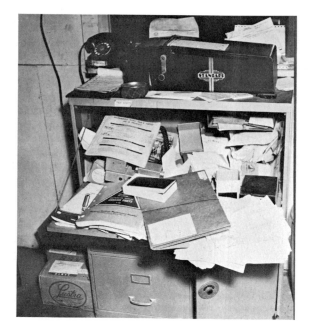

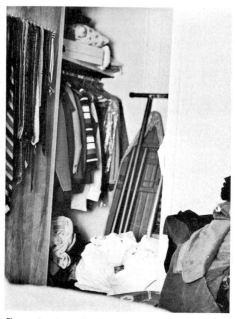

Figure 9 — Ransacked rooms (above and above left)

Figure 10 — Close-ups showing "jimmy marks" on doors (left)

Additional shots should be made of special features, such as foot and tire impressions; broken branches; buttons; torn clothing or other personal property; used matches and booklets of matches; disturbances of rocks, foliage, and other natural features; and displacements of other objects from their normal positions.

An indoor crime scene may also contain evidence of a struggle which should be photographed. Fin-gerprints, if any are found, must be photographed with a fingerprint camera.

PHOTOGRAPHS OF THE SUSPECT

An examination of a suspect by a physician and the assigned investigator may reveal evidence of the criminal act which will link him to the scene. It

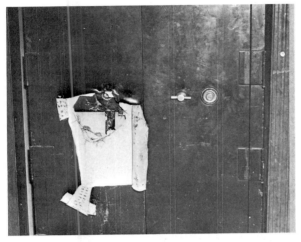

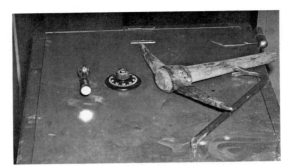

Figure 11 — Tools left at crime scene

Figure 12 — View of attempt to enter safe

is desirable to photograph such evidence in the position in which it is found. The suspect's body may show evidence of the physical struggle, such as scratches or bruises. Foreign hairs, pollen granules, or fibers may be discovered by the physician. The garments of the suspect may reveal bloodstains, semen, or traces of grass stain or mud. (Since semen fluoresces, it can be shown easily by ultraviolet photography.) The trouser cuffs may contain weed seeds or soil. Similarly, if the crime took place indoors, materials peculiar to the premises may be found on the suspect's person or clothing. When photographing the physical evidence, include a data sheet and a ruler.

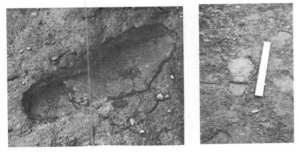

Figure 13 — Footprints

PHOTOGRAPHS OF THE VICTIM

Evidence of resistance to the criminal act is particularly important in sex offense cases involving adult victims. Thus, marks and discolorations of the body in general (color film is excellent for this); the condition of specifically affected parts; and the presence of foreign hairs, fibers, and biological stains are significant. Traces associating the victim with the crime scene, such as those described in the preceding section are also important in some cases to corroborate the victim's account of the occurrence. In photographing the person of the victim, permission should ordinarily be obtained previously, preferably in writing, from the victim or from the parents or guardian if the victim is a minor. It is recommended that the victim's physician be present when such photographs are made.

BURGLARY AND BREAKING AND ENTERING

The burglary investigator should always try to take photographs with the thought in mind of how he is going to use these pictures to prove that the suspect was the one who committed this crime. However, he must realize that most of the pictures of a burglary will be used mainly in assisting a detective to solve the case. Rather than take a suspect around the city to show him some of the homes which were broken into to refresh his memory, detectives can show him photographs to help him recall whether he was involved in any of those jobs. A good set of pictures of burglaries can save the detective a great amount of work and time.

Photographs are also necessary for the prosecutor's office to successfully argue a case. Many cases are lost because the prosecutor is not given the right kind of evidence for him to use in court. The prosecutor's objective is to show that a particular crime was committed and that the accused perpetrated the act. The prosecutor must establish the elements of the offense and produce evidence associating the defendant with the crime scene and events.

For example, in a burglary, the elements of breaking and entering would suggest photographs of the exterior of the building with close-ups of the window, showing where the jimmy had been applied. Views of the ransacked room or the rifled safe would aid in showing the intent of larceny. Photographs of footprints and fingerprints would tend to link the suspect to the scene (See Chapter 12.)

PHOTOGRAPHING A BURGLARY

It is up to the officer taking the pictures to decide how many to take. Usually, for the routine burglary, six to eight shots should suffice. In planning a series of photographs, the elements of the offense can dictate the kind and number of photographs to be taken.

When covering a burglary photographically you should include at least the following shots in your set, photographing in color if possible.

1. The exterior of the building in which the burglary occurred.

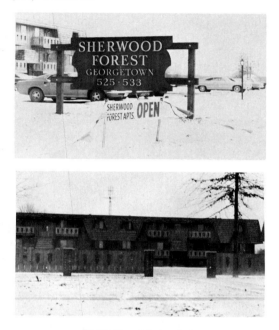

Figure 14 — Exterior shots

2. The point of entry. Just as you did in the homicide case, begin with a distant shot, and then work yourself in to get your close-up shots to show the forcible entry. (Figure 7.) Many times you will have to look the house or building over very carefully to find how the criminal did enter. Look in the window wells of the basement, check all doors and windows, and don't forget the milk chute.
3. Each room in the house or building which is disturbed should be photographed. If you have a wide-angle lens, use it. Take shots from all four corners of the room which is ransacked. Usually two pictures, one from each diagonal corner, should suffice.
4. Take shots of all the furniture or articles which show evidence of being ransacked. (Figure 9.) If the articles cannot be brought back to your laboratory, then photograph each article separately. The lab man will check each article you bring back to the lab for fingerprints, and pho-

tograph each article. When this is done, be sure to identify each item as to where you got it, the date and your name. Get in the habit of identifying any item you are going to work on.

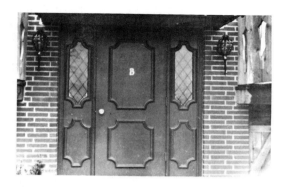

Figure 15 — Don't overlook the front door as a point of entry

5. If you can determine how the criminal left the home, photograph his exit.
6. Many times, when the burglar is in a home, he will be surprised by someone. In his haste to leave the home he may leave something behind, such as a hat, gloves, scarf, cigarette butts or burned matches. (Figure 8.) Most of these articles are usually found at the scene and they should be photographed.
7. All available physical evidence, such as fingerprints, footprints, tire prints, crepe sole prints, heelprints and tool marks and tools should be photographed.
8. If the merchandise which was stolen is recovered, it should be photographed. If you recover some of the merchandise later in the suspect's home or apartment, this should be photographed where it was recovered.

ARSON

Arson is the most difficult crime in the code book to prosecute because the evidence, especially the materials used by the arsonist, is usually destroyed by the fire. But if the fire were photographed and investigated properly, most arson cases could be solved.

The photographer should go to the scene of every fire. He should be the first man to arrive at the scene, so that he will be able to begin photographing the scene even before the fire trucks arrive. He should have all his photographic equipment ready and start shooting immediately. He should shoot the entire operation of the fire as it progresses, taking factual pictures and leaving the sensational photographs for the newspapermen.

HOW TO PHOTOGRAPH A FIRE

One of the best methods of taking fire photographs is to take them from a distance with a camera that is equipped with a telephoto lens. The use of the telephoto lens avoids emphasizing one part of the fire over another. Pictures taken from a distance with a telephoto lens will often reveal important details that would appear insignificant in a picture taken at close range. Also, the great amount of smoke present will not fog a telephoto lens at a distance.

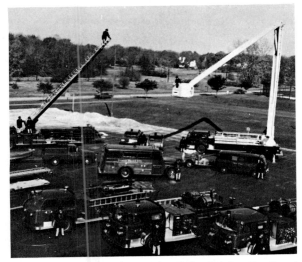

Figure 16 — Fire equipment of the Shaker Heights, Fire Department

As a rule, you will not have conditions made to suit you. Look over the entire scene and try to discover the best position (preferably a high position). Today with the large snorkel ladder trucks, the photographer should be able to get up and shoot the scene from above. (Figure 16.)

While the fire is burning, be sure to photograph as many of the spectators as you can. It is common knowledge that most of the arsonists get their kicks out of watching the fires and may be in the crowd.

Figure 17 — Photographs taken with telephoto lens showing suspicious action in the vicinity of the fire

If you will photograph all the spectators of a fire, and print so that most of the people are recognizable, you can compare the photographs of one fire with another. If you spot a spectator present at most of your fires, you would have a good suspect to quiz and investigate further as to whether he is an arsonist. (Figure 17.) This is a tough job to do, but don't hesitate to try. It could turn out to be a very rewarding effort.

After the fire is extinguished, take exterior views of the scene from diagonally opposite corners of the building. Also get up high on a ladder and take more pictures of the ruins of the fire to show the entire extent of the fire. The immediate vicinity of the fire should also be photographed after the fire to show the location of the building in relation to other buildings of the neighborhood. In major fires it would be advisable to shoot some shots after the fire from high adjacent buildings or even from a helicopter. Today most large cities in conjunction with a radio station have a helicopter to broadcast the traffic reports. You could probably make arrangements to have that man fly you around above the fire scene and take these most useful shots.

PHOTOGRAPHS AFTER THE FIRE

If the photographer for the fire department is not a trained fire investigator, then the fire department should combine both jobs, so that the man who is the fire investigator can also be the fire photographer. These jobs easily supplement one another. If, however, the fire department has a photographer who is not a trained fire investigator, and they have another man who does this work, then after the fire these two men should get together and go over the shots they will want. Nothing should be moved unless whoever is in charge knows about it. This is similar to police photography in a crime scene.

When the destruction is only partial, the fire investigator will probably want photographs of the interiors of every room showing either damage by fire or smoke or evidence of a planned fire. (Figure 18.) These should be taken before any clean-up work is started. Pictures taken from two diagonally

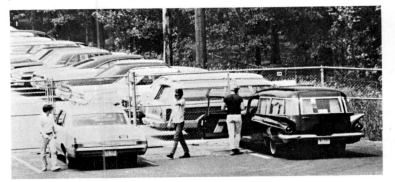

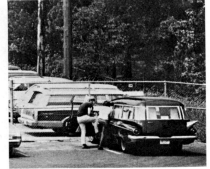

opposite corners of each room with a wide-angle lens will show most of the conditions in which each room was left by the fire. Sometimes, however, the photographer will have to take pictures kneeling, sitting, or even lying down to photograph the ceiling. For this task, a pair of coveralls is almost as essential as a camera.

An indication of forcible entry, such as a broken window or door locks, demands close-up photography because such things are often signs that the fire was started to conceal another crime. All clocks that have stopped should be photographed as the time shown may indicate the approximate time of the start of the fire.

After the photographs have been made to show conditions immediately after the fire, photograph the debris being screened or sifted for evidence. (Figure 19.) Every step of this screening process should be photographed to show in what manner the evidence was collected. This screening or sifting process may take days or weeks before it is all completed. When the point of origin of the fire or explosion is located close-up, photographs should be made immediately of any bits of evidence uncovered. After being photographed, such items should be turned over to the police department laboratory.

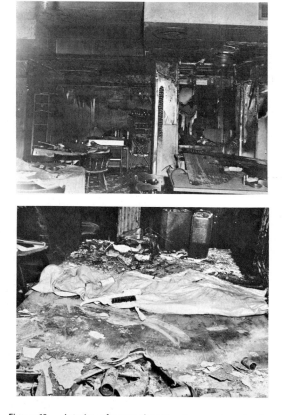

Figure 18 — Interior of room showing damage done by fire

EQUIPMENT FOR ARSON PHOTOGRAPHY

The photographer must have a good tripod, for there will be many times when he will be shooting with color film and, due to the weather, may have to shoot at slower speeds. Also, because lighting is tricky at best when photographing a fire, a light meter is essential to arson photography.

LIGHTING FOR FIRE PHOTOGRAPHY

Lighting is particularly troublesome when photographing burned interiors because it is difficult to illuminate charred areas sufficiently. Some photographers use floodlights and move them about during long exposures to produce the effect of "painting with light." Others find photoflash illumination suitable. In partially burned rooms when the ceiling is not blackened a type of photoflash lighting known as "bounce flash," produced by pointing the flashgun toward the ceiling often will produce good results.

FILM FOR FIRE PHOTOGRAPHY

For black-and-white pictures of fire and explosion scenes use a fast panchromatic film such as Kodak

Tri-X or Kodak Royal Pan Film, Estar Base. With this fast film, short exposures can be used which will be excellent for producing shadow detail. This is particularly important when photographing fire scenes which usually contain many large, blackened areas. The exposure may have to be on the long side in order to show as much detail as possible in the charred areas.

Color photography can be done with Professional Ektacolor or, if the photographer is using a 35mm camera, a fast Ektachrome Film.

IMPORTANCE OF COLOR PHOTOGRAPHS DURING A FIRE

The extent to which the investigator can conduct a preliminary investigation during the actual burning will vary with the nature and severity of the fire. General observations can, of course, be made from an appropriate distance and certain examinations of the nearby areas can sometimes be made at this stage. Much of the information suggested below can also be obtained from eyewitnesses later. Using color film and recording the events of the fire properly will be invaluable later. Below is some of the evidence that can be obtained from a fire, which can help win or lose a case.

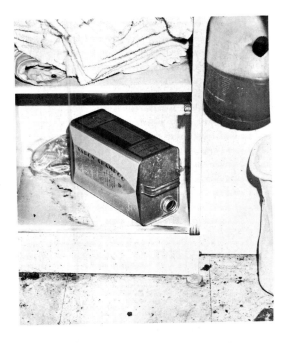

Figure 19 — Flammable liquid container in position found after the fire (above) and moved from cabinet (below)

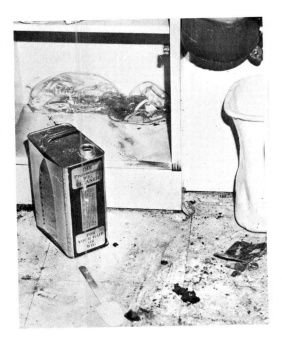

Steam and smoke. The presence of steam indicates that humid substances have come in contact with the hot combustible substances. The water present in the humid substance is evaporated before the substance begins to burn.

White smoke is given out by the burning of phosphorous, a substance which is sometimes used as an incendiary agent.

Grayish smoke is caused by the emission of flying ash and soot in loosely packed substances such as straw and hay.

Black smoke is produced by either incomplete combustion or the preponderance in the burning material of a product with a petroleum base such as rubber, tar, coal, turpentine, or petroleum.

Reddish brown or yellow smoke indicates the presence of nitrates or substances with a nitrocellulose base. Thus, smoke of this color can be emitted from the burning of nitric acid, nitrated plastics, film or smokeless gun powder. A number of these substances are suitable as accelerants.

Color of flame. The color of the flame is indicative of the intensity of the fire and sometimes of the nature of the combustible substances present. The temperature of the fire may vary from 500 to 1500 degrees centigrade with the color of the flame ranging from red, through yellow, and finally becoming a blinding white. Some accelerants may give a characteristically colored flame. For example, burning alcohol is characterized by a blue flame. Red flames may indicate the presence of petroleum products.

Size of fire. The size of the fire should be noted at the time of arrival and at subsequent intervals thereafter. This information may be significant in relation to the time at which the alarm was received. An unusually rapid extension of the fire is indicative of the use of accelerants or some other method of physical preparation. A thorough knowledge about the construction of buildings is essential to the man who wants to be a good photographic-fire investigator.

Direction of travel. Since hot gases rise and fire normally sweeps upward, the direction of travel of a fire is predictable from a knowledge of the construction of the building. It will be expected that the flames will tend to rise until on meeting objects they project horizontally to seek other vertical outlets. The extent and rate of travel in the horizontal direction will depend primarily on the direction of the wind and on ventilating conditions, such as open doors and windows. The spread of fire in an unusual direction or at an exceptional rate should

Smoke and vapors. The characteristics of the smoke, steam or other vapors which emanate from the fire are useful indications in determining the nature of the burning substances, including the accelerants used. In the following list the color of the smoke is related to the most common incendiary agent which may emit it:

arouse suspicion as to the presence of accelerants or a prepared arrangement of doors and windows.

Location of flames. The photo-investigator should note carefully whether there is more than one apparent point of origin and should try to estimate the approximate location of each. Unrelated fires in different places are indicative of arson. The incendiary may, for example, arrange timing devices in different places with the result that the separate outbreaks of flames will be apparent.

Order of searching. The area immediately surrounding the burned property should now be more thoroughly examined for evidentiary traces and

Sketching and photographing. A photographic record should be made of the destruction accomplished by the fire and of physical evidence uncovered by the search. The photo-investigator should follow the order of the search, photographing each area of significance to the investigation prior to the search. When the point of origin is located it should be thoroughly photographed to show such points as the type and extent of "alligatoring" and charring and the remains of any incendiary device. As each piece of evidence is discovered it should be photographed in its original condition and in its position when it is completely uncovered. In addition to the photographs a sketch of important areas should be made, showing the location of the

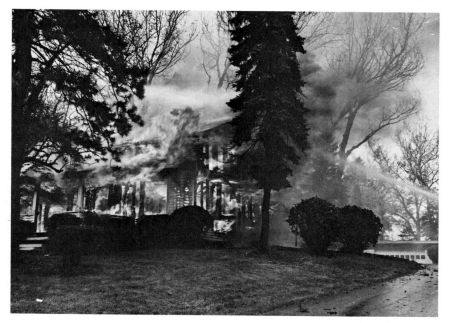

Figure 20 — Photograph taken of fire in progress to illustrate direction and color of smoke

clues. The doors and windows of the building should be studied for evidences of a break, particularly if the premises are normally locked during the period in which the fire took place. Tool impressions, broken window panes, and forced locks are the obvious marks of such a break. The photo-investigator should now progress to the interior, directing his observations to the charred remains of the fire primarily for evidence of the accelerants or other incendiary devices. Assuming that the burning has been extensive, the following order will normally be followed:

1. the outer shell of the remains
2. the first open area or floor from the point of entry
3. the first inner shell or wall of an inside room
4. the general area suspected of being the point where the fire first broke out.

various articles of evidence. As an aid in the construction of this sketch the photo-investigator will find the blueprints of buildings maintained in the files of housing and building departments particularly useful in giving the dimensions and other details of the structure.

PROBLEMS AND CAUTIONS FOR ARSON PHOTOGRAPHY

The greatest scourge to the fire photographer is lens fogging produced by contact with heat and steam. The photographer must wait for the air to cool somewhat before attempting to photograph indoor damages. Smoke also forms a barrier which light sometimes cannot penetrate.

Be careful when using flash units which may explode in the atmosphere surrounding a fire.

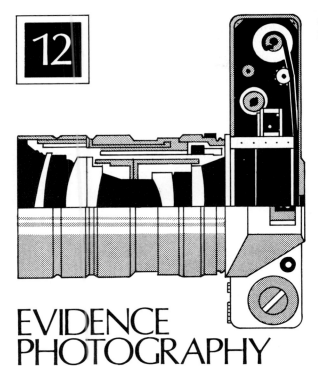

EVIDENCE PHOTOGRAPHY

scene, photographs should be made of items of physical evidence as follows:

1. Objects which serve to establish the fact that a crime has been committed, or the corpus delicti.

2. Evidence relating to the manner in which the crime was committed, or the modus operandi of the criminal.

3. Objects which might provide a clue to the identity of the perpetrator.

4. Clues which would connect a suspect with the crime.

5. Anything which has any bearing on the crime, such as blood splashes, signs of a struggle or any indications of drinking or drugs. Any mark, no matter how slight, should be photographed.

6. Fingerprints found at the scene.

If a body is taken to the morgue it should be photographed there as directed by the pathologist. The body should be photographed with clothing on and then without clothing. When photographing a body at the morgue, color film and a strobe unit should be used. The electronic unit will deliver light at a consistent color temperature.

PROCEDURES

Three photographs of an item of evidence should be made. One should be from a distance sufficient to show the object against the background of its setting so that it can be located and referred to in the over-all crime scene photograph. The other two should be taken close-up and with a fairly large image size to clearly show the nature of the object and its identifying characteristics.

A small ruler should be included in one of these close-ups and omitted in the other (some attorneys may object to the ruler and claim that it changes the scene.) Paper or cloth rulers can be purchased which include room for the date, case number, department, and officer's name.

Shots should also be taken from the viewpoint of the witness or witnesses, if any, to show that, from where they were standing, they could see all that was going on.

Extreme close-ups may be needed, but they involve specialized techniques and are made at the police laboratory or at the morgue.

Many articles of value as evidence will be found at the scene of a crime. Each object should be photographed individually and in relation to other objects at the scene. Three purposes are served by this procedure: (1) a permanent record is made of the original appearance of the object; (2) the photographs can be used in place of physical evidence to supplement the case report; and (3) each article is preserved from unnecessary handling which might cause the evidence to deteriorate or otherwise become altered.

Whenever possible, some or all of the evidence sample should be retained to be photographed in the laboratory where one has all the needed equipment to photomicrograph and macrophotograph the evidence (see page 125.)

As a general rule, a photograph should be made at the scene of any piece of evidence which might deteriorate, change with time, or any evidence which cannot be moved from the scene or which might be damaged by handling. Typical objects which require individual photographs are tools, weapons, clothing, and contraband. Close-up photographs should be made with color film (when possible) of wounds, bruises, scratches, and identifying marks on a body, and skin punctures in the skin of a narcotics addict.

PHOTOGRAPHS AT THE SCENE OF THE CRIME

In addition to the over-all shots of the crime

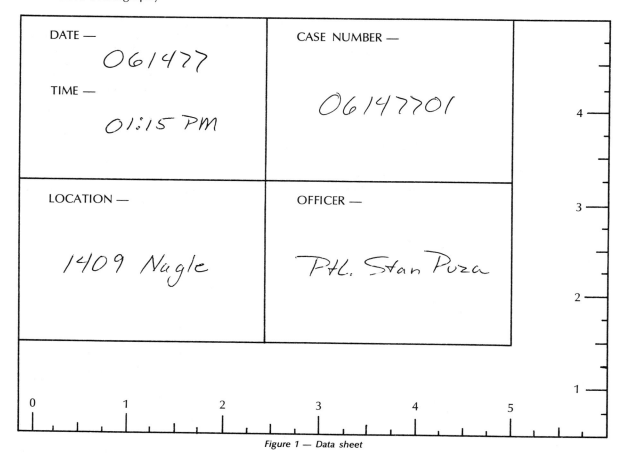

Figure 1 — Data sheet

DATA SHEET

A data sheet must be included in every evidence photograph. The following procedure is becoming uniform throughout the country.

The data sheet should include: date, time, case number, location and officer's name. Dates should be written in digits in the following order: month, day, year. January is written 01, February 02, etc. so that all months are written as two digits. In the same way, days should be written as follows: 01, 02, 03 . . . 31. Years are abbreviated to the last two digits: 77, 78, 79 etc. Thus, every date will be composed of six digits; January 15, 1977 is written 011577.

The time should be written in the following form — 01:15 PM. Case numbers should mean something. In small departments which handle less than one hundred cases a day, the case number can be written as the date plus a two digit number indicating the number of the case for that day. The third case handled on January 15, 1980, would be written: 01158003. This system can also be used for mug shots.

The location should be given as an address where the crime took place and the last space should be filled with the photographer's name.

FOOT OR SHOE IMPRESSIONS

The imprints of shoes in soil are quite often found at or near crime scenes. Before reproductions are made by plaster casting, the impressions should be photographed. The camera, placed on a tripod, should be directed so that the camera axis is perpendicular to the plane of the impression; that is, the lens board and film should be parallel to the ground. The height of the camera should be adjusted so that the whole impression is included in the film with a fairly large image size. A ruler placed at the side of the impression will indicate size. If a particular area of the impression contains any peculiar characteristics which may be helpful in identifying the foot or shoe, a closer shot should be taken so that this area (including the ruler) fills the picture and the desired information is given in clear detail. Kodak Panatomic-X film is recommended.

Oblique lighting (lighting that is low and to the side of the impression) is used when photographing impressions. The low light emphasizes the impression by creating shadows wherever there are ridges in the soil. Photographs made in daylight should be taken with photoflood, strobe or photoflash placed obliquely to counteract the flattening effect of direct sunlight. Indoor shots and night shots should be made with photoflood whenever possible since this lighting can be so easily controlled. Flash may provide too much light: if necessary, the flash should be cut by covering it with a handkerchief.

CLOSE-UP PHOTOGRAPHY

Evidence of all kinds must be photographed close-up to show details. The single-lens-reflex camera is best for this kind of work because of its size and because parallax is avoided. The photographer can add to a good SLR lens any of three powers of close-up lenses, or pair them as needed. The powers of close-up lenses are measured in diopters. A +3 diopter lens is the strongest. When two close-up lenses are used together, the stronger lens (the one with the highest number) should be next to the lens of the camera.

Close-up lenses, simply, allow the photographer to get closer to his subject. By adding a lens of +1 strength, he can get within 20 to 40 inches of the subject; a pair of +3 lenses will reduce the working distance to about six inches, which would cover a field not more than 4½ × 3 inches.

Depth of field is practically nonexistent in close-up photography. There is no margin for error and focusing must be accurate within a fraction of an inch. Working distances should be measured from the front of the close-up lens to the front of the object being photographed. If the camera is on a tripod, a yardstick can be used to position it at a specific distance from the point of focus.

Extension tubes or bellows can be used for large images at medium to close working distances. Bellows extensions are bulkier than tubes but are more versatile and of course more expensive. These units vary greatly and generally are used with cameras which have focal plane shutters.

Basic exposure is subject to change with extension tubes or bellows, since they actually alter the lens-to-film distance. The light-transmitting capacity of a lens diminishes in relation to the length of the tube, necessitating a longer exposure for a given f/stop than the basic lens position requires. This obviously includes a reduction in the maximum "speed" of the lens.

A rigid camera support is essential for close-up work which usually requires slow shutter speeds or time exposures. When using bellows or extension tubes, the camera may become very heavy, making it susceptible to jarring and to vibration, especially during long exposures.

LIGHTING FOR SMALL OBJECTS

Special equipment is needed to light very small objects to enhance texture or to create special effects. Most close-up exposures require maximum illumination in place where shadows are cast by the equipment being used. Standard floodlights, if placed too near an object, are likely to light it too evenly and flatly; furthermore, if the evidence is perishable, the heat from the floodlights may destroy it.

A 150 watt miniature spot is a good lamp to use for lighting close-ups. A metal tube called a snoot can be added to the spot for a narrower beam.

Reflectors are useful for intensifying the main light. For fill-in light, a mirror can be used in the deep shade. For simple softening of shadows, an ordinary white cardboard reflector is good.

MACROPHOTOGRAPHY AND MICROPHOTOGRAPHY

Macrophotography, also called photomacrography, is basically the same as close-up photography, although the lens is usually closer to the subject than in most close-up work. The photographer who must do a great deal of macrophotography should have a permanent set-up with lighting and a floating table to minimize vibration. Contrast filters used with panchromatic film will help to bring out certain stains which are not visible to the naked eye.

Microphotography, or photomicrography, is photography which makes use of a microscope and is used to record such minute evidence as powdered debris, stains, hairs, and fibers.

WOOD PHOTOGRAPHY

Criminal cases often involve wood as evidence. Very seldom are large pieces of wood recovered. Usually the wood is in the form of splinters, sawdust or other small fragments. In the Lindbergh child kidnapping case, a large piece of wood was taken from an attic floor and a ladder was made from it. This proved to be the downfall of Bruno Hauptman, for the piece of wood in the ladder was proven to have come from the attic of his home. Large pieces of wood are of help to the police for their macro-characteristics. Small fragments of wood are found in housebreakings where they are broken from the window, door frame, or from the furniture. Also, in cases of safe-breakings, the wood packing between the inner and outer walls of the safe which is used to insulate the safe can be used as evidence. If the wood cannot be brought into the laboratory it should be photographed at the scene with oblique lighting.

METAL PHOTOGRAPHY

Metal is replacing wood in most construction, particularly in homes which now have metal storm doors and windows. Metal should be photographed using the same procedure (oblique lighting) used for wood. The high reflectability of some metals may make them difficult to photograph. Calm, which can be purchased in a spray can, can be applied to the object (although some attorneys may object to its use) or reflectors can be used to subdue lighting. Cardboard covered with crinkly foil can be used to photograph silvery objects; crinkly gold foil should be used to photograph gold objects.

DUSTY SHOE PRINTS

It is particularly important to photograph any shoe impressions in interiors, such as on floors or counter tops, because these cannot be reproduced readily in any other manner. (Figure 2.) When there is little contrast, it may be necessary to lift the latent footprints before photographing them. For this purpose, a new material, called "Lift Print" is suggested. This flexible rubber matrix is laid down over the print and rolled lightly with a photographic print roller. The dust forming the footprint sticks to the matrix and can be photographed 1:1 on Kodalith film. The Lift Print material is washable and can be used over and over again. For further information write to the West American Rubber Company, 410 North Avenue 19, Los Angeles, California 90031.

Another method to use on a shoeprint is to desensitize a sheet of 8 × 10 photographic paper by putting it into a hypo solution, then letting it dry. This desensitized photographic paper is placed over the imprint and it will lift the print very well. Sometimes, it is better to do this than to photograph it if there is not enough contrast.

TIRE IMPRESSIONS

The procedure for tire impressions is quite similar to that described for shoe impressions. A length of the tire track which shows a clear pattern should be shot several times close-up to give maximum information. In each, the full width of the impression should almost fill the film. One of these should show the class characteristics that will identify the type of tire. Areas which reveal defects, such as cuts, may also serve to identify the individual tire.

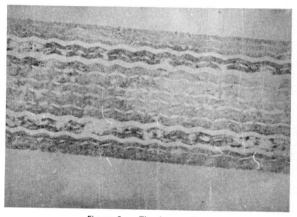

Figure 3 — Tire impression

It is also important for evidence purposes to photograph, in sections, a sufficient length of each tire impression, if available, to provide pictures which correspond to the complete circumference of each tire. After photography, these same areas should be reproduced in plaster casts.

As in photographing shoe impressions, oblique lighting is a must, even in daylight, to create shadows and emphasize the characteristics of the impression. Several shots should be taken with the light source in different places so that each area of the impression will be lighted in at least one photograph.

BLOODSTAINS

In homicides and serious assaults, it will sometimes be necessary to photograph in detail the pattern and color of bloodstains. (Fig. 4) The location,

Figure 2 — Shoe print on linoleum; ruler added to indicate size

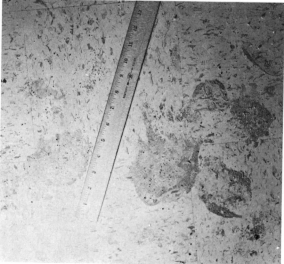

area, and tapering of the stains may indicate the positions and actions of the assailant or the victim.

Blood is often difficult to detect because the color of blood depends upon its age, the temperature, time of year and the material on which it is found. Blood may appear colorless, reddish-brown, green-brown, light olive green and rose; the photographer cannot, therefore, look only for red spots. He should look in out-of-the-way areas for stains such as the bottom side of dresser drawers or table drawers which the suspect may have touched.

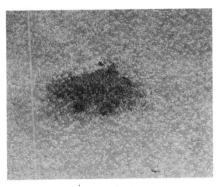

Figure 4 — Bloodstains on rug

A portable ultra-violet light is good for detecting blood stains, as are the various tests such as the Luminol test, the Phenolphthalin reaction test, the Leuco-malachite Green reaction test, and the often used Benzidine reaction test. Further study by the photographer of blood detecting tests will aid him immensely. Photographs of the stain should be taken both before and after the solution is applied.

Close-up photographs of blood stains will record the evidence most graphically. A diagram or sketch of the stains should also be made so that the individual stains can be identified.

Whenever possible, color film should be used to photograph bloodstains. When shooting with black and white film, use Kodak Panatomic-X with a blue filter or Kodak Commercial Film without a filter for stains on a light background. To obtain contrast of stains on a dark background, use Kodak Panatomic-X with a red filter.

Bloodstains photographed under ultraviolet light appear black; even after the fabric has been washed, leaving scarcely a trace of the stain, the blood can be photographed under ultraviolet light.

BULLETS, CARTRIDGES AND SHELLS

In any crime involving firearms, a thorough search is made at the crime scene for bullets, cartridges, and shells. If found, comparison photographs can be made which will be used by a ballistics expert to identify the actual gun used in the commission of the crime. Comparison photographs are a composite of a photograph of each of two bullets. One of the bullets was shot in the course of the crime, the other by a ballistics expert. If they match up, it can be proved that the bullet fired at the crime came from the suspect's gun.

Comparison photographs should be made with a comparison microscope — a specialized camera with automatic features which should be mounted on a floating table to minimize vibration. Comparison photographs can also be made in a small department using macrophotography, but this requires a great deal of patience and hard work.

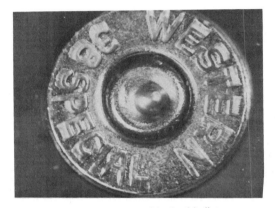

Figure 5 — Close-up of back of bullet

— Cartridge shells or bullets can be compared for marks of similarity by use of the comparison microscope. Here a shell (left) found at the crime scene is matched up to a shell fired from a suspect's gun

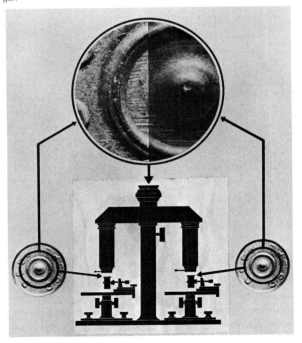

PARTICLES AND OTHER SMALL SPECIMENS

Small quantities of clue materials, such as glass fragments, paint flakes, soil particles, fibers and other substances are often carried from the scene unknowingly by the perpetrator. Their location on the suspect's clothing and at the crime scene should be documented carefully by close-up photographs for comparison purposes. Where such traces are minute, the evidence will be invisible in the over-all crime-scene photographs; hence, considerable care should be exercised to obtain a sharp close-up which will reveal clearly the appearance of the substance in its original position. The location of the close-up can be indicated on the over-all view by an overlay.

Identifying a hit-and-run vehicle can be done by matching paint fragments. A paint fragment found at the accident scene may correspond with an area of a suspected vehicle from which paint is missing.

If the case warrants it, clothing should be photographed with ultraviolet photography, to bring out any invisible marks on the clothing.

PHOTOGRAPHING AT THE IDENTIFICATION BUREAU

The identification photography performed at the crime scene to show the appearance of small objects of evidence can usually be supplemented or improved by photographs taken at the identification bureau or the police laboratory. Here under the more carefully controlled conditions of the laboratory, the photographer can arrange the object so as to present the most informative view to the camera lens.

Photography will also be required for recording the appearance of evidence delivered to the laboratory or identification bureau by a police officer for special processing. Since the analysis, physical testing, or processing of evidence frequently results in a change of appearance or a decrease in quantity, a record of the original condition of the article or substances submitted should be made in anticipation of any questions which might be raised in court concerning the identity or nature of the evidence. A standard lighting and photographic arrangement can usually be used for this type of photograph. However, some materials may require experimentation with lighting to obtain the best results.

Every piece of clothing brought into the laboratory should be photographed on the body before undressing, then photographed individually. Be sure to put a data sheet in each photograph.

PHOTOGRAPHIC TECHNIQUE

Several methods can be used to photograph small objects in the laboratory. If the purpose of the picture is simply that of an identification photograph, the objective of the photographer should be an image that is sharp in all details, free from confusing shadows, and large enough to show all important details of the article of evidence.

If the object is small, make a natural-size photograph. Larger objects and groups of small objects should be arranged symmetrically and framed so that the image almost fills the ground glass.

Focus on a midpoint in the field and stop down the lens opening until both ends of the object are in acceptable focus. For groups of objects, focus on the central object and stop down the lens opening until the objects at the borders are in sharp focus. If an aperture smaller than f/22 is necessary for good focus, increase the lens-to-object distance. The smaller image size should give the required depth of field. Include a ruler and data sheet in all evidence photographs of this type.

Often the aim in small-object photography is to show texture and give an impression of depth of field in a surface by means of contrasting shadow. This may be achieved by the use of grazing, or oblique light with a black background. The lighting arrangement is deceptively simple; actually, the success of the photograph depends on a careful balance between the distances of the illuminant and the reflector from the subject.

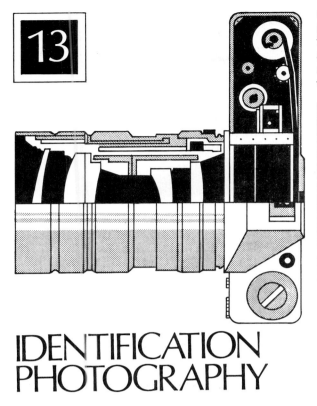

IDENTIFICATION PHOTOGRAPHY

recognized by witnesses or police officers. The photographer should strive to reproduce every freckle, mole, scar, or other blemish which might aid in identifying the subject. Close-ups of head and shoulders with a generally flat front lighting will accomplish this.

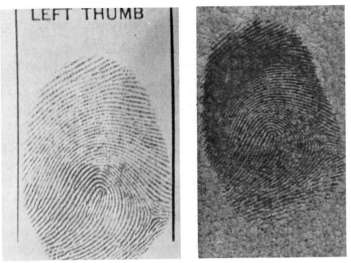

Figure 1 — Single print, known (left) and unknown (right). The unknown print has been taken from the scene of the crime

Figure 2 — Multiple prints, known (top) and unknown (bottom)

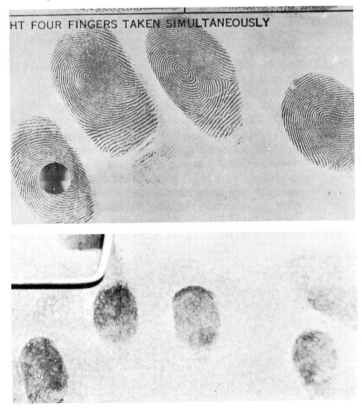

Photography has played a big part in the important role of fingerprints in police work. Were it not for photography, it would be impossible to bring the fingerprints found at the scene of a crime into a courtroom and present them to the jury. There are times when fingerprints are not visible to the naked eye, but by using powder on the latent prints the images of the ridges can be brought out and photographed. These can be enlarged to a size big enough to be seen properly by the jury. The known fingerprint can be placed alongside the unknown fingerprint and a minute fingerprint comparison made of the two prints, along with their individual characteristics. (See figures 1 and 2.)

Photographing fingerprint impressions found at the scene of a crime is a rather difficult chore, demanding an immense knowledge of photography in order to do a good job. It requires a man who has been thoroughly schooled in the science of photography.

The importance of identifying individuals in police work is obvious; identification photographs, like fingerprints, are one of the best means. Using photographs to preserve the personal appearance of an individual at a given time is necessary. The advantage of the police "mug shots" is their unflattering realism, and the ease and economy with which they can be produced.

An identification photograph should be an accurate likeness of the subject, from which he can be

Identification photos are placed on file, together with the prisoner's record and other useful data, such as his height, weight, age and a description of his significant characteristics. Files of such photographs are found to be extremely valuable in crimes involving an unknown perpetrator who was observed by witnesses. The witness is requested to visit police headquarters, where he is shown a number of photographs of criminals selected on the basis of the descriptions given by observers. He is asked to examine the pictures at his leisure and to select any which may resemble the perpetrator of the crime. To aid in searching the files, special classifications of photographs are set up. For example, the file may be arranged according to the crime — namely, burglary, forgery, robbery, and so forth. In such crimes as burglary, an additional sub-classification may be made according to the modus operandi, or method of operation, of the criminal. Thus, under burglary, the use of a pass key, climbing through transoms or skylights, using an electric drill on safes, and many other criminal techniques can be used to classify the photograph.

Another use of identification photographs is for circularizing other police departments with pictures of wanted criminals. Some of the larger police departments provide their officers with albums of "most wanted" criminals. Such pictures enable investigators to become familiar with the facial characteristics of known criminals and can lead to many arrests which might otherwise never be made. The mug shot itself is hardly sufficient proof of identity, but it is proof that may be taken into consideration when accompanied by other evidence, such as fingerprints.

EQUIPMENT FOR FINGERPRINT PHOTOGRAPHY

Fingerprint technicians use a specially built camera for their normal fingerprint work. They use what is called a fingerprint camera. (Figure 3.) It is equipped with an anastigmat lens set for 1:1 reproduction and with an extension in the front of the lens equal to that between the optical center of the lens and the film. The camera opens in the middle; inside there are usually eight batteries, along with lights built into the front so that you can place the camera directly over the surface which bears the fingerprints. Because the lens-to-subject distance is set, the camera does not need to be focused. The film size of these fingerprint cameras is usually 2½ × 3¼ inches. This is a good workable size for one or two prints, but usually four or five prints are found on an object. It is always best to try and get as many fingerprints as possible. Many of the fingerprint men have demanded a 4 × 5 fingerprint camera, which is now available.

It is not recommended that the smaller police departments have a fingerprint camera, because they do not use the camera enough. The batteries weaken with disuse, making correct exposures very difficult. For the large departments that use the fingerprint camera daily, it would be useful. In addition, the batteries may be removed and the camera adapted for electricity with one cord. (See Figure 3.) It can be plugged into a cigarette lighter of a car by means of another cord.

The 4 × 5 camera with the Faurot Foto Focuser attachment (Figure 3) is highly recommended for use especially by the smaller police departments. Every time a picture of a fingerprint is taken, it is done with a flashbulb or a strobe unit, so that the amount of light is constant. With continued use of this Faurot Foto Focuser, a man can become very proficient with it. This gives the benefit of a 4 × 5 negative with which to work, large enough for a full hand of fingerprints.

Using a 35mm camera to lift fingerprints is acceptable, but there are certain limitations. Only one fingerprint can be recorded on one 35mm size film. Of all the miniature cameras for this work, the Instatech is recommended (Figure 3). There are four "Y" shaped brackets which can be attached to the camera, making it possible to take a picture from 1 inch to 15 inches from the subject. For the smaller police department it is a tremendous value. Many of the jobs of the small police department can be done with this inexpensive Instatech camera.

The Polaroid Company has a camera called CU5 Close-up camera (Figure 3) which can be used for fingerprint work. It has a built-in electronic flash making it good to obtain pictures free from blur caused by vibration. Although designed specifically for use with polaroid film it can easily be adapted for use with Panchromatic film packs. This can be done by using the outer frame of a used Polaroid film pack and inserting in it a standard 3¼ × 4¼ film pack. The pack and frame is then loaded in the camera in the usual manner.

Most good fingerprint men usually carry two cameras with them at all times; one would be a 4 × 5 camera with a Faurot Foto Focuser attachment, the other would be either the 35mm Instatech or the Polaroid CU5 Close-up camera. With these cameras the fingerprint expert can photograph properly almost any fingerprint at the scene.

FILMS AND FILTERS

Whatever powder is used to develop a latent fingerprint, nothing will lead to success as much as the choice of film, and (when necessary) the choice of filters. In the courtroom an exhibit of a finger-

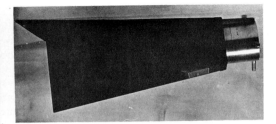

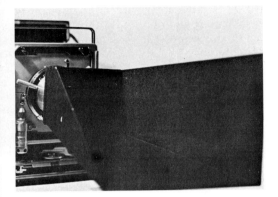

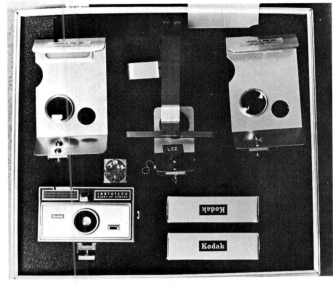

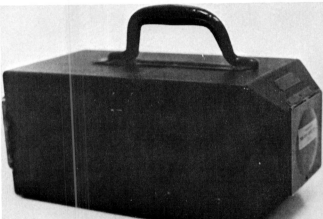

Figure 3 — Fingerprint cameras (clockwise from below) Polaroid CU5 Close-up camera with strobe; fingerprint camera hooked up for electrical and auto current; fingerprint camera; Instatech camera and attachments; Faurot Foto Focuser; and Faurot Foto Focuser on 4 × 5 camera

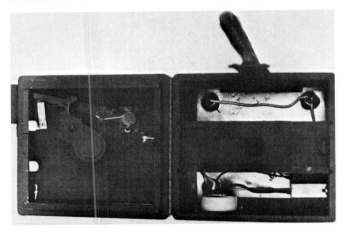

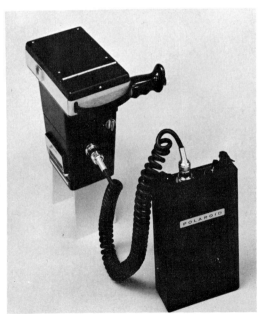

print is one form of law enforcement photograph in which black-and-white photographs are as good as color photographs. In presenting a fingerprint case, an unknown print will be compared with a fingerprint taken from the suspect under ideal conditions.

For courtroom exhibits, fingerprints taken from colored objects should depict a black fingerprint on a white background. The judge and jury will have an easier time concentrating on the pattern of the fingerprint itself on a plain white background.

Fine grain panchromatic film of medium contrast,

along with some high contrast process panchromatic film, should always be used to photograph latent prints. If the lines of a fingerprint are even in density the process panchromatic film will probably produce the best result because it will produce as much contrast between the print and the background as it is possible to obtain. But many times the fingerprint lines are uneven and not clear and process panchromatic film may not be the best choice because it will accentuate the unevenness, causing the lighter portions of the print to be invisible in the finished photograph. A medium speed panchromatic film should be used in this case. A Panatomic-X Film is a good medium speed film to use. It will not produce as much contrast, but if properly exposed and developed it will preserve all the lines in the print even though they are not of equal density.

The following films are recommended for routine black-and-white fingerprint photography at the scene of a crime. Ansco: *Versapan*; Kodak: *Panatomic-X, Contrast Process, Panchromatic* and *Kodalith*.

Most of the time, fingerprints will be found on colored objects, which will usually require the use of filters to obtain the maximum use of panchromatic film. Filters are not needed when photographing impressions on white surfaces such as bathroom fixtures, or on gray or black surfaces such as some gun barrels.

The fingerprint expert must know how to use filters to control lightness or darkness of colored surfaces upon which fingerprints are found. Ordinarily he can make a colored background photograph either dark or light at will. His decision as to how a given colored surface should be made to photograph will depend upon the tone of the fingerprint. If the fingerprint will photograph light gray or white, the surface upon which it appears must be made to photograph as black as possible. (Figure 4.) Conversely, if the fingerprint will photograph dark gray or black, the background must be made to photograph as white as possible. A yellow filter is good for bringing out the definition of the print. A medium yellow filter needs as much exposure as a weak yellow-green filter. But the deep yellow filter gives a more effective picture of this same exposure. When using the filters, the exposure must be trebled. Any time a filter is added, the exposure will have to be much longer. Most exposures with fingerprint cameras are usually long exposures anyway, so adding a filter and extending the exposure should be considered worthwhile.

When photographing black fingerprints on colored objects, the photographer must make the colored background photograph as light as possible in order to provide the greatest possible contrast with the black fingerprint. A panchromatic process film and the proper filter should be used if the fingerprint is of even density; a medium speed panchromatic film and the proper filter if the fingerprint should be used is uneven and patchy. To photograph a black fingerprint on a colored background, a filter having the same color as the background is good. A filter that transmits the color of the object and absorbs other colors will usually solve the problem. (See Chapter 8.)

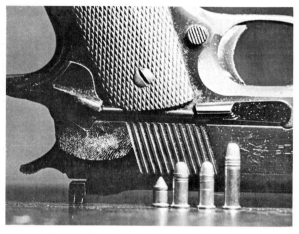

Figure 4 — White fingerprint on black object

Because of the way light strikes it or because it has been developed with white powder, a fingerprint may appear white. To photograph these on a colored surface, a filter should be used that will absorb the color reflected by the object while letting light of other wave lengths through to expose the film. The student should take a good set of fingerprints from some individual, and photograph them first with no filter, then photograph with a yellow, red, blue, green, and orange filter. The letter of the filter used should be put in to identify the filter type in the finished print. This is the best way to learn how to use filters.

For photographing fingerprints found on multicolored objects any filter used will eliminate certain colors but emphasize other colors in the background. It would be best to eliminate all the colors in order to produce a plain background that will contrast well with the prints.

Sometimes fairly satisfactory results can be obtained by using panchromatic film without a filter of any kind when photographing fingerprints on multicolored backgrounds. This will not eliminate the background but it may subdue it, especially if the fingerprint is on even density so that process panchromatic film can be used.

Often it will be necessary to resort to either ultraviolet or infrared photography to photograph fingerprints on a multicolored background. Results obtained from them are very unpredictable. Ultraviolet and infrared photography is much more difficult than people would have you believe. See Chapter 14.

EXPOSURE FOR FINGERPRINT PHOTOGRAPHY

It is difficult to name any certain exposure for any shot; no one knows what the particular circumstances are at the time a certain job has to be done. A man in this field has to do a great amount of experimenting with his camera, film, filters and other tools of the trade. By experimenting with all his filters in combination with different films, and keeping a record of everything he is doing along with the results he obtains, he can figure out just what the camera, film and filters will do for a particular job. Using panchromatic process film and filters he will find that his exposures must be correct within very narrow limits.

When using the fingerprint box camera, exposure results can be predicted by past experience because of the fact that the lamps are always the same position from the subject. The usage of the batteries does wear them down, however, and this affects the exposure. A good record must be kept on the length of exposures made under the various conditions encountered. The photographer can be fairly certain of good results with the fingerprint box camera within the limits of its capabilities.

When using a 4 × 5 camera with the double extension, a photoelectric light meter should be used to obtain exposure. The light meter should be placed as close to the surface bearing the fingerprint as possible without casting a shadow. The camera is extended double when making full size reproductions and, therefore, the exposure must be four times as long as that required when the camera is used for view work. To allow for this difference automatically one can divide the recommended film speed by four. For instance, when using the ASA speed ratings, Kodak's Panchromatic Process Film now has a speed of 80. For fingerprints natural size, however, the listed film speed should be divided by four giving us the ASA speed rating of 20. There are other ways of arriving at the effective aperture and speed by working close to the subject. The above method will eliminate calculations when making life size pictures.

In addition to allowing for the fact that the bellows of the camera is extended double, one must remember to allow for the additional exposure required when a filter is used.

FINGERPRINTS FOUND ON WOOD

When going through a home searching for fingerprints, many times fingerprints will be found on wood surfaces, such as a kitchen or dining room table, dressers or bed, or on other pieces of wooden furniture. There are usually three kinds of wood used to make household furniture, oak, walnut and mahogany. One of the biggest problems confronting the fingerprint man is whether to use black or white powder. The answer depends on whether it is best to make the stained wood photograph light in order to contrast with a black fingerprint or whether it should be photographed dark in order to contrast with a white fingerprint.

It is best to develop fingerprints on dark stained woods with white powder and to photograph them with panchromatic process film and a blue filter. But, if a court exhibit must be made that will show the ridges as black lines on a white background, it is necessary to make an intermediate transparency from the original negative and print from the intermediate transparency. Fingerprints on light oak should be developed with black powder and photographed on process panchromatic film through a red filter.

FINGERPRINTS FOUND ON GLASS

Visible fingerprints found on glass must always be photographed before applying powder to them. Latent fingerprints found on sheet or plate glass sometimes can be photographed without the use of developing powders, by oblique lighting from behind the glass, and against a black background. Here again the ridges will show up as white lines against a black background unless the court exhibit is printed from an intermediate transparency made from the original negative.

Glass bottles and tumblers many times yield fingerprints. Even though the print consists only of colorless perspiratory secretions, it may be photographed successfully without the use of powders by filling the bottle or tumbler with a dark liquid such as grape juice and photograph with oblique lighting. The floodlight must be adjusted with great care because the convexity of the bottle or tumbler will cause disturbing reflections when the lamp is in certain positions. With a dark impression, the bottle or tumbler should be filled with a white liquid, such as milk, before it is photographed.

Fingerprints which are found on a mirror can be photographed if great care is given to focusing and lighting. Lack of care in these particulars will result in a blurred photograph. If it is possible to do so, the job will be made easier by scraping the silver off the back of the mirror.

If fingerprints are detected on both surfaces of a glass plate, it is necessary to develop them separately. First, the print on one side is treated with white lead, then photographed, and finally colored black by allowing the vapors of ammonium sulfide to act on it for a few minutes. Then the print on the opposite side is covered with the white lead powder, a dark colored paper is applied against the print previously blackened, so as to render it invisible, and a photograph of the second print taken.

FINGERPRINTS FOUND ON PAPER

Fingerprints found on paper should be treated with powders, fumes, or liquid reagents to bring out the fingerprints so they are clear enough to be photographed. One of the best developers for fingerprints on white paper is powdered antimony; also the magnetic powders which come with the Magna brush are very good. Another method of bringing out latent prints on paper is with the iodine fuming process. Some fingerprint men use the silver nitrate process: after being treated with the solution, the paper is dried and then exposed to sunlight or high intensity illumination until any prints present are visible. Then the developed fingerprints are photographed without delay.

fingerprints developed with powders probably will last indefinitely, especially if protected with a plastic cover.

ENLARGING FINGERPRINT PHOTOGRAPHS FOR TRIAL

A fingerprint photographer must have his case well prepared to present it before a judge and jury. In testifying to comparisons between fingerprints, the expert witness should utilize some graphic representation of the facts presented, such as enlarged photographs. For this purpose, enlarged photographs of prints from corresponding fingers

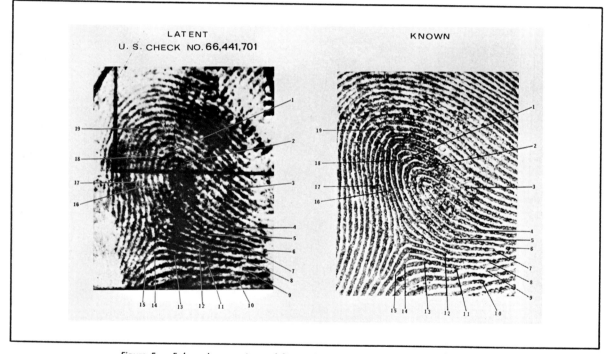

Figure 5 — Enlarged comparison of fingerprint properly prepared for court exhibit.

PHOTOGRAPHING LIFTED FINGERPRINTS

Fingerprints which have been lifted should always be photographed as soon as possible or the lifting material bearing the prints should be used as transparent positives to make an enlarged negative.

Many fingerprint men find the lifting process so easy that they have a tendency to lift prints when it is not necessary. Rarely should fingerprints be lifted when they can be photographed successfully while still on the original surface. Fingerprints have the highest value as evidence while they remain on the objects in which they are found. It is true that latent fingerprints may disappear in some instances but

may be mounted side by side. The degree of enlargement is not important, so long as both photographs are enlarged to the same degree, and the ridges of both prints are distinguishable. Generally, enlargements of five to six times natural size will be found best. Smaller enlargements are difficult to see over a few feet away, while larger ones lose some of their contrast between ridges and background. A white border of at least 1½ inches should be left for numbering purposes. An enlargement to about 22 × 30 inches should be made to serve as a demonstration exhibit to the court, and 11 by 14-inch exhibits for each member of the jury.

The corresponding ridge formations in the two prints should then be similarly numbered and indicated with straight lines drawn from the characteristic to a numbered point on the margin. Care should be taken that lines are drawn to the characteristic to be indicated, not short of nor beyond it. (Figure 5.)

When the degree of enlargement is great (25 to 30 diameters) it is well to draw a circle around the characteristic and to draw the line from the circles to the number in the margin. In such cases the ridges will be much larger than the illustrating lines.

Since the enlarged photographs appear in black and white, it is preferable to use an ink other than black or white to line the chart. The ink used should be translucent, so that it will be possible to see the details of the ridges that cross it.

A cleaner, neater, and more pleasing appearance is obtained if the numbers are evenly spaced and made to follow a sequence, as by placing them in a clockwise or counterclockwise order. Some states do not permit numbering on these exhibits. A clear sheet of plastic placed over the exhibit and then numbered will avoid this problem. Art stores have Prestype lettering and numbering outfits, which are excellent for lettering and numbering to be done on fingerprint exhibits for court. They make a nice clean job, enabling anyone to print and number like a professional.

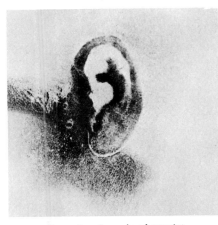

Figure 6 — Example of earprint

EARPRINTS

The literature of criminal investigation generally mentions ears when discussing the problem of personal identifications. Ears are but one factor of several employed in the systematic, verbal descriptions of a person used in personal appearance files.

These earprints were taken by pressing a piece of paper against the subject's ear. This latent earprint was then brought out with the use of standard fingerprint powder. These prints were taken at f/16 at $\frac{1}{100}$. (See Figure 6.)

THE IDENTIFICATION PHOTOGRAPHER

Most police departments in cities with a population of more than 15,000 possess an "Identification Bureau" or at least a skilled photographer assigned to identification work. However, because the importance of photography in law enforcement is so well recognized, many smaller towns are now training selected police officers to do photographic work. It will often be found that the identification photographer in a small community is required to deal with a greater variety of tasks than is his counterpart in the large city. The latter will tend toward specialization in one particular branch of identification work. For example, in a city with a population of a million, several police photographers may be occupied exclusively with "mug" shots, while others will perform only "on-the-scene" photographic tasks.

The typical responsibilities of an identification unit with respect to photography are the following:

1. Photographing prisoners charged with serious crimes.
2. Photographing deceased persons in homicide cases.
3. Photographing the scenes of serious crimes, fires, and accidents.
4. Dusting and photographing fingerprints.
5. By photographic methods, reproducing checks, documents, and other evidential papers.
6. Copying and reproducing photographs.
7. Reproducing official records and notices.

IDENTIFICATION PHOTOGRAPHS

There are four basic ways of shooting identification photographs: 1) the front and side view, 2) the front, and two three-quarter face views, 3) the front, side and standing view, 4) the color front and side view.

1. *The front and side view.* Most of the police departments photograph their prisoners with a front view and a profile (or side) view. (Figure 7.) The front view permits ready recognition of the individual, but the side view is necessary for certain identification. Persons are so often viewed from the front that it is quite possible, at first sight, not to recognize someone if a profile photograph is shown. The public can recognize front view photographs much more readily than they can the profile view. Usually the trained police officer will prefer the side photograph when attempting to identify an

individual. The front and side view identification photograph can be taken with a 4 × 5 camera with a split-back attachment.

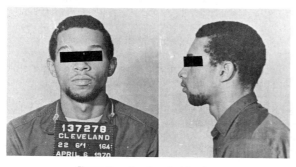

Figure 7 — Front and side view

2. *The front and two three-quarter face views.* This type of identification photograph has proved to be quite satisfactory. Many times identification can be made more easily from the three-quarter face view when the front and side method fails. For this method, a specially designed identification camera is used, which is equipped to make three separate exposures on one 4 × 5 sheet of film. (See Figure 8.)

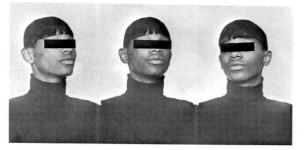

Figure 8 — Front and two three-quarter face views

3. *The front, side and standing view.* This is the preferred method, since the stand-up view can be most helpful in identifying a suspect. This may be done in one of two ways. The first is the easiest. This involves a special camera known as the Deardorff camera for identification which will be discussed in greater detail in a following section. The second method is much more complicated, but is possible if this type of identification photograph is wanted without using the Deardorff camera.

A special back will enable the photographer to take three exposures on one 4 × 5 sheet of film. The Milwaukee Police Department has a setup as follows which allows them to photograph by this method: they take a front and side view with one camera set at approximately five feet away from the suspect, then they move the subject into another room

which is equipped with a camera to take a stand-up shot. This camera is situated approximately twenty feet from the subject. The stand-up view is exposed on the remaining third section of the film. This method allows for the difference in focal length between the close-up and stand-up views.

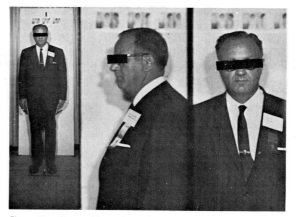

Figure 9 — Front, side and standing views taken with Deardorff camera

4. *The color front and side view.* Color identification mug shots can be taken with almost any good quality 35mm camera. In this method, each view must be taken on an individual film. They can be put on the same sheet of paper in the enlarging process by use of a color print easel with a wallet-size mask.

FILM

Using the same film for identification and most other purposes simplifies photography for the smaller department. Kodak Royal Pan Film, because of its high speed, is well suited to police work. It can also take good identification pictures and is, therefore, so used by many departments.

An increasing number of color photographs are being taken for identification. These can be made on color reversal film to produce slides or on color negative film to make prints. The negative material may be preferable in that its exposure is less critical: prints and enlargements are simpler to make than those from color slides. Black-and-white prints and color slides can also be made from 35mm color negatives. 35mm Kodacolor Film is increasingly used. However, no particular process or film size has been adopted as standard.

LIGHTING

In identification work, it is particularly important to be consistent in all of the photographic procedures. Changing the lighting arrangements, for example, can produce markedly different facial contours. Hence, a standard lighting arrangement should be selected and adhered to strictly in all photographs. In this way, lighting, image size, and exposure can be fixed for standard poses with a great saving of time and effort. The operation can easily be made one of routine procedure in exposing, developing, and printing the negative.

The flat lighting provided by two No. 1 photoflood lamps with diffusers will be found satisfactory for this work. They should be placed close enough to the subject to permit the use of a fast shutter speed, but not so close as to become oppressive because of heat and glare. Using two No. 1 photoflood lamps with diffusers, an exposure of 1.50 second at f/11 will be satisfactory with Kodak Royal Pan Film.

Electronic flash lamps are becoming popular for "mug" shots because their very short exposure times eliminate danger of subject movement. With units of medium power, an aperture of f/32 with the shutter at 1/50 second should be adequate with either Kodak Royal Pan or Kodak Royal Ortho Film.

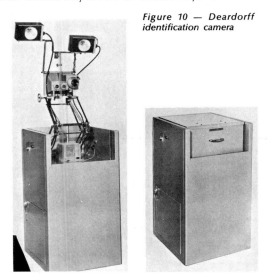

Figure 10 — Deardorff identification camera

THE DEARDORFF CAMERA

The Deardorff identification camera is a fixed focus camera which takes three poses on one sheet of 4 × 5 black-and-white or color sheet film, or 4 × 5 Polaroid film packet (Figure 10). The camera has two lenses; a 3½ inch focal length lens used in taking the full length picture, and a 9½ inch focal length lens employed in taking the side and front or three-quarter face views. For all three pictures operating distance from the back of the camera to the subject's nose is about eight feet, a distance that produces pleasing perspective. Image reduction of the full length picture is 24 to 1 and of the bust pictures 8 to 1. Illumination is supplied by two

electronic flash lamps that freeze almost any possible movement of the subject and provide sufficient light to use the lens stopped down.

The three pictures the Deardorff identification camera takes are made on one sheet of film and involve just two exposures. (Figure 9.) The full length and the front picture are made simultaneously by tripping both lenses at the same time. Hence, the bust front view is really the same picture as the full length but on a larger scale. After the two front views are taken the back of the camera is shifted once and the subject is turned to the side for the profile picture.

STANDARDIZATION OF IDENTIFICATION PHOTOGRAPHS

The International Association for Identification, along with Mr. Harris B. Tuttle, former Law Consultant for the Eastman Kodak Company, tried for years to standardize the format for "mug" shots to a 3 × 5 inch size, but were unsuccessful. With so many schools originating Police Science courses all over the country, this is the ideal time for everyone to start standardizing their "mug" shots. The police could then exchange their identification photographs with other police departments and everyone would be able to file them in a uniform 3 × 5 inch file.

Along this same line, it is suggested that the "mug" shot backgrounds be black or dark-maroon for white individuals and gray or off white for black individuals, thus providing the best contrast.

Further in this area it is suggested that identifying plaques be standardized. They should contain the following information:

1. The name of the police department.
2. The number of the case or individual. The first two digits of this number should indicate the year.
3. The date of arrest.
4. The height, weight and age of the individual.

IDENTI-KIT PHOTOGRAPHY

Many police departments are using the Identi-Kit to aid in identifying a person from a verbal description. Making of multiple pictures from the original is usually a complicated job. By using the fuming process, the pictures will not last long and will turn brown. The following method proves to work better. Set the Identi-Kit board with the composite and take a picture of it with the 4 × 5 camera. Use the negative obtained in the enlarger along with a

Saunders color print easel. It is not very difficult to make many pictures this way and they can be distributed to the cruisers and detectives. Figure 11 shows how four shots can be printed on one 8 × 10-inch piece of paper. If the subject is really "hot" and you want to make an 8 × 10 of the Identi-Kit composite, it can be done very easily by this same method.

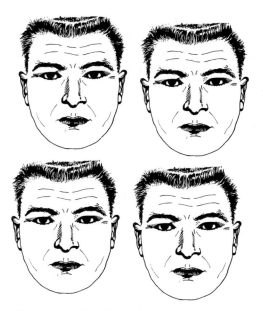

Figure 11 — Four shots of Identi-Kit composite printed on one 8" × 10" sheet

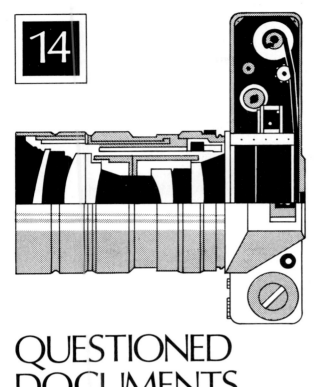

QUESTIONED DOCUMENTS

One specialized form of evidence photography is the photographing of questioned documents. Photography is an indispensable aid to the document examiner not only in detecting alterations in documents (such as checks) but also in presenting proof.

A major part of document examination is concerned with making legible or clarifying any writing (any markings on paper) which has been obscured. Wills, insurance policies, licenses, checks, or official records may be altered for some criminal purpose. Documents may also become illegible through exposure to fire or water or through deterioration or fading with time. The document examiner must do two things: first, he must decipher the writing; second, since a question of proof is involved, he must convince the court of his findings.

The photography of questioned documents can be divided into two general classes: (1) documents where it is obvious that an erasure or visible alteration has taken place, and (2) documents which appear satisfactory, but where forgery by alteration is suspected. In the first case, the erasure or alteration may be poorly executed and quite evident to the trained investigator, but acceptable to the untrained eye. In the second case, the work of bleaching, erasing, and altering may have been so cleverly done that there is no evidence visible even to the trained eye of an experienced investigator.

The procedures for the various types of examinations, photographic and other, can be found in standard reference works on questioned documents. Some of the more common applications of photography are described here.

Document examiners rarely give the court an opinion concerning a handwriting or typewriting comparison or an alteration without supporting their statements with photographic exhibits. Even though the questioned-document specialist may see clearly that a forgery or alteration has occurred, he still must photograph these irregularities and obtain enlargements for possible court use. In no other type of expert examination is photography used so extensively in explaining points of proof to jurors.

REPRODUCTION FOR CASE STUDY

A good photographic copy of the document should be made as soon as possible. To prevent soiling or mutilating the document, this photograph, rather than the document, should be used by the examiner whenever practicable. For example, in comparing handwriting specimens, the examiner will usually find it necessary to cut off sections of the enlarged photographs of questioned and known writings so that the significant parts of the writings or characteristics of individual letters can be placed side by side for comparison. (Figure 1.)

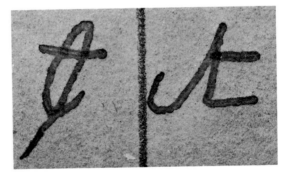

Figure 1 — Comparison of handwriting specimen

COPYING 1:1

Copying is somewhat like portraiture — it demands a great deal of technical skill and patience. Special cameras and elaborate set-ups are used by professionals for copying. The best camera for this work is similar to a view camera and allows the photographer to see the image through a mirror on a ground glass screen. An SLR camera will suffice; however, it will reveal any lighting glare which might need correcting and also simplifies measurements of the image size. For serious copy work there are attachments, adaptors, and various extension bellows designed for small cameras.

To make a good-quality 1:1 copy of a document, the board or easel on which the document is placed should be exactly parallel to the planes of the lens and the camera back, and in a fixed position.

A lighting arrangement that provides uniform illumination over the whole surface is of great importance. A set of four bare lamps or two lamps properly diffused can be fixed permanently to a wooden frame and attached to the camera stand. Mark the 1:1 position of the lens board, the camera back, and any other movable parts of the set-up so that a document can be photographed rapidly as a routine procedure, and a copy obtained in which all parts of the document are in a sharp focus.

After copying, put the document in a glassine envelope. This type of envelope will permit the document to be seen and studied, and yet protected at all times.

FILM AND DEVELOPERS

The correct degree of contrast is most important in documentary work. Faintly visible details require high contrast. On the other hand, where detail is required in both ink and paper, high contrast would "block up" one or the other, so moderate contrast is better. The best contrast for a given problem is often a matter of experiment — both in film contrast and choice of printing paper. Generally, ortho films are used unless the document requires a lighter rendering of reds by use of a filter, when pan films are needed.

Proper exposure is important. A series of exposures should be made, each one stop apart. One negative may be best for one part or one aspect of the document, another for another part. Composite prints can be made from several negatives.

While black-and-white is usual in document photography, do not overlook color photography. Same-size or enlarged Ektacolor prints for Ektacolor or Kodacolor negatives show the document realistically. Color prints can show color differences better than black-and-white can; for example: black ink from a check writer and red ink of a bank endorsement.

ERASURES

Writings which have been erased, that is, removed from the paper by mechanical or chemical means can often be photographed using one or another arrangements of lighting. If the writing appears to have been removed completely, there may be little hope of restoring it.

Visual methods should be tried first. A small lamp, such as a microscope illuminant, whose intensity and direction can be controlled, is very useful. By experimenting with the lighting angle, one may be found that will enable the photographer to read the writing. (Figure 2.) The document is then set up on the copying camera and lighted in the same way. Kodak Contrast Process Panchromatic Film is best for great contrast and Kodalith Film for extreme contrast. Where faint traces are visible, a contrasty film such as Kodalith will emphasize the details and sometimes exaggerate the traces so they are readable.

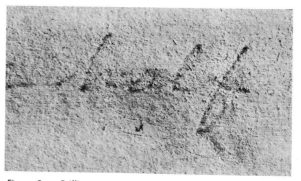

Figure 2 — Brilliant contrast and Kodalith film are used here to bring out erased pencil writing

The correct lighting for deciphering erasures is determined by experiment. As a general guide, these steps should be tried:

1. *Ordinary lighting.* Obviously, the first step is to look at the document by ordinary reflected light.
2. *Side lighting.* Try lighting from various angles. An extremely oblique angle will often be found useful. If some particular lighting and viewing angle make the erasure visible, duplicate the setup for the camera.
3. *Transmitted light.* Look at the document with the light coming through it. Turn the document over and repeat.
4. *Magnification.* Examine the paper with a magnifier, such as a hand glass or a low-power binocular microscope. Magnifications up to about 10X are most useful.
5. *Polarized light.* Light the document with polarized light, using a Kodak Pola-Light, for example, Examine it through a Kodak Pola-Screen.
6. *Filters.* Look at the document through various filters — either separate filters or the viewing filters in the Kodak Master Photoguide.

CHEMICAL METHODS

If sufficient traces of ink or graphite remain in the paper, it is sometimes possible to read the original writing and even to show it photographically if a chemical treatment is used. An erasure can be brought up with iodine fuming. Iodine fuming is a general procedure which (1) reveals the presence and extent of an erasure, (2) restores some of the writing, and (3) delineates any area that had previously been wet.

A fuming tube, similar to one used for fingerprints, is warmed with the hand and warm breath is blown through it. Moisture from the breath is removed by a layer of calcium chloride or other desiccant and the dry fumes of iodine stain disturbances in the paper caused by writing. This should be photographed immediately.

OTHER METHODS OF PHOTOGRAPHING ERASURES

Some inks and some bleaches fluoresce, so any time there is a brightness difference between visible and invisible writing or bleaching or between different inks, this can be photographed by ultraviolet light (See Chapter 16.)

Infrared photography will also reveal any significant difference between absorption of infrared radiation between the original writing and that used to obliterate it. Erasures, obliteration, or indented writing (ghosts) from pen, pencil or typewriter inspected and photographed with grazing light. (See Chapter 16.) A comparison microscope is used to compare writings. These same comparison microscopes can be used to photograph the questioned and known material to be examined.

OBLITERATED WRITING

If the writing has been obscured by markings, such as a series of typed X's, over writing, or a

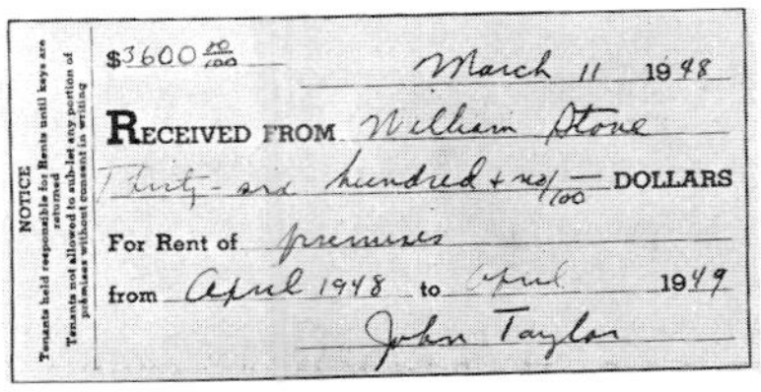

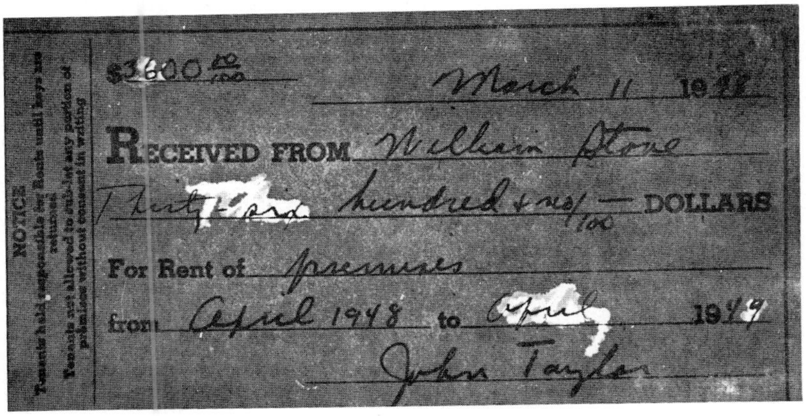

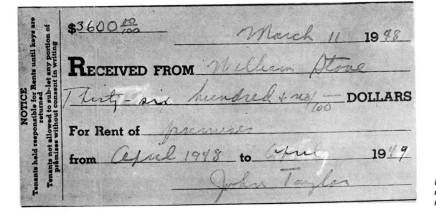

Figure 3 — Detection of forgery by ultra-violet radiation. The rent receipt is (top left) in ordinary light (top left) and by fluorescent method under ultraviolet light

Figure 4 — A photograph of the same receipt, this time photographed by reflected ultraviolet radiation

haphazard scratching of lines (Figure 5), the problem of deciphering the underwriting can sometimes be solved by one of the following methods:

1. *Filters*. If the upper markings and underwriting differ in color, use a filter of the same color as the top layer to photograph the writing with Kodak Contrast Process Panchromatic Film. To select the correct filter, view the obliteration through filters of different color or through the series found in the Kodak Master Photoguide.

2. *Oblique lighting*. Differences in the reflecting characteristics of the upper and lower layers may permit the decipherment of the obscured writing. The pressure with which the lower layer was impressed is also important. If great pressure was used, a legible, indented outline may be seen from the front or the back. Oblique lighting should be used. Direct a light at varying angles and with varying intensities across the writing. If the writing can be read at a selected angle, photograph it with Kodak Panatomic-X or Kodak Contrast Process Panchromatic Film.

3. *Infrared photography*. This sometimes shows up alterations. It can also show up obliterated writing if the obliterating ink is a dye, since most dyes transmit infrared. Infrared film is required, and a red or deep-red filter must be used. While the Kodak Wratten Filter No. 25 usually works, the deeper Wratten No. 87 is preferable. Ordinary tungsten lamps are used.

4. *Ultraviolet radiation*. Differences in the fluorescence characteristics of obliterated writing as seen under an ultraviolet lamp can be helpful. The difference may be one of color or of intensity. The reflected-ultraviolet method may also prove useful.

5. *Wetting method*. Occasionally, the obliteration is made by pasting paper over the writing. To leave the paste-over intact, try wetting the reverse side of the original document with a volatile fluid, such as benzene. The writing will appear for a few seconds and again become invisible as the fluid evaporates; photograph it as soon as the image appears. Use Kodak Panatomic-X Film with strong lighting and a wide aperture. This wetting method is sometimes successful with ordinary obliterations.

INDENTATIONS

The impressions left upon a pad of paper by writing on an upper sheet which has been removed will sometimes provide a legible copy of the message written on the missing page. (Figure 6.) This kind of evidence is commonly found in connection with gambling arrests. The sheet bearing the original record of the bet will have been removed by the time the police officer makes the arrest. The officer must rely on the paper pad found in the defendant's possession to supply the needed corroboration. By directing a beam of light from the side (almost parallel to the plane of the paper), the indentations can be brought into relief and the writing revealed. No special treatment of the paper is required; in fact, the investigating officer should be instructed to leave the paper untouched before photography.

> The date could not have been later than the ▬▬▬▬▬▬▬▬ since the notes which were taken at the time seem to indicate that there was full knowledge of the facts and that subsequent investigation (i.e., after ▬▬▬▬▬▬▬ could not

> The date could not have been later than the **15th of October**, since the notes which were taken at the time seem to indicate that there was full knowledge of the facts and that subsequent investigation (i.e., after **October 15**) could not

Figure 5 — Kodak infrared and a Kodak Wratten filter No. 87 were used to decipher obliterated writing and to render it as shown in the lower photograph

The camera is focused by visible light. Best infrared focus differs from that for visible light. For 1:1 focus, try extending the back of the camera by 0.5 percent of the focal length. Best focus can be found by trial.

Figure 6 - Moderate contrast, combined with side lighting, help to decipher illegible indentations on paper

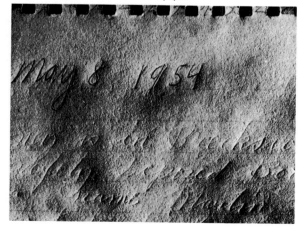

The photograph should be made at natural size (that is, in 1:1 ratio) on Kodak Commercial, Kodak Contrast Process Panchromatic, or Kodalith Film. If the outline is faint, use the film of greatest contrast. It is sometimes impossible to obtain in one photograph a satisfactory image of all the writing, because different areas of the paper require different angles of illumination. In these instances, a series of photographs should be made. Pairs of pictures made by lighting one from the right and the other from the left side of the paper are helpful in some cases. By offsetting very slightly the two negatives obtained in this manner, and printing them together, the writing can sometimes be made more distinct.

CONTACT WRITING

Other techniques of discovering the nature of writing on a missing sheet of paper rely on the traces of ink which may have been passed from one sheet to another. Although there are chemical methods for the detection of these traces, the simpler and often effective technique of fluorescence under an ultraviolet lamp should be tried first. A faint fluorescence may be discernible from the ink traces transmitted by contact from the missing sheet.

CARBON PAPER

A carbon paper discarded after the typing or writing of a document will reveal the original message. Try:

1. *Oblique writing*. With the carbon side of the paper facing the lens, direct a single lamp from the side until the light appears to be reflected from the writing. This method is especially useful if the carbon has been used only once or twice. Kodak Commercial Ortho Film should be used.
2. *Carbon as a negative*. A much-used carbon that is thin and evenly perforated in spots may be used on the contact printed as a negative. The writing is then printed directly on photographic paper. This usually requires a long printing exposure.
3. *Transmitted light*. By illuminating the carbon from the rear and using a red filter (Kodak Wratten No. 25) a satisfactory photograph of the writing on carbon paper can be obtained with Kodak Contrast Process Panchromatic Film.

DIFFERENTIATING INKS

In some types of forgery the criminal adds writing to the check or other document by using an ink of the same color, but with different constituents than that used originally. Since the added writing is usually limited in quantity — often only a single stroke — the use of chemical methods to prove a difference in inks may be risky. A photograph of the fluorescence under ultraviolet radiation or an infrared photograph is often helpful in these situations.

A blotter applied by the suspect to his ink writing sometimes picks up a legible copy of the text. It should be photographed with Kodak Panatomic-X Film. If the blotter is colored, use a filter of the same color. Since the blotter writing is a mirror image of the original it is necessary to reverse the image by printing with the emulsion side away from the paper.

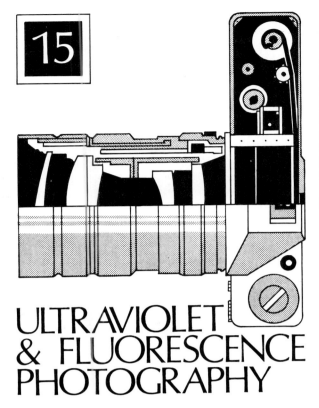

15

ULTRAVIOLET & FLUORESCENCE PHOTOGRAPHY

This chapter has been divided into two distinct parts, one on "Ultraviolet Photography" and the other on "Fluorescence Photography." The purpose of this division is to emphasize the fact that two types of photography are involved. It has often been considered that ultraviolet photography is also fluorescence photography. Although it is common technique to use ultraviolet radiation to produce fluorescence, this is not the only radiation which can be used for the purpose. Also, since it is possible to photograph an object completely by ultraviolet with no fluorescence produced, the reason for the division is further justified. If an object is photographed by ultraviolet reflected from it or transmitted through it (as in microscopy), the technique should be called ultraviolet. In the latter case, however, involving a microscope, the technique is sometimes referred to as ultraviolet micrography. If certain radiations (including ultraviolet) are used to excite fluorescence in an object, the recording of the resultant fluorescence is called fluorescence photography.

ULTRAVIOLET PHOTOGRAPHY

The main purpose of ultraviolet photography is to provide information about an object or material which cannot be obtained by other photographic methods. Obviously, if differentiation between two substances is produced in photography with visible light or infrared radiation, there is little need to resort to ultraviolet photography. If the first two methods fail, however, there is always the possibility that the third might succeed. In many cases, it is worth a try.

Ultraviolet photography is usually accomplished by reflected radiation, and depends upon the premise that two (or more) elements of an object will reflect or absorb ultraviolet differently. Techniques in visible and in infrared photography operate on essentially the same principle — except, of course, that in most visible-light photography the elements of an object may show color contrast.

Some materials will absorb ultraviolet, while others will reflect these radiations. Some have partial absorption and partial reflection. These effects can be recorded photographically by using ultraviolet radiation.

ULTRAVIOLET RADIATION

Ultraviolet cannot be seen by the normal human eye and is often termed "invisible," as are all other electromagnetic radiations except those in the short visible range. Photographic emulsions, however, are sensitive to most wavelengths of ultraviolet. By using a filter that absorbs all visible light but passes ultraviolet, it is possible to make a photographic exposure with just ultraviolet. This technique is called "ultraviolet photography."

For practical photographic purposes the ultraviolet spectrum is arbitrarily divided into three very narrow bands: long wave ultraviolet, middle ultraviolet, and short wave ultraviolet. Another band, called "vacuum ultraviolet," also exists but is not usable in photography.

RADIATION SOURCES

Sunlight. Sunlight is probably the most common source of long-wave ultraviolet radiation. Although the long and some middle waves of ultraviolet pass rather freely through the atmosphere, the short waves are attenuated by scattering and by absorption due to moisture and gases in the atmosphere. A sufficient amount of long-wave ultraviolet is usually present, and bright sunlight could be used to illuminate rather large areas with ultraviolet radiation, particularly on a dry day. For ultraviolet photography with sunlight, a filter is placed over the camera lens. This filter should transmit long-wave ultraviolet freely and absorb *all* visible light. The filter should be closely fitted to the camera lens so that no visible light enters the lens.

Fluorescent tubes. Fluorescent tubes are often used in the photographic lab to provide visual illumination over a large area. Special tubes of this type can be used to provide ultraviolet radiation for photography. Ultraviolet is produced in such tubes by a

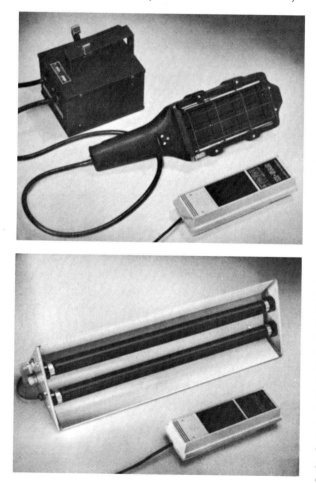

Figure 1 — Typical ultraviolet lamps

discharge of electricity through a carrier gas, such as argon. This gas ionizes enough to cause a glow, and develops enough heat to cause mercury in the tube to vaporize. As the mercury vaporizes, it is ionized by the electrical discharge and gives off vis-

ible light (mostly green and blue), but also emits ultraviolet, both long wave and short wave. Since long-wave ultraviolet is most wanted for ultraviolet photography, this tube is coated on the inside with a phosphor that absorbs short wave and emits long-wave ultraviolet. The glass of the tube usually contains a chemical salt as a filter. It is opaque to most visible light but freely transmits the long-wave ultraviolet. Tubes of this type are often called "black light" tubes, since they appear visually black. (Figure 1.) They can be otained in several lengths, up to 48 inches long, so they can be used to illuminate large areas with ultraviolet light. They can be operated in standard fluorescent light fixtures, with the standard starter coil and ballast. Tubes of this type are called "low pressure" mercury vapor lamps.

Mercury vapor lamps. Mercury vapor lamps of "high pressure" consist of small, tubular, quartz envelopes, in which mercury vapor is produced under a pressure of several atmospheres. These lamps require high electrical current for operation, with a considerable output of long-wave ultraviolet. They also, however, emit some middle-wave and short-wave ultraviolet. They are of particular advantage in illuminating reasonable small areas with high ultraviolet brightness. Special mercury vapor lamps of this type, and of high wattage, are of particular interest in both ultraviolet photomicrography and ultraviolet spectrography. Mercury vapor lamps produce extremely bright spectral lines in both the ultraviolet and the visible range. Special transformers are usually required for operation, and a warm-up period of several minutes is necessary for highest brightness.

Arc lamps. Arc lamps are also used on occasion to produce very intense ultraviolet radiation, either medium wave or long wave. The cored carbon arc is probably the best-known lamp of this type. An arc is produced by impressing electricity across two electrodes of carbon in close proximity, and in air. Since the carbon is consumed in the process, a mechanical means is necessary to maintain a constant separation between the electrodes. In a similar manner, electrodes of cadmium can be used to produce an extremely bright line at 275 millimicrons. The xenon arc is enclosed in a small glass tube containing metal electrodes in a high-pressure atmosphere of xenon gas. Although this arc lamp emits some long-wave ultraviolet, its primary use is in visual-light photography and photomicrography. A continuous spectrum is produced in the ultraviolet, visible and infrared spectral ranges.

Electronic flash lamps. Electronic flash lamps vary considerably in ultraviolet output, depending to some extent on the type of gas contained within the tubes. A tube containing a high percentage of krypton or argon emits more blue and long-wave ultraviolet than one in which xenon predominates. All electronic flash lamps, however, emit some long-wave ultraviolet and can be used in reflected ultraviolet photography. Those lamps in which the tube and envelope are composed of quartz also emit some shorter wavelengths of ultraviolet.

Wire-filled flash lamps. Wire-filled flash lamps are also suitable for reflected ultraviolet photography, since these light sources, either blue-coated or clear, emit enough long-wave ultraviolet for instantaneous exposures at near subject distances.

ILLUMINATION FOR ULTRAVIOLET PHOTOGRAPHY

As previously stated, there are many sources which emit ultraviolet radiation. The selection of a source for ultraviolet photography depends primarily upon certain factors — such as availability, cost, convenience, object size, and source emission. Sunlight, of course, is most readily available, costs nothing and provides a broad source of illumination. On the other hand, the intensity of ultraviolet available is quite variable due to changes in light conditions and by attenuation of ultraviolet by scatter and absorption in the atmosphere. A bright, sunny, dry day is best.

To control illumination conditions more satisfactorily, ultraviolet photography is usually done indoors. The most readily available ultraviolet source is the "black light" fluorescent tube. (See Figure 1.) Tubes of this type can be obtained from all major electrical supply firms (General Electric, Sylvania, Westinghouse, etc.). These tubes can be fitted to, and used in, regular fluorescent light fixtures. They can be obtained in short or long lengths to suit the size of object to be illuminated and are reasonably inexpensive. Since the glass for each tube contains a visibly opaque filter element, it is usually necessary to illuminate the subject temporarily with an auxiliary light source (such as a tungsten floodlamp). Long tubes of this type are excellent for ultraviolet illumination of large areas, as in the photography of large documents.

Mercury vapor lamps of the "high pressure" type are usually small and are most suitable for illuminating small objects in close-up photography, in photomicrography, and in spectrography.

Carbon-arc lamps are not generally suitable for ultraviolet photography. They can be erratic and inconvenient. Also, they provide no principal advantage over previously mentioned light sources. They can be used for specific purposes, however, in photomicrography by transmitted or reflected light,

and in spectrography. The xenon arc can be used for long-wave ultraviolet photography by filtering the visible emission.

Electronic flash lamps provide a broad source of visual illumination, with some ultraviolet emission. The efficiency of ultraviolet illumination is limited, however, by the type of gas contained in the tubes, and by the percentage of reflection of ultraviolet from the reflector. An aluminum reflector provides a high percentage of ultraviolet reflection. Enough ultraviolet is emitted from any electronic flash to permit instantaneous exposures with a hand-held camera, provided that the subject distance is not too great.

Wire-filled flash lamps are probably the least expensive and most convenient long wave ultraviolet sources of all. They are available in a wide variety of sizes, representing various light intensities; can be easily procured; and can be used with most cameras. Even the smallest lamp (AG-1, AG-1B, or Flashcube) provides a high enough ultraviolet brightness for instantaneous exposure with a hand-held camera at a subject distance of six feet or closer. Lamps of this type, however, could not be used for medium-wave and short-wave ultraviolet photography, since these radiations are not transmitted through the glass envelope.

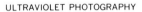

ULTRAVIOLET PHOTOGRAPHY

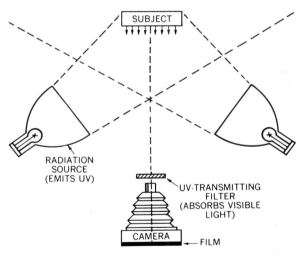

Figure 2 — Typical set-up for reflected ultraviolet photography

FILTERS

Regardless of the source of illumination, a filter *must be placed over the camera lens*. This filter should have a high transmittance of ultraviolet, and should *not* pass any visible light. Exposure by ultraviolet only is the aim point of ultraviolet photography. Ultraviolet transmitting filters are usually made of glass in which coloring agents are contained to control transmittance. Most types of glass will transmit long-wave ultraviolet, but will absorb all medium-wave and short-wave ultraviolet. This is not a disadvantage in general ultraviolet photography, since lenses used in cameras are made of optical glass, whose transmittance is also limited to long-wave ultraviolet. There are *no* gelatin filters suitable for this type of photography.

Kodak Wratten Filter No. 18A is a glass filter with high percentage transmittance of long-wave ultraviolet, particularly the 365 millimicron line of the mercury spectrum. It is currently available in both 2- and 3-inch squares, and as a 4-inch square on special order. It can be obtained through regular photographic supply dealers. This filter or its equivalent is highly recommended for long-wave ultraviolet photography.

A No. 18A filter (very difficult to get) can be attached to a camera lens by means of a Kodak Gelatin Filter Frame Holder and a suitable adapter ring. A Series 6 holder will accommodate a 2-inch square filter; a Series 8 holder, a 3-inch square filter; and a Series 9 holder, a 4-inch square filter. The 2-inch square filter is adequate for most 35mm cameras. The larger sizes are appropriate for view-type cameras. When a glass filter is mounted in front of a camera lens, it is imperative that all visible light be excluded, possibly with some kind of light seal around the filter.

Ultraviolet-transmitting filters can also be obtained from other filter manufacturers. It is suggested, however, that filter transmittance curves be obtained and examined for efficiency of both ultraviolet transmittance and visible light absorption. Filters for this purpose should have no visible light transmittance.

FILM

All photographic emulsions contain silver halide, which is inherently sensitive to blue and ultraviolet. Sensitivity in the ultraviolet actually extends far into this region, but the response of a film or plate is somewhat limited, due to absorption of ultraviolet by gelatin, the medium in which silver halide crystals are suspended. For long-wave ultraviolet photography, most any film or plate can be used to record an image; the choice is almost unlimited. Only black-and-white films need be considered, since color film has no advantage. In 35mm ultraviolet photography with long-wave radiation, Kodak Panatomic-X Film, Kodak Plus-X Pan Film, and Kodak Tri-X Pan Film are all quite suitable, and are easily obtainable through photographic dealers. Panatomic-X Film is especially recommended because of its extremely fine grain, which permits great enlargement. All the above films are

currently available in 20- or 36-exposure rolls in camera magazines and in 100-foot rolls.

If a high-contrast 35mm material is needed, Kodak High Contrast Copy Film can be used. This film is available both in 100-foot rolls and in 36-exposure rolls in magazines. If a color-blind film (sensitive only to blue and ultraviolet) is desired, Eastman Fine Grain Release Positive Film, Type 5302, is suggested. It is available only in 100-foot rolls, but can be handled and processed under a light-red safelight (Kodak Safelight Filter No. 1A). Panchromatic films must be handled and processed either in total darkness or under a deep-green safelight (Kodak Safelight Filter No. 3) according to direction provided.

If a view camera is to be used, sheet film is indicated. Again, a wide variety of films are suitable because all films have ultraviolet sensitivity. A film of medium to high contrast, with very fine grain, should be the first choice. Although film-speed ratings are given only for visible light, a fast film is preferred to minimize exposure time. Films such as Kodak LS Pan (Estar Thick Base), Kodak Panatomic-X, Kodak Plus-X Pan Professional (Estar Thick Base), and Kodak Tri-X Pan Professional (Estar Thick Base) are quite suitable. They have extremely fine to very fine grain, although their contrast is moderate. For medium to high contrast, one could use either Kodak Contrast Process Ortho Film (Estar Thick Base) or Kodak Contrast Process Panchromatic Film.

Images formed with ultraviolet usually present low contrast. Therefore, if a high contrast film is not used, medium to high-contrast development should be practiced for best effect. This can be achieved either by extending development time in recommended developers or by using developers which produce elevated contrast.

FILM SPEED

The rated speed for any film is determined for visible light, and does not apply for ultraviolet. An arbitrary ultraviolet film speed can be determined by test exposures; this speed rating can then be applied in setting the meter to indicate exposure to ultraviolet. The ultraviolet speed will be considerably lower than the visible-light speed. For example, one film has a speed of ASA 400 for visible light; exposures to ultraviolet, however, indicated that the effective speed was only about ASA 10.

A specially designed meter can be obtained from Ultra-Violet Products, Inc., San Gabriel, California 91778, for making reading of ultraviolet intensity. It is called Blak-Ray® ultraviolet intensity meter, and is a hand-held device for measuring the intensity of emission from ultraviolet sources and the radiation incident on a surface from a source. Visible light has no effect on the meter. Two sensors are available, one for long-wave ultraviolet and another for short wave. Meter readings are in microwatts per square centimeter, which can be correlated to exposure time in ultraviolet photography. The meter requires no batteries, electrical supply, or other source of power.

If an exposure meter is not available, or not adequate, exposure must be determined by a series of test exposures. In general, exposure time will be considerably longer than if visible light were used (for one aperture setting). A test series could therefore be made at a small f/number, with variations in exposure time over a wide range — starting with a short exposure time and increasing by a factor of 2. An approximate series could be 1/10, 1/5, 1/2, 1, 2, 4, 8 seconds, etc. If all exposures are too long, then overexposure will result, and shorter times are indicated. Conversely, if all exposures are too short, under-exposure results and longer times are necessary. Once a reasonable exposure time is determined for a given set of conditions, exposures for different conditions can probably be estimated. A shorter test series can be applied. Of course, if a film of higher or lower speed is used, another test exposure series must be made.

FOCUS

Although a camera lens is specified as having a definite focal length, this characteristic pertains to visible light only. When infrared is used to form an image, the focal length of the lens is longer than specified; when ultraviolet is used, it is shorter. An image in sharp focus visually may be quite unsharp in a photo taken by ultraviolet. For ultraviolet photography, a good technique is to achieve focus visually and then to decrease the lens aperture to obtain more depth of field. The amount of aperture decrease is a function of normal focal length. Lenses of short focal length inherently have more depth of field, and will require less aperture decrease than those of long focal length. In 35mm photography, lenses usually have short focal lengths (38mm, 45mm, 50mm, etc.). A lens-aperture decrease of at least 2 stops below wide-open will usually suffice. Test exposures at various apertures, however, will definitely establish the largest aperture for sharp focus in reflected-ultraviolet photography.

EXPOSURE

The methods by which exposure can be determined in reflected-ultraviolet photography are using an exposure meter, making test exposures, or establishing a guide number when flash lamps are used.

Most conventional exposure meters have some sensitivity to ultraviolet. The incident-light type of meter, however, is the most convenient. If the cell can be covered with a Kodak Wratten Filter No. 18A (or equivalent) so as to exclude all visible light, the meter will give an indication of ultraviolet intensity. The intensity will vary, of course, as the distance from radiation source to subject is varied. The source should be positioned so that the entire area to be photographed is well illuminated. If a mercury vapor lamp is used, no filter is necessary in front of the lamp, and the visible light emitted will ascertain efficiency of illumination. If the lamp contains an ultraviolet transmitting filter which cannot be removed, the coverage and evenness of illumination must be determined by ultraviolet intensity alone.

FLASH

The determination of exposure with flash lamps is simplified, since a guide number can be determined from one test exposure series. The duration of a flash is fairly constant, so a fixed shutter speed (1/25 or 1/30 second) can be used for the series. All exposures in the series should be made at the same lamp-to-subject distance. The test series should include exposures at all available lens-aperture settings.

Here is an example of a test series: A 35mm camera with an f/2.8 lens is used to make a test series on Kodak Tri-X Pan Film. With the shutter set at 1/30 second, exposures are made at f/2.8, f/4.0, f/5.6, f/8, f/11, f/16, and f/22. Ordinary flashcubes are used, and a Kodak Wratten Filter No. 18A is placed in front of the lens. The subject in front of the camera is 6 feet away. After the film has been processed, the frame showing good exposure is determined by examining the strip. In this case, the exposure at f/4 looks to be best. Since a flash guide number is equal to the subject distance multiplied by the lens-aperture number, 6 (distance) is multiplied by 4 (f/number), and a guide number of 24 results. This figure can be used for future exposure determination when the same camera, film, and flash are used. For instance, if the distance were changed to 4 feet, the new f/number would be 6; if the distance were 2 feet, the f/number would be 12, etc. With this technique, a flash guide number can be determined for any combination of film and flash. The same technique applies whether electronic flash or wire-filled flash lamps are used.

BLAK-RAY CRIMINOLOGY AND DETECTION KITS

Under ultraviolet light many clues will reveal a good deal of important information about the crimi-

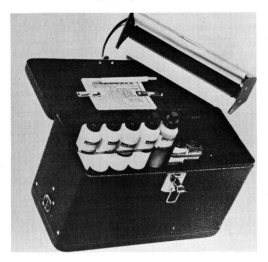

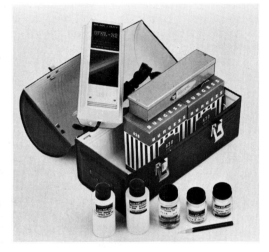

Figure 3 — Blak-Ray criminology kit (above) and detection kit (below)

FLUORESCENCE PHOTOGRAPHY

LUMINESCENCE

When certain materials (solids, liquids, or gases) are subjected to short-wave electromagnetic radiation, they will emit another radiation, of longer wavelength and very often in the visible spectrum. The exciting radiation may be X-rays, gamma rays, electrons, ultraviolet, or even some visible wavelengths. This phenomenon of induced light emission is called luminescence, of which there are two distinct types, known as fluorescence and phosphorescence.

FLUORESCENCE

If the luminescence ceases within a very short time (8 to 10 seconds) after the exciting radiation is removed, the phenomenon is called fluorescence. Although fluorescence is commonly produced by excitation with ultraviolet light, other radiations can also be used in some applications. It is also possible to stimulate fluorescence with some visible wavelengths. Blue light, for example, stimulates green fluorescence in some compounds.

There are many thousands of materials which exhibit the phenomenon of fluorescence, and fluorescence photography has numerous applications because it will provide information that cannot be obtained by other photographic methods.

Just the fact that a substance will fluoresce is an important characteristic. The particular radiation that excites fluorescence and the specific position of that fluorescence in the visible spectrum can be clues to the identity of a substance. Also, contrast between the elements of a material can often be produced by fluorescence, even when they otherwise appear similar.

nal that is not apparent when the clue is observed under ordinary light. Lipstick traces, for example, too minute to be seen under white light, will fluoresce under ultraviolet. Oil and grease spots have a distinctive fluorescent glow as do sputum and semen. Crimes can be detected by placing an invisible fluorescent powder or paste on such objects as money, fire alarms and coin boxes.

Ultra-Violet Products, Inc., San Gabriel, California 91778 produces a criminology kit and a detection kit (see Figure 3) that can be used for a variety of detection methods. Some of them are as follows: inspection of clues, detection of persons sounding false alarms, detection of tampered documents, inspection of documents, autopsy assistance, coin box tampering, trailing, illegal money transactions, use of firearms and weapons, repeated burglaries, petty theft and shoplifting, sex crimes, narcotics, espionage, kidnappings, forgeries and altered checks, censorship and detection of psychics and mediums.

PHOSPHORESCENCE

Although fluorescence ceases almost immediately after the exciting radiation is removed, there are some substances which continue to emit luminescence for some time, even hours, after removal of the exciting stimulus. This phenomenon is called phosphorescence and is produced in compounds called phosphors. Phosphorescence, like fluorescence, is stimulated by many radiations, but in fewer substances. The image on a television screen, for example, is produced by phosphorescence.

INFRARED LUMINESCENCE

Although most luminescence appears in the visible spectrum and is excited by either ultraviolet or short visible wavelengths of blue, it is also possible to excite luminescence in the infrared by irradiation of certain materials with blue-green light. The phenomenon is referred to as luminescence, instead of fluorescence or phosphorescence, because it is not known whether or not the effect ceases immediately after the exciting stimulus is removed.

EXCITATION SOURCES

The most common radiations used to excite fluorescence are the long ultraviolet wavelengths, and many of the radiation sources used for ultraviolet photography or micrography can also be used for fluorescence recording. Some shorter visible wavelengths are used occasionally to produce fluorescence, either at longer visible wavelengths, or in the infrared.

Although it would be possible to use sunlight as a source of ultraviolet or visual light to produce fluorescence, it is not a practical procedure. Artificial radiation sources are preferable because they are constant, easily procurable, and convenient to use.

Mercury vapor lamps. All of the mercury vapor lamps, both high-pressure and low-pressure, have application in fluorescence photography. The selection of a lamp depends to a great extent on the application. If the subject is large, then a source is needed which can illuminate a large area with the desired radiation. If a small subject is to be irradiated, then a small, intensely bright source will be advantageous. All mercury vapor lamps, however, emit long-wave ultraviolet, and if the tube is made of quartz, then the shorter waves of ultraviolet may also be emitted.

Electronic flash. It was stated in the section on ultraviolet that electronic flash lamps are suitable for ultraviolet photography since they emit long-wave ultraviolet. They can also be used for recording fluorescence, excited by ultraviolet, in close-up applications such as photographing fingerprints dusted with fluorescent powder. A flash-tube with high intensity output should be obtained for this purpose. One of the difficulties encountered in using electronic flash is that resulting fluorescence is not visible during the short flash interval. A continuous ultraviolet source is often necessary for preliminary inspection to ascertain the presence of fluorescence.

Visual light sources. Fluorescence can be excited in certain materials by irradiation with blue or blue-violet light, and occurs at a longer wavelength in the visible spectrum, often green or yellow-green. A light source having a high intensity with continuous emission in the blue region of the spectrum is needed for this application. The xenon arc is probably the most suitable light source, although electronic flash might also be used. Carbon arc lamps also emit light of high intensity, but they can be quite erratic unless a mechanical (or electrical) means of maintaining electrodes in a constant position is available.

There are several light sources which could be used for producing infrared luminescence. This phenomenon is exhibited in some materials by stimulation with blue-green light. Although it is possible that infrared luminescence may also be stimulated by irradiation with specific wavelengths of blue or green, it is suggested that a source having continuous emission in the blue and green spectral regions be obtained. High-wattage tungsten lamps, the xenon arc, or even ordinary fluorescent lamps could be used for this purpose.

PHOTOGRAPHIC TECHNIQUE

When fluorescence is stimulated either with ultraviolet or visible wavelengths, there are several factors which must be considered for efficient photography. The subject must be illuminated with the exciting stimulus, and this is accomplished by selecting a suitable source which emits the necessary radiation. A filter is used with the source to screen out other radiations and to transmit the exciting radiation. Another filter, usually placed between the subject and camera, absorbs any residual exciting radiation and transmits the fluorescence. The fluorescence is then recorded on a suitable photographic material.

ILLUMINATION

One of the main factors influencing the brightness of fluorescence is the intensity of the exciting radiation. Fluorescence brightness is generally of very low order compared with image brightness in other types of photography. It is important, therefore, that the radiation source be as close to the subject as possible, while furnishing even illumination over the area to be photographed.

The size of the subject must be considered in selecting an appropriate source of illumination. When a large subject is to be photographed, the source should cover a large area with as bright an illumination as possible. The long fluorescent tubes (low-pressure mercury vapor lamps) are quite suitable. High-pressure mercury arcs are also useful, but are small sources. If they are used to illuminate a large area, there may be a sacrifice in fluorescence brightness, resulting in extremely long exposure times. If the long tubes are selected, two or more (in suitable reflectors) can be placed on each side of the subject to provide a considerable quantity of exciting radiation. If the subject is large and flat, such as a large document, the tubes should be placed so that the incident illumination angle is less than 45 degrees. Make sure, however, that no direct light from the source is "seen" by the camera. The lamp reflectors can be oriented so that this condition does not occur.

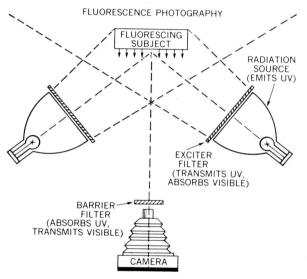

FLUORESCENCE PHOTOGRAPHY

Figure 4 — Typical set-up for fluorescence photography using ultraviolet

High-pressure mercury-vapor lamps are excellent for illuminating small objects or small areas. One lamp, however, is usually not adequate, since illumination is then provided for one side only. At least two lamps should be used, one on each side of the subject, especially when the subject is three-dimensional.

Electronic flash lamps are especially useful when living subjects which exhibit fluorescence are to be photographed, since instantaneous exposures are possible. Although one lamp may be sufficient, two lamps (one on each side of the subject) will provide twice as much light and will allow smaller lens apertures for increased depth of field.

The illumination of the subject should consist only of the radiations needed to excite fluorescence. All ambient illumination (room lights) and all other illumination from the source must be excluded from the subject. Fluorescence photography is most often accomplished either in a darkened room or in a light-tight enclosure.

EXCITER AND BARRIER FILTERS

At least two distinct types of filter are used in a fluorescence photography system. The first, called an exciter filter, is placed between the subject and the radiation source. It transmits the radiation needed to excite fluorescence. The second, a barrier filter, is placed in front of the camera lens (or somewhere behind the objective lens in a microscope), to remove any residual exciting radiation and to transmit the fluorescence.

The filter used with the radiation source is called an exciter filter, and its purpose is to transmit the exciting radiation efficiently and absorb all, or almost all, of the other radiations emitted from the source. When ultraviolet is the radiation used to excite fluorescence, the exciter filter should pass a high percentage of the ultraviolet radiated from the source. If visible blue or blue-green light is used to excite fluorescence, then the exciter filter for this purpose should transmit either of these radiations freely and absorb all others.

Fluorescence brightness, as previously stated, is usually of low intensity, and if any other than the exciting radiations are incident on the subject, they will be higher in brightness and may mask the fluorescence.

The exciter filter in front of the light source transmits the radiation necessary to excite fluorescence. Not all of this radiation is used, however, and some residual radiation still exists — reflected from, or transmitted through, the subject. If this residual radiation is not removed, it will record on film. Since it is usually of higher brightness than the fluorescence, it will cause more exposure than the fluorescence. Another filter must be used, usually in front of the camera lens, to prevent the residual exciting radiation from causing exposure. This filter acts as a barrier to the exciting radiation, and is logically called a barrier filter. An efficient barrier filter absorbs all radiation transmitted by the exciter filter, and transmits only the wavelengths of light evident as fluorescence. If ultraviolet is used to excite fluorescence, then the barrier filter must absorb ultraviolet. If the exciter filter passes both ultraviolet and some short visual blue, then the barrier must absorb both ultraviolet and blue.

For further information on selection of exciter and barrier filters, refer to the Eastman Kodak Company Publication *Ultraviolet and Fluorescence Photography*, Kodak Publication No. M-27.

FILMS

All photographic emulsions are inherently sensitive to blue and ultraviolet. This is why all blue and ultraviolet transmitted by the exciter filter must be absorbed by the barrier filter. Otherwise, the film will be exposed to these radiations, which may cause greater photographic effect than the fluorescence. If a color film is used, any ultraviolet reaching the film will record as blue, seriously degrading the record of fluorescence colors. Similarly, any unwanted blue light passing through the barrier filter will degrade the fluorescence record.

Color film, of course, presents the greatest advantage in recording fluorescence colors. Daylight-type color film is especially recommended because of its balanced sensitivity to the blue, green, and red regions of the visible spectrum. Color film balanced for tungsten illumination is seldom recommended, since it has higher blue sensitivity than the daylight type.

Roll color films, especially in 35mm size, are usually recommended for recording fluorescence because they have the highest speeds, are more readily available, are less expensive, and are more conveniently handled and processed than sheet color films.

Although there is no question about the advantage of using color film in recording fluorescence colors, there are applications for which a black-and-white film may be perfectly satisfactory. Usually the black-and-white film should have panchromatic sensitivity and high speed.

Infrared luminescence is best recorded on an infrared-sensitive film such as Kodak Infrared Film or High Speed Infrared Film.

EXPOSURE DETERMINATION

Because of the very low brightness of fluorescence, the most practical method of determining exposure is by test. The beginner should make several exposures, increasing time at a fixed lens aperture by a factor of 2, in successive steps, over a wide range. Lens apertures could also be varied by using a fixed time, but this technique would cause a variation in depth of field that might not be desirable. Once the exposure time has been determined, however, the lens aperture can be changed to achieve the appropriate depth of field. As in all other photographs, if lens aperture is changed, exposure time must be changed in inverse proportion. When a constant source, such as a mercury arc lamp, is used, exposure time will be several seconds, or even minutes if the fluorescence is extremely low in brightness. Extremely long exposures result when large subjects are to be photographed and illumination is spread over a large area. Extremely long exposures can also result when image size is greater than object size, as a photomacrography.

It is seldom possible to use an ordinary exposure meter to read fluorescence brightness, but an extremely sensitive meter can be used. If one is available, its cell should be protected with a barrier filter which absorbs ultraviolet. Otherwise, the meter will indicate ultraviolet rather than fluorescence brightness. Ultraviolet reflected from or transmitted through the subject will be much higher in brightness than fluorescence, so an erroneous indication of exposure time will be obtained.

When electronic flash is to be used (as in close-up fluorescence photography), an experimental guide number can be determined for a specific subject, flash unit, and film. If the subject is changed, however, the guide number might or might not apply, since fluorescence brightness might change. In this case, exposures should be bracketed. Exposure time will be constant, so changing the lens aperture is the only practical means of varying exposure.

No matter how exposure is determined, it is a good idea to make a record of all exposure conditions for future reference. These conditions include the subject, the radiation source, the exciter filter, the barrier filter, the position of the source, the film, the exposure time and lens aperture, and any other details pertinent to fluorescence photography.

FOCUS

When fluorescence occurs in the visible spectrum there is no problem involved in obtaining correct focus. It can be achieved by a distance setting on the camera, by means of a rangefinder, or by adjustment on a ground glass (as in a view-camera).

Recording infrared luminescence, however, involves an invisible image, and lens focal length is longer for infrared than for visible light. The use of a small lens aperture is a practical means of obtaining correct focus. Usually the image is focused with visible light; the lens aperture is decreased to at least two stops below the wide-open position; the infrared-transmitting filter is placed in front of the lens; and the exposure is made. The exact lens aperture would be determined by the depth of field necessary to record a satisfactory image.

APPLICATIONS

Since there are many thousands of substances which exhibit fluorescence when excited by specific radiations, it is reasonable to expect that there are many photographic applications in which this phenomenon is of particular interest. Like any type of photography, the photography of fluorescence is practiced to supply information that cannot be ob-

tained by other means. Just the fact that a sub-stance does fluoresce is enough to differentiate it from one which does not. When two substances both fluoresce, they may differ in fluorescence color, or their fluorescence may occur in distinctly different portions of the spectrum – visible or invisible. Most fluorescence occurs in the visible spectrum with long-wave ultraviolet excitation. Fluorescence can also occur, however, in long-wave ultraviolet (or in the visible spectrum) with short-wave ultraviolet excitation. It can also occur in the long-wave visible region with blue light excitation. Finally, some materials, as stated, produce infrared luminescence when excited by blue-green light.

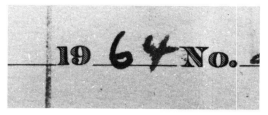

Figure 5 — (A) This check appears to be dated 1964 in the original photograph, but (B) when ultraviolet photography is used, it shows that the check was originally written in 1960

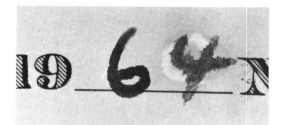

QUESTIONED DOCUMENTS

An outstanding application of fluorescence photography is in the field of law enforcement — most particularly in the examination of questioned documents. When other photographic methods fail to

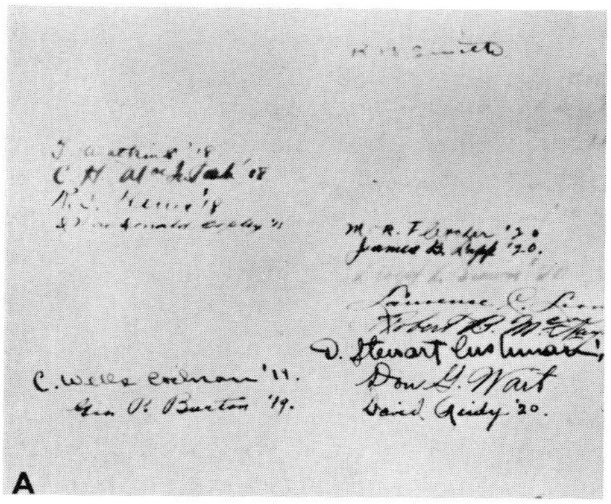

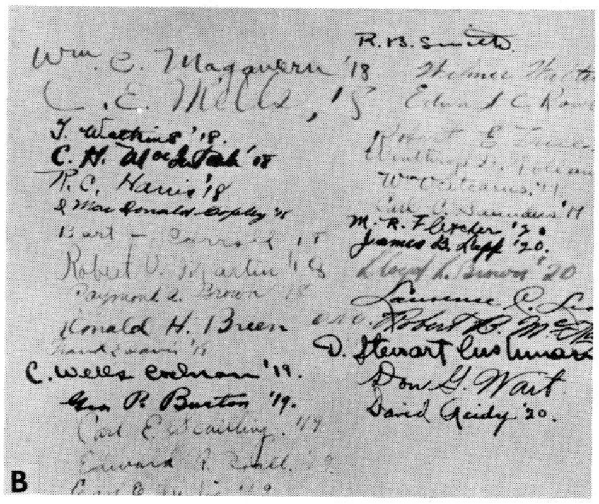

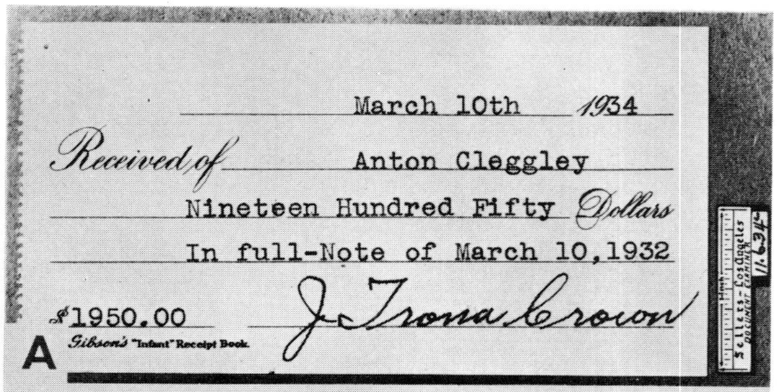

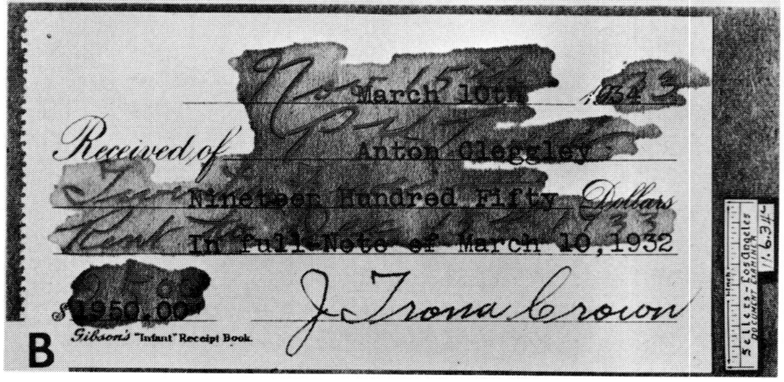

Figure 6 — Typewritten receipt (above, A) looks bonafide, but ultraviolet fluorescence shows it to be a fraud (above, B)

Figure 7 — Faded signatures in document (left, A) are made visible with black light (left, B)

reveal suspected alterations in, or addition to, a document (check, letter, will, etc.) it is always possible that a fluorescence technique will provide fruitful results. Many inks may show a difference in visible fluorescence. The effects of bleaching or erasures can also often be detected by this means.

Most papers on which documents are written or printed contain cellulose fibers. These fibers often fluoresce brightly when the paper is illuminated with ultraviolet in a darkened room. Erasures will alter this fluorescence; the effect can be recorded and enhanced on a high-contrast black-and-white film. If inks have been bleached, as with an "ink eradicator," the bleach material still in the paper may show a typical fluorescence color. If it does, the effect can be recorded on either black-and-white or color film. (Figures 5, 6, 7.)

Since visible fluorescence may be produced by excitation with either long or short wave ultraviolet, photographs should be made by both methods.

To produce fluorescence by short-wave ultraviolet, a radiation source is needed which emits this wavelength. A high-pressure mercury arc in a quartz envelope emits several spectral lines of ultraviolet, including the short wave ultraviolet at 254 millimicrons. A filter which passes only short radiations must be placed in front of the source to provide only the necessary excitation. Narrow-band "interference filters" can be used for this purpose and are available from some firms.

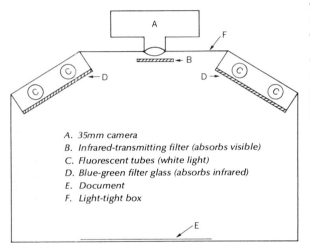

A. 35mm camera
B. Infrared-transmitting filter (absorbs visible)
C. Fluorescent tubes (white light)
D. Blue-green filter glass (absorbs infrared)
E. Document
F. Light-tight box

Figure 8 — Suggested technique for photographing infrared luminescence in questioned documents

Different inks may show different "infrared luminescence" when irradiated with visible blue-green light. This may prove invaluable in detecting alterations in documents. The following is a method of illuminating a document in a light-tight box with blue-green light (provided by fluorescent tubes) and photographing the resultant infrared luminescence. (Figure 8.) A box of this type can be constructed of wood (or other material) to accommodate average-size documents, such as checks and letters. Since the camera is reasonably close, special close-up lenses are usually necessary if a camera with extendible bellows (or extension tubes) is not available. The box should be light-tight so that no ambient light containing infrared is incident on the surface of the document. A Kodak Wratten Filter No. 87 (or No. 88A), which transmits infrared but absorbs visible light, is suggested in front of the camera lens. Focus is accomplished first, however, with the blue-green light. The lens opening is decreased to a small aperture to assure good focus

in the infrared. The blue-green filter in front of the lamps can be Corning Glass No. 9780, available from the Corning Glass Works (Corning, New York 14830). A long, narrow size is suggested for use in front of the fluorescent tubes. Information about available sizes and prices can be obtained from the above firm. Since this type of luminescence is very low in brightness, Kodak High Speed Infrared Film (35mm) is suggested for photography. Even with this high-speed film, however, exposure times may be of several seconds, or even minutes, duration.

The exposure box just described could also be adapted for regular close-up photography of visible fluorescence in documents or other objects. "Black light" fluorescent tubes, which emit ultraviolet, could be used in place of the white light tubes, and the infrared-transmitting filter on the camera lens could be replaced by a barrier-type filter to absorb the ultraviolet reflected from the subject. Fluorescence photographs could be made either on color reversal film or on black-and-white.

The same equipment could also be used to photograph documents by reflected ultraviolet. In that case, the "black light" tubes would remain in place. A Kodak Wratten Filter No. 18A could then be used in front of the camera lens to transmit only ultraviolet radiation to a suitable black-and-white film.

The size of the box would be governed by the length of tubes to be used and the sizes of documents to be photographed.

FINGERPRINTS

Photographing fingerprints with visible light is a well-known, long-established procedure. Latent fingerprints on a dark surface are dusted with a light or white powder; those on a light surface, with a dark or black powder. In this way a high-contrast effect is produced, which can be photographed on a black-and-white film. As long as the surface is smooth and uniform in color or density, no problem exists. If a surface is multicolored or of alternate light and dark areas, however, neither a light nor a dark powder will give satisfactory contrast. Visualization of an entire fingerprint may be difficult. In this case, the area containing a latent print can be dusted with a powder which will fluoresce brightly when irradiated with long-wave ultraviolet in a darkened room. The background will usually appear very dark, with little or no fluorescence, so the fingerprint stands out, and excellent contrast is achieved. (Figure 9.)

A suggested technique for photographing such fingerprints is to use a single-lens reflex camera (35mm) focused on the area suspected of containing a fingerprint. (Figure 10.) An electronic flash unit attached to the camera with a long synchronizing cord will provide adequate ultraviolet intensity to produce very bright fluorescence. The flash unit is placed at one side and directed at the area. A Kodak Wratten Filter No. 18A (or equivalent) can be taped in place on the front of the flash to provide only ultraviolet, the exciting stimulus, and exclude all visible light from reaching the subject. The dusting powder could be "Magna-Glo," a commercial powder (available from MacDonald Associates, Box 1111, Corning, New York 14830) made for the purpose, which fluoresces a bright yellow-green. Anthracene, a chemical compound which fluoresces a bright blue-white, could also be used.

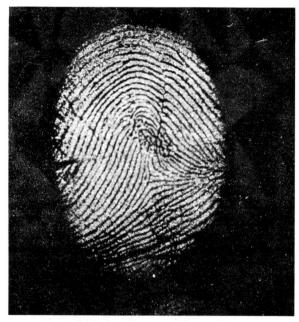

Figure 9 — Fluorescent fingerprint

A barrier filter must be placed in front of the camera lens to prevent reflected ultraviolet from exposing the film. A Kodak Wratten Filter No. 2A is suggested for this purpose. Focus and composition can be accomplished in room light, which is extin-

guished for the fluorescence exposure. The camera should be placed on a small tripod or bench clamp, since exposures are made in a darkened room. Kodak Tri-X Pan Film can be used for recording the

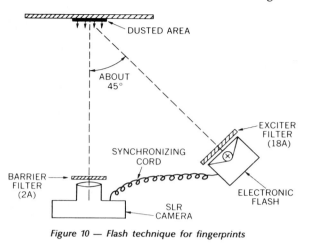

Figure 10 — Flash technique for fingerprints

image of the fingerprint. If higher contrast is desirable, Kodak High Contrast Copy Film is suggested. Color film is neither necessary nor desirable, since the goal is to record the fingerprint with good contrast against the background. Exposure time is fixed at the flash duration, so it is usually necessary to vary test exposures by changing lens apertures (f/numbers). The actual lens aperture used will depend upon the brightness of the source and its proximity to the subject. An exciting source of relatively low intensity would necessarily have to be very close to the subject, but would produce a fluorescence brightness high enough for the instantaneous flash to cause adequate exposure on the film.

If an electronic flash lamp is not available, the dusted area can be illuminated with long wave ultraviolet from any typical source that emits this radiation. In any case, the exciting source should be placed very close to the area in order to produce the highest fluorescence brightness.

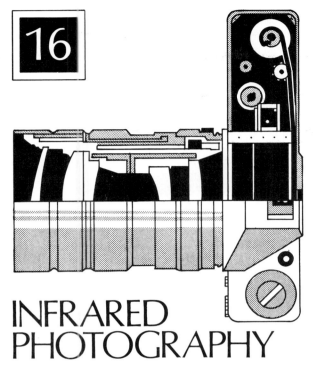

16

INFRARED PHOTOGRAPHY

Infrared photography has found many applications in the field of criminology. These applications include the detection and deciphering of erasures and forgeries; deciphering of charred documents or those which have become illegible as the result of age or abuse; differentiation between inks, and pigments which are visually identical but which represent different compounds; detection of gunshot-powder burns (Figure 1), stains, and irregularities in cloth; examination of cloth, fibers, and hair which are dyed too dark to be easy to study by visible radiation; study of fingerprints; examination of the contents of sealed envelopes; detection of certain kinds of secret writing; determination of carbon monoxide impregnation of victims of gas poisoning; and photography in the dark, especially in surveillance or trapping of a burglar.

CAMERAS

Any type of view camera regularly used for ordinary photography can be used for infrared photography. Because much of the work, especially indoors, deals with small specimens, the camera should be adaptable for close-up photography.

The most useful 35mm equipment is a single-lens reflex camera with an automatic diaphragm. It is well suited to hand-held operation with infrared color film. Also, when opaque, infrared-transmitting filters are placed over the lights instead of over

the lens; this camera can also be hand-held for black-and-white infrared photography. But when such filters have to be placed over the lens, a camera with a viewfinder is needed.

If the camera has a through-the-lens exposure meter, the meter should be turned off when an opaque filter is employed. Some work can be done, especially outdoors, with a red filter and with the meter in operation. The camera should be set for *the film speed rating without a filter*. However, a red filter will affect the spectral response of the meter and may indicate an incorrect exposure for automatic operation. Tests will indicate the need for setting a dummy film speed.

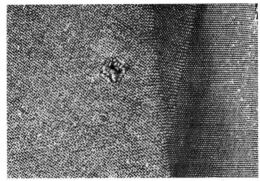

Figure 1 — From the visual appearance (above) of this garment it was not possible to determine the cause of the hole in it. The infrared photograph (below) reveals the powder and burn marks of a firearm

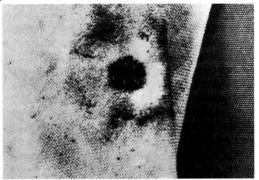

CHECKING THE CAMERA

The photographer should be alert to a possible radiation leak through the leather bellows or the camera body, or through a plastic lens board. Should obscure streaks show up on negatives, such a defect is a probable cause. A camera can be checked by placing unexposed film in it and then moving a strong tungsten light around in front of it for about a minute. Any density that occurs on the film is due to an unsafe bellows, lens board, or camera body — provided that the shutter and film holder are safe.

To rule out the shutter, the lens should be covered with a metal cap when the test is done. Then the shutter blades do not become a factor. For sheet-film cameras, load the film into the holder in the dark and insert the holder into the camera in the dark, too. The dark slide of the holder is thus taken out of consideration.

There is little chance that the blades of most current shutters will cause trouble. However, some older ones were made of hard rubber and some later ones of black plastic. Using them for infrared photography would be like employing blades of almost clear plastic for ordinary photography. A check can be made by focusing the camera on a light bulb. Then, in essence, a film is exposed with the shutter closed. About a minute at f/8 should be sufficient time. If no image of the bulb appears on the negative, the photographer can proceed with confidence.

To check a dark slide for leaks, leave it in position over a loaded film. Then place a large coin upon the outside of the slide and hold the light over the holder for about a minute. If neither streaks nor a shadow image of the coin appear after development of the film, the slide is safe. (Streaks coming in at the edges of the negative would indicate, in the absence of a coin shadow, that the holder may not be safe for panchromatic photography either.) Wooden and some hard rubber slides transmit infrared rays readily and should not be used. Eastman Kodak Company and Graflex Incorporated have placed five raised indicator dots (instead of a lower number) on dark slides that are safe. Special-composition slides and metal slides are in this class.

LENSES

Unless a lens has been especially achromatized for infrared photography, there will be a difference between the infrared focus position and the visual-focus position. Usually, this difference causes no serious problems for the photographer, yet it ought to be investigated. Some good lenses have a red dot on the focusing scale to indicate an average correction for infrared photography.

In the field of document copying, a lens of high quality should be used because fine detail is often needed.

FOCUSING

Focusing for an infrared image is often difficult. An infrared image, even when focused correctly, will not be as sharp as a panchromatic image because aberrations in the camera lens have been corrected for panchromatic photography. Many infrared images (particularly those of biological subjects) are formed from details which are not on the visible surface of the subject. Also, many images will have a translucent, scattering medium interposed between their outlines and the lens. Thus, a misty appearance may result from the most carefully focused image.

When focusing for a panchromatic image, it is customary to shift back and forth across the sharp-focus position. For a correct infrared focus, this action should be stopped just when the image of the subject goes slightly out of focus and the lens-to-image distance is being *increased*. For simpler focusing, sharp detail should be sought in the subject. Lacking this, a comb, ruler or some other marker can be placed in the scene to facilitate focusing, and then removed for the photograph.

For most subjects, the lens must be stopped down to at least f/11 so that sufficient depth of field will be provided. This procedure also helps to offset the difference between visual and infrared focus. Specimens should be positioned and trimmed, if possible, to present a minimum of depth in the image.

INFRARED CLOSE-UP PHOTOGRAPHY

Cameras with nonextendable lenses can be used conveniently for photographing small specimens if the various close-up attachments and supplementary lenses are used. When supplementary lenses are used, it is not necessary to make any compensation in the exposure for close-up work, since the effective f/value remains unchanged. However, for best definition, the lens should be stopped down to f/11 or f/16.

APERTURE COMPENSATION

When small specimens are photographed, and a considerable camera bellows extension is involved, the effective aperture becomes considerably less than that marked on the lens. The effective f/value for all close-up work can be computed from this formula:

$$\text{Effective f/value} = \frac{\text{Indicated f/value} \times \text{lens-to-film distance}}{\text{Focal length}}$$

The lens-to-film distance is the focal length plus the lens extension from its position at infinity focus. This aperture compensation can be readily computed with the Effective Aperture Computer in the *Kodak Master Photoguide*, or with the tables in the

Kodak Master Darkroom Dataguide or *Kodak Color Dataguide*. The plane of the diaphragm is usually a close enough reference point for distance measurements.

For 35mm cameras with lenses which must be extended for close-ups, the figures in Table 1 may be used for bellows corrections by measuring the length of the included subject area that will fill the length of the frame. Table 1 applies to the full-frame 35mm film only.

a surge of heat from an electronic flash unit. Therefore, only rarely must the photographer employ special lighting for infrared photography.

Visible light intensity need not be greater for infrared photography than for panchromatic photography. Photographic exposure-meter reading for various setups with photoflood and similar lamps can be directly related. However, the fundamental exposure has to be based on exposure tests in order to obtain negatives of a desired quality.

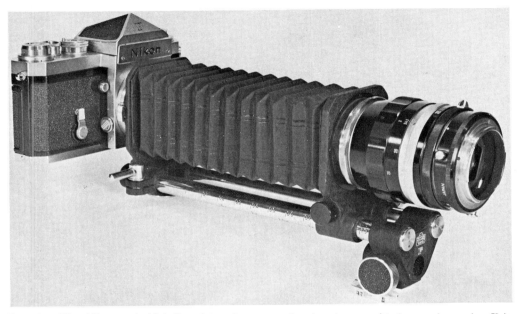

Figure 2 — Micro-Nikon used with bellows for maximum extension. Lens is reversed to increase image size. E2 is added at the end for semi-automatic diaphragm control

Table 1—Aperture compensation for close-ups

Length of subject area (inches)	12	6	3-1/2	2-1/2	2	1-1/2	1-1/4	1
Open the lens by (stops)	1/3	2/3	1	1-1/3	1-2/3	2	2-1/2	2-2/3
Or multiply the time by	1.3	1.6	2	2.5	3	4	5	6

LIGHTING

Photographic lights of all kinds have high emission in the infrared region of the spectrum. Infrared emission is closely related to heat radiation; thus, heat from a lamp indicates that infrared emissions are present. Any photographer who has come inadvertently in contact with a hot lamp or who has taken a flashbulb out of a reflector too soon after it has been fired will attest to the presence of heat, and therefore the emission of infrared, from ordinary photographic lights. It is even possible to feel

It is wise to check the evenness of the spot of illumination from any lamp, because variations will be exaggerated by the somewhat contrasty infrared technique. This can be done by photographing the spot of light itself on a sheet of cardboard or on a wall. Also, shadows from indistinct images of filaments or dirty condensers in spotlights should be guarded against.

Photoflash lamps. It is practical to coat a dark red, infrared-transmitting envelope over photoflash lamps in manufacture, because they are used only once. Other sources of light are usually too hot for such treatment. Flashbulbs of this kind are designated "R."

They are valuable when bright visible light has to be withheld from living subjects, as well as from the emulsion. For instance, they may be used for photographing actions of a suspect in the dark. The use of the "R" flashbulbs would eliminate the need for special lamphouses with windows covered by large sheets of filter material. The practicality of changing bulbs for each exposure must be considered.

The only type of infrared photoflash lamp now manufactured is the General Electric No. 5R. Many photographic dealers do not stock it, but they can order them from the manufacturer. The photographer may have to accept a case lot because of the relatively low demand for these lamps.

Guide numbers published for these bulbs apply to photography indoors. For outdoor work it is necessary to open up the lens an additional f/stop.

Those who wish to coat their own photoflash bulbs are referred to Morris and Spencer (1940). The dyes given in their paper are made by British manufacturers; however, large dye companies in other countries supply suitable equivalents.

Clear photoflash lamps should be used for routine laboratory work. The optimum filtering is then done at the lens or over the lamp reflector.

Electronic flash lamps. Electronic flash units have many advantages in the photography of living subjects. Their benefits of coolness and short exposure time are extendible to infrared photography. The amount of infrared radiation emitted in electronic flashtube setups is comparable, exposurewise, to the intensities in photoflash setups that would be employed for photographing the same subjects. Another advantage of these units is that they are more readily obtainable with compact reflectors than in tungsten flood equipment. Preferably, they should be equipped with modeling bulbs. Low-voltage lamps have a higher proportion of infrared radiation than the high-voltage units.

Lamps for infrared color photography. Electronic flash illumination is best for indoor infrared color photography. Photoflash bulbs are not suitable. Photoflood and quartz halogen lamps should only be used when circumstances demand, and then only with special filtering, discussed in the section on filters. It is necessary to employ heat-absorbing glass or a gelatin cyan filter.

It is worthwhile to make every effort to utilize electronic flash illumination in this technique. Not only can simpler filtering be achieved, but also the advantages of coolness and quick exposure times can be gained.

FILTERS

Since infrared emulsions are sensitive to the blue region of the spectrum as well as to part of the red and to the near infrared region, filters are needed for infrared records. Filter factors are given in the Data Sheets.

In an emergency, black-and-white photographs can be made with infrared-sensitive materials without a filter, but the rendering will be more like that of a blue-sensitive film. The quality will usually be less satisfactory than that produced by either an orthochromatic or a panchromatic film. Reds, greens, and yellows will be reproduced darker than normal.

Infrared color photography calls for particular filtering methods. In some black-and-white and color techniques, absorption filters are needed for the illumination.

Eastman Kodak Company supplies infrared-interference filters for highly specialized techniques, manufactured to customer specifications on special order only. These filters come in three main types: short-wavelength pass (cut-off), long-wavelength pass (cut-on), and band pass (1.5 to 11.0 microns). They are described in *Kodak Publication No. U73.* For further information, write directly to the Special Products Sales Department, Kodak Apparatus Division, Rochester, New York 14650.

Filters for black-and-white photography. Several considerations govern the choice of filters. The following Kodak Wratten filters will absorb violet and blue for black-and-white photography: No. 15 (G, orange); No. 25 (A, red); No. 29 (F); No. 70 (deep red); and No. 87, 88A, and 87C (infrared opaque visually). Wratten filters 87 and 87C are often difficult to find. The red filters can be used when the camera has to be hand-held or when circumstances like activity on the part of a live subject make the adding of an opaque filter after focusing impractical. It ought to be noted again that critical focusing through the red filter is somewhat difficult.

Kodak Wratten Filter No. 89B has been designed for aerial photography. It produces records quite similar to the No. 25 filter. However, it affords additional penetration of haze with only a slight increase in exposure time. For aerial photography, filters should be mounted in "B" glass; unmounted gelatin filters are likely to result in poor definition.

All Kodak Wratten filters are available in unmounted 2-, 3-, 4-, and 5-inch gelatin squares, and the commonly used ones mounted between optical glass in the first three sizes. Large unmounted sheets, up to 13 × 18 inches, can be obtained on special order for windows in light boxes or for placing over lamp reflectors. Gelatin filters are particularly useful when techniques are being worked out. Once a procedure has been established, it is convenient to order glass-mounted filters to fit the lens attachments that are available for the particular camera in use. This type of filter may be obtained in some circular sizes from your dealer's stock; other sizes will have to be procured by him. For information, write Industrial Photo Methods, Eastman Kodak Company, Rochester, New York 14650.

For black-and-white infrared photography in some specialized applications, sharply selective filtration may be necessary. Experimentation should be carried out when there is reason to expect that using the red or longer-wavelength portion of the infrared spectrum might lead to significant differentiation. Exacting work involving such band separation is beyond the scope of this book. Jones and Tuttle (1939) describe some of the useful filter combinations.

Filters for photography in the dark. Most individuals can detect a slight red glow through a No. 87 filter with scotopic vision when they happen to be looking directly at the source during an exposure. Bouncing the radiation off a low ceiling, a reflector, or a wall is often helpful, when a subject might see a tell-tale glow as photographs are made in the dark. Alternatively, a No. 87C filter should be considered. The filter coating on the "R" infrared flashbulb cuts just beyond the visible region. Since the cut is not sharp, a glow can be detected. Still, such bulbs do away with the need for an infrared filter over the lens when the scene is in darkness or when ambient or observation illumination is so low as not to affect a synchronized exposure.

Those who wish to construct a light-tight ventilated illumination box, with an enclosed tungsten lamp and an infrared-transmitting window for cinematography, should note that the No. 87 filter can withstand two weeks of exposure to a 1000-watt lamp at two feet. The gelatin sheet can be clamped loosely to glass on the lamp side but left free to radiate in front; a cooling fan can be directed onto it. In a laboratory this filter withstood 5 hours' exposure to a 500-watt reflector photoflood at 1 foot. No closer location should be considered and a hot, focused beam must be avoided. The Corning Glass Color Filter, C.S. No. 7-69 (2600) molded, provides a similar filter, but it is a little more sensitive to cracking from heat than the gelatin filter.

Filters for infrared color photography. While Kodak Ektachrome Infrared AERO Film, Type 8443, 35mm, 20-exposure rolls, does not call for the use of an opaque filter for the infrared color photographic technique, a Kodak Wratten Filter No. 12 (minus blue) should be used over the camera lens. This filter absorbs the violet and blue to which the emulsion is sensitive. The color balance of the film is such that no other filter is normally needed under illumination of daylight quality.

For outdoor use, a Kodak Wratten Filter No. 12 ought to be used, although a No. 8 or No. 15 filter can be utilized for special effects. However, for scientific photography, the No. 12 filter must be used outdoors and indoors as well. Here, every effort should be made to employ electronic flash. Flashbulbs are not suitable. Special filters have to be used for illumination of photoflood (3400K) quality.

A Kodak Color Compensating Filter CC20C and a Corning Glass Filter C.S. No. 1-59 (3966) (specify diameter) provide a good balance for photofloods. A filter factor of 2 should be tried. (In some applications a CC50C-2 filter alone may suffice.)

The unfiltered quartz halogen lamp is useful in the photographic laboratory. It can be utilized for infrared color photography. Since the iodine vapor in these lamps absorbs some infrared, this type of incandescent source does not radiate quite as much excess infrared as that emitted by the photoflood lamp. Accordingly, a head-absorbing glass filter may not be needed over the lens. Schneider (1967) stated that a Kodak Color Compensating Filter, CC50C sufficed in the light beam of his photomicrographic setup — in conjunction with the usual Kodak Wratten Filter No. 12. For general infrared color photography, the CC50C-2 filter should be employed with the 3200K and 3400K lamps. A filter factor of 2 is required.

FILMS

The characteristics and availability of Kodak films for infrared photography are presented in detail in the Data Sheets. General suggestions for using the films are given in the following sections. Since black-and-white negatives can be made from color transparencies, anyone embarking on a color program can publish in color or in black-and-white.

Black and white. Specific data on film speeds, exposure, and reciprocity effects for Kodak black-and-white infrared films are given in the Data Sheets.

The indoor speeds of these films are low. However, a tripod is almost always used in routine laboratory photography, so film speed presents no great problem. Photoflood lighting can be used without causing undue discomfort to living subjects, but electronic flash illumination is more convenient, cooler for living subjects, and allows more depth of field. It should be used whenever possible.

As a general rule, a black-and-white infrared negative should look fairly dense. Grass and trees, particularly, appear much darker than they do in a panchromatic negative. The main features of the subject and areas that photograph dark (light on the negative) should be recorded on the straight-line portion of the sensitometric curve. Small black shadows, of course, will have to be blank, because serious overexposure should be avoided. A shadow density of about 0.3 above fog for sheet film, and 0.5 for roll film, yields good separation.

Kodak High Speed Infrared Film is available in 35mm, 100 foot rolls. The method of loading it into cassettes is described in detail in the instructions. Its major use is in the luminescence technique, where it permits time exposures that are reasonably short for the faint emissions encountered. Nevertheless, the high speed film is also valuable for photographing living subjects with hand-held single-lens reflex cameras or for making records of action in the dark when it is not practical to provide a high level of radiation for the exposures. It can be loaded into motorized 35mm cameras that accept film for a large number of exposures.

Color. Kodak Ektachrome Infrared AERO Film, Type 8443, is very fast. It is available for scientific photography in 35mm, 20-exposure cassettes. This makes it excellently suited to photography with a hand-held, miniature, single-lens reflex camera in numerous applications.

CHECKING THE DARKROOM FOR INFRARED SAFETY

All infrared films not placed in cassettes by the manufacturer should be loaded in the dark. Naturally, the darkroom must be light-tight. Also, an electric space heater with exposed heating elements or a cowling that becomes sizzling hot,

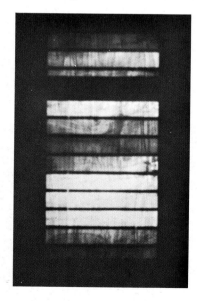

Figure 3 — Darkroom door photographed with infrared film shows image of panels, indicating unsafe door

should not be turned on. Even though the heater may not produce enough visible glow to affect panchromatic films, it could fog infrared emulsions. The temperature associated with steam pipes and radiators, though, is not high enough to worry about during the handling times of loading and processing film.

Some wooden doors for interiors may leak infrared radiation through their panels. This can happen when the panels are thin and unpainted. Also, there is a type of door constructed from thin sheets of plywood bonded over a framework. Infrared is very likely to be transmitted through the air cells so formed. If a door is suspected as a source of fog, a photographic test should be made. (Figure 3.) An attempt to photograph the door is made on infrared film — from inside the darkroom and in the dark, but with full illumination outside. No filter is placed over the lens and an exposure of 30 minutes at f/5.6 is used. If no image of panels or air cells appears on the film, the door is safe.

PROCESSING INFRARED

Development of black-and-white infrared film is best carried out in the dark, although a safelight can be employed to provide personal orientation or enough light to read a clock. (See Data Sheets). Infrared films are carried through the development procedure like any other films. However, it is not advisable to develop a batch of sheet films in a tray by the leaf-over-and-over system. This could easily cause abrasion. Two sheets of infrared film can be developed in a smooth tray by handling them back-to-back. However, they should first be thoroughly wetted in a tray of clean water so that their backings do not stick together in the developer.

Developers and average processing times are shown in the Data Sheets. Development contrast can be varied within certain limits to provide negatives of more, or less, contrast. For records of faint patterns, film can be developed for a 30 percent increase over the average time, if moderate developers are used. The additional fog is negligible and the resultant pattern is strengthened. Consistent development contrast is imperative in making comparable serial records.

Some applications call for negatives of the highest practical contrast; they can be obtained with very active developers. The use of such developers is attended with some increase in graininess and requires a concomitant reduction in exposure. For some flat-surfaced subjects such as imbedded fossils or faint texts, where surface contours do not introduce lighting contrast, an increased development contrast can be beneficial in strengthening faint patterns.

Rinsing, fixing, washing and drying of black-and-white infrared films are carried out in the fashion usual for similar noninfrared materials.

Directions for processing Kodak Ektachrome Infrared AERO Film, Type 8443, for scientific applications are given in the instruction sheet packaged with the film. No safelighting or infrared inspection equipment is tolerable during processing. The photographer will usually have to do the work himself. Any custom-processing laboratory accepting rolls of infrared color film must be advised of the above restrictions.

COPYING WITH INFRARED

The infrared copying technique has been widely used in numerous applications — often in conjunction with other non-destructive methods of examination, such as ultraviolet photography and radiography. One of the categories which has a broad application for police science is in the investigation of illegible documents — censored, deteriorated, or forged. The infrared color method is valuable when inks and pigments that appear to have the same color can be differentiated photographically. The following sections review broadly the representative copying work done in various fields and does not pretend to be all-inclusive. Particular aspects of technique are given in context. Where technical factors are not included, it can be assumed that only the general procedures are needed.

Kodak Wratten Filter No. 87 is usually employed in copying applications. When the photographer feels the need for a stronger infrared effect or greater differential penetration, he can try the No. 87C filter.

ILLEGIBLE DOCUMENTS

The most important application of infrared photography in copying is the deciphering of indistinct writing. The text may have been made illegible by: charring; deterioration as a result of age or the accumulation of dirt; obliteration by application of ink by a censor; invisible inks; deliberate chemical bleaching; or mechanical erasure and subsequent overwriting.

Inks and pigments. Inks, pigments, and other materials that appear identical to the eye are frequently rendered quite differently by an infrared photograph. If an ink transparent to infrared is applied over one opaque to it, the underlying ink will show up in an infrared photograph. (Figures 4 & 5.) The original inks used in writing documents that have

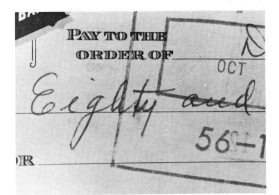

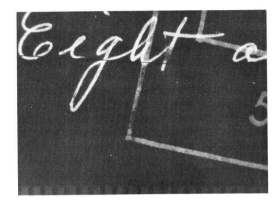

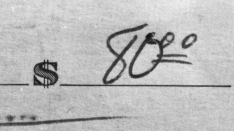

Figure 4 — Check for eighty dollars (above) when photographed with infrared method. Shows the "Y" to be added later

Figure 5 — The same check (left) photographed with infrared (below)

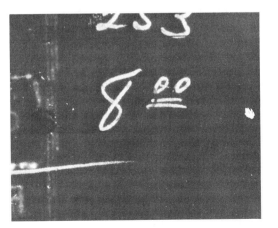

become blackened may be revealed by infrared photography, although success will depend on the condition of the paper. Writing that has been mechanically erased may be revealed in an infrared photograph by virtue of the traces of carbon or other pigment left embedded in paper fibers. Chemically bleached writing often is deciphered by infrared photography. The reaction of the bleach with the ink absorbs more infrared radiation than the surrounding paper. Especially useful results have been obtained in deciphering of certain falsified documents by photographing infrared luminescence induced by exposure to blue-green light or, in some instances, to ultraviolet radiation. The infrared luminescence technique involves the use of a special "glow powder" coupled with the infrared film. There are several light sources which could be used for producing infrared luminescence. This phenomenon is exhibited in some materials by stimulation with blue-green light. Although it is possible that infrared luminescence may also be stimulated by irradiation with specific wavelengths of blue or green, it is suggested that a source having continuous emission of the blue and green spectral regions be obtained. High-wattage tungsten lamps, the xenon arc, or even ordinary fluorescent lamps could be used. This technique should be tried when the reflection method (use of flood lamps, flashbulbs, or electronic flash) does not supply all the information hoped for.

Charred, aged, and worn writings. Documents that have become charred by fire — and those blackened by age, dirt, or stains — can sometimes be deciphered in an infrared print. The investigation of papers surviving wilful attempts to burn them and of forged documents is very important. Sometimes wear will obliterate writing so that it can no longer be seen with the naked eye or photographed with panchromatic film. Yet traces may remain that can be picked up by infrared photography.

PHOTOGRAPHING IN DARKNESS WITH INFRARED

The capability of making infrared photographs "in the dark" is extremely pertinent to the area of surveillance in law enforcement, because evidence can be gathered without the knowledge of those committing the offenses.

It is relatively simple to rig infrared photoflash setups, or to utilize them in flashguns, to make still photographs in the dark. Human subjects can be photographed without their realizing it. This is of special value in trapping burglars at safes, cash drawers, etc.

For photographic traps and for many laboratory setups, cameras usually have to be preset and the flash fired by circuits triggered with infrared detectors. It is necessary for the photographer to know where his subject is going to be. No lens filter is needed.

The use of coated flashbulbs entails some precaution when photographic traps are rigged. A dull red glow may be visible, especially if the subject happens to be looking in the direction of the flash. Visibility can be reduced by directing the flash-holder toward a light-toned wall or ceiling to provide bounce irradiation and to preclude direct viewing by the subject. The maximum working distance indoors for an infrared-coated No. 5R lamp, Kodak Infrared Film (35mm), and an f/3.5 lens is 20 feet. The approximate distance must be decided beforehand, and the focusing scale set accordingly. The lens diaphragm must also be set according to a guide-number calculation involving this distance: Divide the appropriate flash exposure guide number by the lens-to-subject distance in feet to find the f/number of the lens opening.

When a great many infrared flash pictures are to be taken, or when infrared-coated flashbulbs are not available, the photographer can use a gelatin or glass filter. A piece of Kodak Wratten Filter No. 87 or 87C can be purchased in a size large enough to cover the front of the flash reflector and can be taped to a single piece of clear glass or sandwiched between two pieces of glass for protection. Since optical quality is not required for this light-source filter, the gelatin filter taped to ordinary glass suffices. A light-tight housing can be devised to hold this filter on the flash gun. The housing should be easy to open so that flashbulbs can be changed after each exposure. Using clear No. 5 or 25 bulbs with a No. 87 filter will result in flash exposure guide numbers of the same range as those given for the No. 5R coated lamps used without a filter. The No. 87C filter gives no tell-tale glow, but it necessitates 1½ stops more exposure.

Electronic flash units can be used similarly, and since the lamp does not have to be replaced after each exposure, the filter holder can be simpler. The filter can even be taped over the reflector or held in place with rubber bands. Guide numbers here are easily determined by the user with a simple trial exposure series. Most of the portable low-voltage units (around 500 volts) yield guide numbers in the 200 to 300 range with Kodak High Speed Infrared Film, and 70 to 120 with Kodak Infrared Film.

Kodak Publication No. M-8, *Criminal Detection Devices Employing Photography*, (available from Dept. 412-L, Eastman Kodak Company, Rochester, New York 14650), gives details on rigging infrared photographic traps and other specific information for those employing photography in law enforcement.

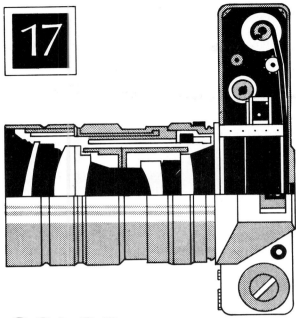

17

There is an enormous amount of literature written about color photography, much more than could possibly be put into this book. This chapter is intended as an introduction to the basics of color. It will be limited to the procedures used to develop color film and printing color prints as it concerns police departments. For further literature on this subject, the photographer should refer to Eastman Kodak Company pamphlets on color photography.

WHAT TO PHOTOGRAPH IN COLOR

COLOR

Most police photography is done in black and white. Yet the evidence being photographed is not black and white; most evidence is composed of one or more colors and sometimes the colors can be very important to a case. With black and white photographs, the officer must often swear to the original color of the evidence; the court must then believe that, if he says the pool of liquid in the photograph was red, it was red.

But if the court is presented with a photograph in color, it can judge for itself whether the officer's red is truly red, that a blue car is truly blue, that the leaves on a tree are truly green.

Judgments of color, according to psychologists, are subjective judgments. One man's sea green may be another man's powder blue and neither one will be lying. The progressive police department must use color photography, then, in the cause of accuracy and realism.

At one time, color photography was prohibitively expensive and, in some jurisdictions, thought to be in bad taste. More and more departments are now turning to color because (1) the process of making a color photograph has become relatively easy; (2) many color processing materials are becoming readily available to the modern police photographer; and (3) color is vital to accurate information.

Color photography has come of age as far as courtroom acceptability is concerned despite repeated efforts by defense attorneys over the years to support their claim that color photographs are inflammatory. They failed in their attempts to disallow the obvious — color pictures convey to the judge and jury a more accurate representation of the facts as they are.

VEHICULAR AND PUBLIC ACCIDENTS

If it is possible, accident photographs should be done in color. They have a more evidential value than black-and-white photographs because they portray the scene more realistically by conveying the true atmosphere at the accident scene. Generally, they are useful for showing whether the traffic lights were operating, the color of the vehicles involved, the presence of blood if the accident involved personal injury and whether or not the headlights and signal lights work properly.

Trees, shrubbery, skid marks, and tiremarks show up much better in color. Taxpayers are entitled to the best possible evidence that can be accumulated for them at an accident scene. At the time of the accident, they are excited and do not know what is going on, but a professional policeman should know what should be recorded as good evidence when the case comes to court.

Color is especially superior to black-and-white in hit and run cases. The color of the car is very important. If paint chips are picked up at the scene, they can be easily matched to the car involved. The vehicle will probably have blood stains on it if the accident involves a pedestrian. If the car is located later and photographed in color, the blood will show very clearly whereas, in black-and-white, it will show up merely as a dark blotch.

Public accidents are a great concern to cities. The cities are being sued daily by persons who fall on city property. To help the city prosecutor, who has to defend the city in these cases, it would be of great value to him if the entire case is taken in color. Shots should include sidewalk, foliage, grass, house along with house number and any other buildings in the vicinity near the spot the person may have fallen.

CRIME SCENE AND IDENTIFICATION

Photographing a homicide scene in color is a must, regardless of how gruesome the scene may be. Color photography is much more effective to show bloodstains and wound markings.

In the case of burglaries, all articles that have been stolen and recovered can be more easily identified if they are done in color.

Arson cases done with color show the color of the flames and smoke much better than black-and-white. Progression of the fire photographed in color may be extremely helpful in the investigation later on. Debris and possible evidence of a planned fire are more realistic if photographed in color.

"Mug" shots photographed in color have the definite advantage over black-and-white because they show the color of the skin, eyes and hair. Unusual identifying marks also photograph better in color. The ultimate achievement for police would be for every department to have color identification photos.

With today's methods and materials, the lack of color in a photograph may be considered an unnecessary distortion of the original scene.

COLOR FILM

There are many types of color film, only two of which are suitable for police work; these two are color reversal (slide) film and color negative film.

Color reversal film yields a color transparency after it has been exposed and processed. If 35mm slides are to be used in the presentation of evidence in court, color reversal film will provide them inexpensively. With this type of film, the negative process is bypassed and only a transparent positive is produced; the positive is mounted in a cardboard frame which can be put into a projector and shown on a screen in the courtroom. Usually these are called 2 × 2 inch color slides, and the actual picture area measures approximately 1 by 1½ inches. These slides can be projected on a large screen in front of the jury or on a smaller daylight screen by using projection from the rear. Hand viewers may also be used. It is recommended, if possible, that the jury look at the same picture at the same time. You can have black-and-white or color prints made from these slides.

The ending "chrome" in a film name, such as Kodachrome, indicates that it is a color reversal film. If the ending is "color," such as Ektacolor, a color negative film is indicated. Most American film manufacturers employ this system of endings.

The other type of color film which is suitable for police work is color negative film, from which a color negative is produced. This negative can be used to make color prints, color slides, black and white prints and black and white slides.

There are some advantages to using color negative film for police photography. First, the exposure latitude is much greater. Filters, except for the usual haze filter, are seldom needed, and color corrections can be made by the photographer if he is doing his own processing.

PHOTOGRAPHIC COLOR-LIGHT RELATIONSHIPS

The color circle as shown in Figure 1 represents the visible light spectrum. The six individual colors — red, green, blue, cyan, magenta, and yellow — are single points on this continuously changing band of light. However, they have special photographic relationships to each other. The Additive Primary Colors (red, green, and blue) added together in approximately equal amounts, as with three projectors aimed at a screen, will produce white light. The Subtractive Primary Colors (cyan, magenta, and yellow) added together in approximately equal amounts, as with three filters on a single light source, will absorb all color and produce black or shades of gray; this is neutral density.

Each primary color on the light-spectrum circle is composed of equal amounts of its adjacent colors, and is complementary to the color directly across the center of the circle. Complementary colors added together also form neutral densities.

The interaction of the additive primary colors, in photographic light sources, and the subtractive primary colors, in the filters, form the controls necessary in color photography. All present-day color films and color printing papers employ three layers of emulsion, each sensitive to one of the photographic *additive primary colors: red, green or blue*.

COLOR PROCESSING

EQUIPMENT

In addition to the standard equipment needed for processing black and white film (see Chapter 5) the following equipment is necessary for color processing:

Color enlarger: For color work, an enlarger is needed that has a color head into which filters can be placed. A good enlarger of this type is the Omega Type D5, manufactured by Simmon Brothers Inc., Long Island City, New York, a division of Berkey Photo Inc., which can be modified for printing color negatives. Color printing filters are

ADDITIVE PRIMARIES

SUBTRACTIVE PRIMARIES

NEUTRAL DENSITIES

COMPLEMENTARIES

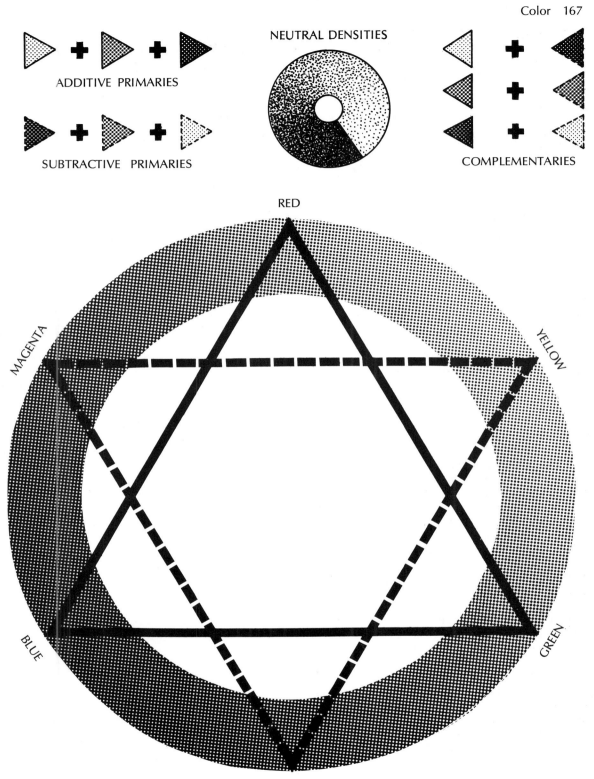

RED

YELLOW

MAGENTA

GREEN

BLUE

CYAN

Figure 1 — Color circle

assembled in a frame and inserted in the drawer below the lamphouse. (See Figure 2.) The Chromega B, manufactured by Simmon Brothers Inc., also, is an enlarger designed for printing color negatives. The dials below the lamphouse are adjustments for the Kodak Video Color Negative Translator, Model 1-K. (See figure 3.)

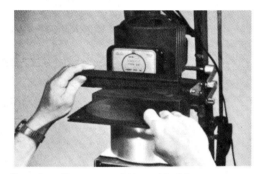

Figure 2 — Omega type D11, modified for printing color

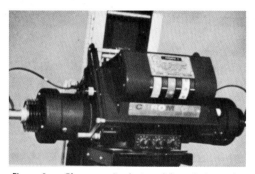

Figure 3 — Chromega B, designed for printing color

Kodak Rapid Color Processor (Model 11 or 16-K).

Filters. One set of CC filters, one set of CP filters and the CP2B filter always used.

Safelight. Kodak Safelight Filter No. 10 (dark amber) 7¼ watt bulb.

Dryer. A large drum dryer with a stainless steel drum.

Thermometer. Temperature is critical in color work and a good thermometer is a necessity.

Timer. Processing times are crucial in color work; a Time-O-Lite or a Gra-Lab timer should be used.

PROCESSING COLOR NEGATIVES

The procedure for processing color negatives is approximately the same as that for black and white (see Chapter 6) but requires more baths and more time. Below is a chart listing the several baths and times for processing color negatives.

SOLUTION	TYPICAL TIME	TYPICAL TEMP.
Water preheat	*1 minute*	*100° F*
total color 1 DEVELOPER	3¼ minutes	100°F
WATER	6 minutes	100°F
total color 2 BLIX	3 minutes	100°F
Optional: STABILIZER	*30 seconds*	*Room Temperature*

Chart 1

COLOR PRINTING

Color prints can be made with any enlarger that can produce black-and-white prints if it has a space between the condensers and the light bulb to place filters. Most enlarging lenses are color corrected and are good for color work. If the enlarger only accepts filters which are placed between the lens and the easel, several possibilities remain open. Conversion kits are available which allow acetate filters to be placed between the light source and the negative.

Enlargers which use cold light heads should be avoided because they emit light of several possible colors. Light from a tungsten enlarger head is yellow, not white. The glass in the enlarger's optical system may add its own color to the light. Light must be corrected because almost every box of color-printing paper varies in relative overall speed and in relative color sensitivity.

Lacking a Dichroic Superchromega enlarger with built in filter wheels, the photographer will have to place filters between the light and the lens. The CP2B filter is inserted to remove ultraviolet radiation. A heat absorbing glass is used to decrease infrared radiation. The CP2B filter may be placed anywhere in a filter pack. The heat-absorbing glass is best placed between the light source and the rest of the pack. In addition, the photographer will need the following basic minimum selection of subtractive filters: one each — CP05M, CP05Y, CP05C-2; CP10M, CP10Y, CP10C-2; CP20M, CP20C-2; and two each — CP40M, CP40Y, CP40C-2. Additional magenta (M), yellow (Y), and cyan (C-2) filters may be acquired if needed, as may CP red (R) filters but the basic filters listed should suffice for most printing. The values 05 through 40 in the filter designation refer to color densities; an 05Y is a very pale yellow; a 40Y is much deeper. Be sure to use a Wratten series 10 safelight for certain steps.

DETERMINATION OF FILTER COMBINATIONS

The determination of filter combinations can also be simplified by thinking of all filters in terms of the subtractive colors in Table 2. Note that a particular red, green, or blue filter may not give exactly the same color adjustment as the corresponding subtractive pane.

The following procedure is based on the relationships in Table 2.

1. Convert the filters to their equivalents in the subtractive colors — cyan, magenta, and yellow — if not already done (for example, 20 R = 20 M + 20 Y).
2. Add the values for each color (for example, 20M + 10M = 30M).
3. If the resulting filter combination contains all three subtractive colors, take out the neutral density by removing an equal amount of each (for example 10C + 20M + 20Y = 10M + 10Y + 0.10 neutral density, which can be removed).

THE KODAK DRUM PROCESS

Small drum processing offers the possibility of getting started in color printing with a minimum outlay for equipment. The Kodak Rapid Color Processor, Model 11, makes it possible to process an 11 × 14 inch print in less than 8 minutes. (Figure 4.) Also available are the model 16-K (Figure 5), which will handle a 16 × 20 inch print in the same time, and the Model 30, which will handle a 30 × 40.

A method employing a new chemical system that works at 100° is one of the major reasons behind the success of the "drum processor." The paper is held stationary against the rotating drum which constantly picks up and transfers fresh solution to the emulsion with vigorous agitation. Only five chemicals are used in this system. All of the CP-5 chemicals are available in the one-gallon size from your dealer. Eight ounces of each chemical are required for one processing run. A small hinged tray receives the chemical or water in proper sequence.

A RED FILTER (absorbs blue and green)	is equivalent to A YELLOW FILTER (absorbs blue)	plus A MAGENTA FILTER (absorbs green)
A GREEN FILTER (absorbs blue and red)	is equivalent to A YELLOW FILTER (absorbs blue)	plus A CYAN FILTER (absorbs red)
A BLUE FILTER (absorbs green and red)	is equivalent to A MAGENTA FILTER (absorbs green)	plus a CYAN FILTER (absorbs red)

Table 2 — Filter combinations

PRINTING PROCESSES

The major difference between color and black and white printing is that, with color, consistency of process is paramount. The photographer must watch the voltage to his enlarger, his water temperature, his cleanliness; he must do each step of his process *exactly the same, every time.*

The major cost of color work is in paper and chemicals, so waste should be kept to a minimum. For most printing, a drum is used for processing which has a capacity of several prints. Trays are also suitable for color work.

SYSTEMS TO PRINT COLOR

Four systems are suitable for police work: the Eastman Kodak drum process, the Unicolor process, the Beseler process, and the Cibachrome process.

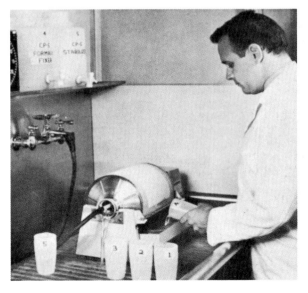

Figure 4 — Kodak Rapid Color Processing Model 11

The change from one processing solution to another is made by tilting the tray, rinsing it, and refilling with new solution.

Uniform processing temperature is maintained by circulating thermostatically-controlled water through the interior of the drum. No special plumbing is required. The processor should be placed in a sink on a platform that will raise the processor to a comfortable working height.

Cibachrome steps are:

1. Develop .... 3 min.
2. Bleach .... 3 min.
3. Fix .... 3 min.
4. Wash .... 3 min.

Another advantage of this system is that it only takes a total of 12 minutes to complete the cycle.

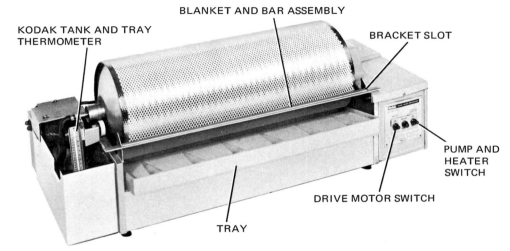

Figure 5 — Kodak Rapid Color Processor Model 16-K

The Unicolor Process. With unicolor chemicals you can develop your film and also print a picture. The following are the steps to processing negatives with Unicolor:

SOLUTION	TYPICAL TIME	TYPICAL TEMP.
Water-presoak	1 minute	105°F
total color 1 DEVELOPER	2 minutes	105°F
WATER	15 seconds	105°F
total color 2 BLIX	1 minute	105°F
WATER	1 minute	105°F
Optional: STABILIZER	30 seconds	Room Temperature

Chart 2

The Beseler Process. The Beseler company distributes a pamphlet called, "A Guide to Simplified Color Printing" which can explain this very simple process.

Write to Beseler Photo Co., 8 Fernwood Road, Florham Park, New Jersey 07932. The Beseler process is an inexpensive way to work with color.

Cibachrome Process. This is a good way of making a color print directly from a color slide.

Cibachrome print material has many advantages over other processes. One advantage of this system is that the temperature is not as critical as it is in many others. The photographer can work from 68° to 82° F.

There are many manufacturers of processing drums for color prints. An 8 × 10 size is one of the most practical drums. The 8 × 10 is a good size enlargement for police work and it also requires less chemicals. The beauty of having a drum is that the print can be taken from the easel and placed directly into the drum, the end is capped, and the lights can then be turned on. The print is presoaked, developed, stop-fixed, bleached, washed and stabilized in the drum.

Trays are not adequate for proper agitation in the development stage of color processing and the proper temperature is not easily maintained. It also requires more chemicals to process a print in a tray than in a drum and also finally, the photographer has to remain in the dark.

There is a certain way to view a color print to determine if the print has an unsatisfactory color balance. With a little self-training, the photographer can view a print through various color filters. When the print begins to appear correct but the balance is still off, corrections must be made.

Eastman Kodak Company has developed the Print Viewing Kit — an essential for the photographer's initial set of color printing tools. The Print Viewing Kit consists of six cardboard-mounted sets of color filters. Each of these cards represents one of the six basic colors of red, blue, green, magenta, cyan and yellow, in three strength densities. This kit is designed to pinpoint color errors and provides instructions on how to correct them.

GLOSSARY OF TERMS

Aberrations: Optical defects in a lens which cause imperfect images.

Abrasions: Marks on emulsion surfaces, which appear as pencil marks or scratches. Usually caused by pressure or rubbing.

Accelerator: The alkali added to a developing solution to increase the activity of a developing agent and swell the gelatin, thus shortening developing time.

Acetate base: The term used to designate a photographic film base composed of cellulose acetate. Also referred to as safety base because of its noninflammability.

Acetic acid ($HC_2H_3O_2$): The acid widely used in short stop-baths to stop the action of the developer before negatives or prints are placed in the fixing bath. Often used in fixing baths.

Acetone (dimethyl ketone): A highly volatile, inflammable liquid, solvent for nitrocellulose, etc.; used as ingredient of film cements.

Achromatic lens: A lens which is at least partially corrected for chromatic aberration.

Acid fixing bath: A solution of hypo to which has been added an acid (usually acetic acid) for the purpose of maintaining the hypo at the proper acidity.

Acrol: Eastman Kodak Company trademark for Amidol.

Actinic light: Light which is capable of causing photochemical changes in a sensitive emulsion. Blue and violet are the most actinic of the visible light rays.

Adapter back: A supplementary back for view cameras permitting the use of smaller film or plate holders than the size for which the camera was designed.

Adapter ring: A device designed to permit using filters, supplementary lenses, etc. of a single diameter in connection with several lens mounts whose diameters differ.

Additive process: Pertains to color photography; it is the production of color by the superimposition of the separate primary colored lights on the same screen. Yellow, for example, is a mixture of red and green light rays in the proper proportion.

Adurol: A form of hydroquinone, which is used as a developing agent. Chemical name is monobromo-hydroquinone.

Aerial perspective: An impression of depth or distance in a photograph by means of progressively diminishing detail due to aerial haze.

Aero: Applied to a lens, camera, or film intended for use in photography from aircraft.

171

Affinity: The chemical attraction of one substance for another. Sodium sulfite has an affinity for oxygen, thereby reducing oxidation of the developing agent in a developer.

Afocal: Applied to a lens system which has both foci at infinity; afocal systems include certain wide angle and telephoto attachments for lenses which do not change the lens extension.

Agitation: The procedure used in processing to bring fresh solution in contact with the emulsion. This may be done by moving the material in the solution, as in tank development, or by moving the solution itself, as in tray development. Agitation may be either constant or intermittent. Agitation is necessary to assure uniform development results.

Air bells: Small bubbles of air which attach to the surface of an emulsion and leave a small area unaffected by the solution. Can be removed by vigorous agitation.

Albumin paper: Sensitive paper, usually printing-out paper in which the silver salts are suspended in albumin instead of gelatin; sometimes spelled "albumen" paper.

Alkali: A substance with basic properties which can neutralize acid. An example of an alkali which is commonly used in developing solutions is sodium carbonate. Alkalies are often referred to as "accelerators or activators."

Anamorphic: A lens or optical system in which the magnification is different in two planes at right angles; used in wide-screen movie processes to "squeeze" a wide image into standard format and to "unsqueeze" it in projection on a wide screen.

Anastigmat: A lens which has been corrected for astigmatism, and therefore focuses vertical and horizontal lines with equal brightness and definition. Anastigmat lenses are also free from other common aberrations.

Angle finder: A veiwfinder containing a mirror or prism so that pictures may be taken while aiming the camera sideways.

Angle of view: The angle subtended at the center of the lens by the ends of the diagonal of the film or plate.

Angstrom unit (AU): A unit of length equal to one ten-thousandth of a micron. Commonly used as a method of expressing length of light rays.

Anhydrous: Refers to chemical salts which contain no water of crystallization. Identical in meaning with "desiccated."

Aniline (Anilin): A coal tar derivative used as a basis for many dyes. It can also be produced by the reduction of nitrobenzene.

Ansco color: An integral tripack natural-color film which can be activity processed.

Anti-halation backing: A coating, usually gelatin, on the back of a film, containing a dye or pigment for the purpose of absorbing light rays, thus preventing the reflection from the back surface of the film base.

Aperture: A small opening, usually circular. In cameras, the aperture is usually variable, in the form of an iris diaphragm, and regulates the intensity of light which passes through a lens.

Aplanat: A lens of the rapid-rectilinear type, sometimes better corrected for spherical aberration, but not for astigmatism.

Apochromatic: Refers to lenses which are most completely corrected for chromatic aberration. These lenses focus rays of all colors to very nearly the same plane.

ASA: American Standards Association rating of film emulsion. For example, Kodak Royal Pan Film has an ASA rating of 400.

Astigmatism: A lens aberration in which both the horizontal and vertical lines in the edge of the field cannot be accurately focused at the same time.

Asymmetrical (non-symmetrical): Applied to a lens having differently shaped elements on either side of the diaphragm, or both.

Autofocal: Self-focusing; applied to enlargers which keep the image in focus when changing the degree of enlargement by raising or lowering the head.

Autopositive: Applied to a film or paper which renders a positive image when exposed to a positive, or a negative image when exposed to a negative, when processed in a single development stage. Distinguished from *direct positive* which produces such images by reversal processing procedures.

Autoradiograph: An image produced on a film or plate by radiations from a radioactive subject in close contact with the emulsion.

Auxiliary lens: A lens element which is added to the regular camera lens to shorten or increase its focal length.

Avoirdupois: The systems of weights and measures used in the United States and Great Britain for dry chemicals (note that U.S. Customary and British Imperial liquid measures differ); abb.: avdp.

Axis of lens: An imaginary line passing through the center of a lens and containing the centers of curvature of the lens surfaces.

Back focus: A trade term often used to designate the distance between the back surface of the lens and the surface of the focusing glass when the camera is focused at infinity. This dimension is used in determining the length of the camera bellows suitable for a given lens.

Back, revolving: A camera back which can be revolved so that either a vertical or horizontal picture may be obtained. Usually found in the heavier types of cameras, such as press or view cameras.

Back, swinging: A camera back which can be swung through a small arc so that the divergence or convergence of parallel lines in the subject can be minimized or eliminated.

Background: Generally that part of a scene beyond the main subject of the picture.

Backing cloth: An adhesive fabric, used to strengthen a photographic print to withstand handling.

Bag, changing: A light-proof bag equipped with openings for the hands, in which films can be loaded or unloaded in daylight.

Barndoor: Folding wings used in front of studio spotlights to aid in directing the light, and to shade portions of the subject from direct illumination.

Barrel distortion: A term applied to the barrel shaped image of a square object, obtained when the diaphragm is placed in front of a simple convex lens.

Baryta: A treated emulsion of barium sulfate. It is commonly used, in the manufacture of photographic paper, to coat the paper stock before the light-sensitive emulsion is coated. It provides a white surface and keeps the light-sensitive emulsion from being partially absorbed by the paper base.

Bayonet lock: A means of quickly attaching or removing a lens from a camera by turning through only part of a revolution.

Bed: The base of a camera, usually carrying the focusing guide rails.

Beer's Law: The optical density of a colored solution is proportional to the concentration of the light-absorbing substance.

Bellows: A folding tube of the accordion type which permits movement for focusing between the back of the camera and the lens and which collapses when the camera is packed. The camera bellows is usually made of leather or black cloth. Modern miniature cameras have a helical-threaded metal tube in place of a bellows.

Bellows draw: The maximum extension of a camera bellows.

Between-the-lens: A shutter located between the front and back elements of a double lens.

Big Bertha: A custom made camera, usually consisting of a 4 x 5 or 5 x 7 Graflex body combined with a powerful telephoto lens. Most important feature is its lens. It is a very bulky camera.

Black body: A theoretically perfect radiator, having no power of reflection.

Blackout (adj.): Applied to photoflash lamps, a lamp having a visually opaque coating transmitting only infrared radiation, and used for photography in total visual darkness.

Bleacher: A chemical compound, usually containing potassium ferricyanide, employed for bleaching or dissolving silver images. Bleachers are used in both reversal and toning processes.

Bleaching: The first step in the intensification of a negative is to bleach the negative until it appears white when viewed from the back of the film or plate. After bleaching, the negative is redeveloped. It is also necessary to bleach bromide prints before toning or developing them into sepia and white prints.

Blisters: Small bubbles forming under an emulsion due to the detachment of the emulsion from its base. Blisters are caused by some fault in processing.

Blocked up: Applied to highlights in a negative which are so overexposed or overdeveloped that no detail is visible.

Blocking out: Painting out undesired background areas on a negative.

Blow-up: Photographic slang for enlargement.

Boom: A stand, usually on wheels, having an extension arm on which a microphone or lamp may be attached.

Bounce light: Flash or tungsten light bounced off ceilings or walls to give the effect of natural or available light.

Box camera: An inexpensive camera, boxlike in form, with either few or no adjustable controls; also referred to as a "simple camera."

Breathing: Movement of a projected picture upon the screen due to buckling of the film in the projector.

Brightness range: Variation of light intensities from maximum to minimum. Generally refers to a subject to be photographed. For example, a particular subject may have a range of one to four, that is, four times the amount of light is reflected from the brightest highlight as from the least bright portion of the subject.

Brilliance: A term denoting the degree of intensity of a color or colors.

Brilliant: A term used in referring to the tone quality of a negative or print.

Bromide paper: A photographic printing paper in which the emulsion is made sensitive largely through silver bromide. Bromide papers are relatively fast and usually printed by projection.

Bromoil: A process for the making of prints in permanent oil pigments on the base of a bromide print.

Bulb: Shutter setting in which the leaves remain open as long as the button is depressed and close as soon as the button is released; marked "B" on cameras.

Burned out: Applied to an overexposed negative or print lacking in highlight detail.

Burning in: A method of darkening parts of a print in which certain parts of the image are given extra exposure while the rest of the image is protected from the light.

Butterfly: Silk gauze or scrim on a frame, used to soften or diffuse a highlight, or to cast a soft shadow on some part of a picture.

Cabinet camera: An automatic camera, usually operated by a coin-slot device; occasionally combined with an automatic developing machine.

Cable release: A flexible shaft for operating the camera shutter.

Camera angle: The point of view from which a subject is photographed.

Camera obscura: A darkened room in which an image is formed on one wall by light entering a small hole in the opposite wall.

Camera, pinhole: A camera which has a pinhole aperture in place of a lens.

Candid photography: A term applied to pictures taken without posing the subject. The object is to catch natural expression.

Candle: A unit of luminous intensity; approximately equal to the intensity of a 7/8-inch sperm candle burning at 120 grains per hour.

Candle-meter-second: A unit of exposure consisting of the light from a standard candle burning for one second at a distance of one meter from the plate.

Candlepower: Luminous intensity expressed in terms of the standard candle.

Capacitor: An electrical circuit element consisting of one or more pairs of plates separated by some insulating material; sometimes called a condenser but the term capacitor is preferred since it is more specific.

Carbon process: Referring to a process using a printing paper the final image of which depends on the thickness of the gelatin layer in which finely ground carbon or other pigment is suspended.

Carbonates: A term applied to certain alkaline salts, such as potassium carbonate and sodium carbonate, used as an accelerator in a developer.

Carbro process: A combination of the carbon and bromide methods for making a print.

Cardinal points: In a thick lens or lens system, the two principal points, the two nodal points and two focal points.

Cartridge: A light-tight container which may be loaded with film in the dark and placed in the camera in daylight.

Cassette: A film cartridge or magazine.

Catch lights: The small reflections of a light source, found in the eyes of a portrait subject.

Celluloid: A transparent film made from cellulose nitrate.

Celsius: The preferred name of the Centigrade thermometer scale.

Centigrade scale: A temperature scale in which 0 degrees represents the ice point and 100 degrees the steam point. Celsius is now the preferred term in technical use.

Centimeter: A measure of length; 1/100 of a meter; abb.: cm.

Cepa paper: A Kodak trade name for a tough tissue paper for diffusion purposes or vignettes.

Characteristic curve: A curve plotted to show the relation of density to exposure. Sometimes referred to as the H and D curve.

Chloride paper: A photographic printing paper in which the emulsion is made sensitive largely through silver chloride. Usually chloride papers are printed by contact and require comparatively longer exposure than bromide or chloro-bromide paper.

Chloro-bromide paper: A photographic printing paper used basically for enlarging. Its emulsion contains a mixture of silver chloride and silver bromide.

Chromatic aberration: A defect in a lens which prevents it from focusing different colored light rays in the same plane.

Cinching: Tightening a roll of film by holding the spool and pulling the free end; invariably results in parallel scratches or abrasion marks.

Cine: Word or prefix referring to motion-picture.

Circle of confusion: An optical term describing the size of an image point formed by a lens.

Circle of illumination: The total image area of a lens, only part of which is actually used in taking a picture.

Clinical camera: A camera especially designed for use in hospitals and clinics.

Clumping: Relates to the effective increase in grain size in the emulsion due to the partial overlapping of grains of silver.

Coating lens: A thin, transparent coating applied to a lens to reduce surface reflection and internal reflection; also cuts down transmission of ultraviolet rays, acting somewhat like a haze filter.

Collage: A composite photograph made by pasting up a number of individual prints.

Collimate: To produce parallel rays of light by means of a lens or a concave mirror.

Collimating lens: A lens so adjusted as to produce a parallel beam of light.

Collinear: The line-to-line relation existing between the corresponding parts of the object and its image formed by a lens.

Collodion: A transparent liquid obtained by dissolving pyroxylin in a mixture of equal parts of alcohol and ether. It is used as the vehicle for carrying the sensitive salts in the wet-plate process.

Color: The sensation produced in the eye by a particular wave length or group of wave lengths of visible light.

Color-blind: Applied to an emulsion sensitive only to blue, violet, and ultraviolet light.

Color contrast: A property by which the form of an object can be recognized by its variation in color, whether or not the brightness of all parts of the object is equal.

Color sensitivity: The response of a photographic emulsion to light of various wave lengths.

Coma: A lens aberration in which a coma or pear-shaped image is formed by oblique rays from an object point removed from the principal axis of the lens.

Combination print: A composite print made from several negatives.

Complementary colors: A color is complementary to another when a combination of the two produce white light.

Composition: The balancing of shapes and tones to produce a pleasing effect.

Compound Shutter: A trade name for an American (or German) shutter similar to the Compur, except that its slow speeds are controlled by means of a pneumatic piston retard instead of a gear escapement.

Compur Shutter: A trade name for a between-the-lens shutter containing independent mechanisms for time (and bulb) exposures and for instantaneous exposures varying from 1 second to as high as 1/500 of a second.

Concave: Hollowed out; curved inward; applied to negative lenses which are thinnest in the center.

Concave lens: A lens having one or two concave surfaces.

Concavo-convex lens: A lens having one concave and one convex surface.

Condenser: An optical system in projection printers used to collect the divergent rays of a light source and concentrate them upon the objective lens.

Contact print: A print made by placing a sensitized emulsion in direct contact with a negative and passing light through the negative.

Contact printer: A box or machine providing a light source and a means for holding the negative and the sensitive material in contact while they are exposed to this light source.

Contrast: Subject contrast is the difference between the reflective abilities of various areas of a subject. Lighting contrast is the difference in intensities of light falling on various parts of a subject. Inherent emulsion contrast is the possible difference between the maximum and minimum densities of the silver deposits with a minimum variation of exposure. It is determined by the manufacturer. Development contrast is the gamma to which an emulsion is developed. It is controlled only by the developer, time, temperature, and agitation.

Contrast filter: A color filter so chosen as to make a colored subject stand out very sharply from surrounding objects.

Contrast paper: Photographic paper having a contrasty emulsion in order to produce good prints from soft negatives; also called hard paper.

Contrasty: Having a great difference between tones; sometimes applied to a print having mostly black and white, lacking in middle tones, correctly called chalky.

Convertible lens: A lens containing two or more elements which can be used individually or in combination to give a variety of focal lengths.

Convex: The opposite of concave; curved outward; applied to a lens which is thicker in the center than at the edges.

Copy board: A board or easel to which photographs or other originals are fastened while being copied.

Corex: A trademark of the Corning Glass Works for a type of glass which is highly transparent to ultraviolet light.

Coupled rangefinder: A rangefinder connected to the focusing mechanism of the lens so that the lens is focused while measuring the distance to the subject.

Covering power: The capacity of a lens to give a sharply defined image to the edges of the sensitized material it is designed to cover at the largest possible aperture.

Crop: To trim or cut away the unnecessary portions of a print to improve composition.

Curtain aperture: The slit in a focal plane shutter which permits the light to reach the film. The slit size may be either fixed or variable.

Curvature of field: The saucer-shaped image of a flat object formed by an uncorrected lens.

Cut film: A flexible transparent base, coated with a sensitized emulsion and cut in sheets of various sizes. Often referred to as sheet film.

Cyan: A blue-green (minus red) color.

Daguerreotype: An early photographic process which employs a silver-coated plate sensitized with silver iodide and silver bromide. After long exposure, the plate is developed by subjecting it to the mercury vapor.

Darkroom: A room for photographic operations, mainly processing, which can be made free from white light and is usually equipped with safelights emitting non-actinic light.

Darkslide: A British term for a plate holder or a sheet-film holder.

Daylight loading: Any arrangement on a camera, a film magazine, or a developing tank permitting insertion of film in daylight without the use of a darkroom or a changing bag.

Decimeter: A measure of length; 1/10 of a meter.

Deckle edge: A rough or irregularly trimmed edge on a sheet of paper.

Definition: The clarity, sharpness, resolution, and brilliancy of an image formed by a lens.

Dense: Very dark; applied to a negative or positive transparency which is overexposed, overdeveloped, or both.

Densitometer: A device for measuring the density of a silver deposit in a photographic image. It is usually limited to measuring even densities in small areas.

Density: A term used in expressing the light-stopping power of a blackened silver deposit in relation to the light incident upon it.

Depth of field: The distance measured between the nearest and farthest planes in the subject area which give satisfactory definition.

Depth of focus: The distance which a camera back can be racked back and forth while preserving satisfactory image detail in focal plane for a given object point.

Desensitizer: An agent, usually a chemical solution, for decreasing the color sensitivity of a photographic emulsion to facilitate developing under a comparatively bright light. The emulsion is desensitized after exposure.

Desiccated: A term applied to chemicals in which all moisture has been eliminated.

Detective camera: An early name for what is now called a candid camera.

Developer: A solution used to make visible the latent image in an exposed emulsion.

Developing agent: A chemical compound possessing the ability to change exposed silver halide to black metallic silver, while leaving the unexposed halide unaffected.

Developing-out paper: A printing paper in which the image is made visible by developing in a chemical solution.

Development by inspection: Development of negatives or prints by inspection, depending on the operator's judgment as to when development is complete.

Diaphragm: A device for controlling the amount of light which passes through a lens. It is usually an iris diaphragm but may be in the form of slotted discs of fixed sizes.

Diapositive: A positive image on a transparent medium such as glass or film; a transparency.

Dichroic fog: A two-color stain observed in film or plates. Appears green by reflected light and pink by transmitted light.

Diffraction: An optical term used to denote the spreading of a light ray after it passes the edge of an obstacle.

Diffusion: The scattering of light rays from a rough surface, or the transmission of light through a translucent medium.

Din: A European system of measuring film speed; little used in this country.

Diopter: A measure of lens power; the reciprocal of the focal length of the lens in meters.

Direct finder: A viewfinder through which the subject is seen directly, such as the wire finder on various cameras.

Direct positive: A positive image obtained directly without the use of a negative.

Dispersion: The separation of light into its component colors created by passing white light through a prism.

Distance meter: An instrument used for estimating the distance to a particular object. Also known as a range finder.

Distortion: Defects caused by uncorrected lenses, resulting in images that are not the proper shape.

Dodge: To shade a portion of the negative during printing.

Dodging: The process of holding back light from certain areas of sensitized material to avoid overexposure of these areas.

Double exposure: The intentional or unintentional recording of two separate images on a single piece of sensitized material.

Double extension: A term used to describe the position of a camera bellows. A double extension bellows has an extended length of about twice the focal length of the lens being used.

Double image: A blurred picture, caused by movement of the camera or of the subject during exposure.

Double printing: Printing from two or more negatives to make one picture; for example, to use a second negative to print clouds into a landscape.

Double weight: The heavier weight in which photographic papers are supplied; abb.: DW.

Dragon's blood: A resin used as an etching resist.

Drop bed: A camera bed which may be lowered to avoid interference with the view of a wide-angle lens.

Drop front: A type of rising front which permits lowering the lens below the center of the film.

Dry mounting: A method of cementing a print to a mount by means of a thin tissue of thermoplastic material. The tissue is placed between the print and the mount and sufficient heat applied to melt the tissue.

Duplicator: A split lens cap used to photograph a person twice on a single film without a dividing line between the two exposures.

Dyes, sensitizing: Dyes used to extend the color sensitivity of an emulsion. Applied during the manufacture of emulsions to obtain selective sensitivity to colored light.

Easel: A device to hold sensitized paper in a flat plane on an enlarger. Generally includes an adjustable mask to accommodate different sizes of paper.

Effective aperture: The diameter of the lens diaphragm as measured through the front lens element; the unobstructed useful area of a lens; it may actually be larger than the opening in the lens diaphragm, owing to the converging action of the front lens element.

Efficiency: As applied to shutters, the percentual relationship between the total time a shutter remains open (counting from half-open to half-closed position) and the time required for the shutter to reach the half-open and the fully closed positions.

Efficiency of a lens: The ratio of the light actually transmitted by a lens to that incident to it.

Efflorescence: The process by which a chemical salt loses its water of crystallization upon exposure to air.

Ektalith: Eastman Kodak trade-mark for a diffusion-transfer system of producing lithographic plates.

Elon: Kodak trade-mark for a popular developing agent.

Embossing: The process by which the central portion of a print is depressed, leaving a raised margin.

Emulsion: The light-sensitive layer, consisting of silver salts suspended in gelatin, which is spread over a permanent support such as film, glass, or paper.

Emulsion speed: The factor which determines the exposure necessary to produce a satisfactory image. This is commonly expressed in Weston, General Electric, or ASA emulsion numbers which have been assigned to the film.

Enlarged negative: A negative made from a smaller one.

Enlargement: A print made from a negative or positive by projecting an enlarged image on sensitized material.

Enlarger: An optical projector forming an image of a negative on a larger sheet of sensitized paper.

Equivalent focus: The focal length of a group of lenses considered as one lens.

Etch: To scrape away some of the density of a negative by means of a knife during retouching.

Evaporation: The changing of a liquid into vapor at a temperature below the boiling point.

Exposure: The product of time and intensity of illumination acting upon the photographic material. Intensity x Time = Exposure.

Exposure indicator: A device attached to a camera to indicate the number of exposures; also to a plate holder to show whether the plate has been exposed.

Exposure meter: An instrument for measuring light intensity and determining correct exposure.

Extension: The distance between the lens and the sensitive material in a camera.

Extinction meter: An exposure meter which measures the light by the minimum visibility of the image or target.

Eyepiece: The lens element of a microscope, viewfinder, or telescope to which the eye is applied in order to view the image.

f-number: A system denoting lens apertures. Example f/5.6; f/11; f/16; f/32

Factorial development: A system of development in which a standard degree of contrast is obtained by developing for a time period, which is estimated by multiplying the time interval (elapsing between the immersion of the negative and the first appearance of its image) by some recommended factor.

Fading: This refers to the gradual elimination, usually of the print image, due to the action of light or other oxidation.

Fahrenheit: A system of calibrating thermometers in which the freezing point of water is taken as 32 degrees and its boiling point as 212 degrees.

Farmer's reducer: A formula, composed of potassium ferricyanide and hypo, used to reduce either negative or print densities.

Far point: The farthest object from the camera which is still acceptably sharp when the camera is focused at a given distance.

Fast lens: A lens which has a large relative aperture. Example f/1.2; f/1.5; f/1.9

Faurot foto focuser: An attachment put in lens of 4x5 camera to take photographs of fingerprints.

Ferrotype plates (tins): Sheets of thin enameled metal, chromium plated metal or stainless steel used in obtaining high gloss on prints.

Field: The area covered by a lens or a viewfinder.

Filament: That part of an incandescent lamp, composed of resistance wire, which becomes luminous when heated by the passage of electric current.

Fill-in: Secondary illumination directed so as to keep shadow areas from photographing too dark; also known as the fill light.

Film: A sheet or strip of celluloid, coated with a light-sensitive emulsion for exposure in a camera. The celluloid support has a nitrate or acetate base.

Film base: The transparent material on which an emulsion is coated.

Film cement: A solution of cellulose acetate or nitrate used to join strips of motion-picture film.

Film cleaner: A liquid used to remove dirt, dust, and grease from a film without injuring the base or the emulsion.

Film clip: A metal clamp used to hold film while processing or drying.

Film hanger: A frame of noncorrodible metal in which film is suspended for processing.

Film pack: A metal case containing a number of films so arranged that films may be changed by pulling out paper tabs.

Film pack adapter: A holder by means of which the film packs may be used in a camera designed for plates or sheet films.

Film sheath: A metal holder in which single sheets of film may be placed and inserted into plate holders.

Film tank: A container holding solutions and films to be processed therein.

Film trimming guide: A metal form designed to allow one to cut the ends of film correctly for loading magazines.

Filter, light or color: A piece of colored glass or gelatin, which is usually placed in front of the camera lens to compensate for the difference in color sensitivity between the film and the eye. Also used to modify or exaggerate contrast to provide primary color separation in color photography.

Filter factor: The number by which the correct exposure without the filter must be multiplied to obtain the same effective exposure with the filter.

Filter paper: A porous paper used to strain impurities from solutions.

Filter ratio: The ratio between the factors of two or more filters used with the same film and illuminant; frequently used in color separation work in preference to the actual filter factors, since no exposure is normally made without filters in such work.

Finder: A viewer through which the picture to be taken may be seen and centered.

Fine-grain developer: A developer of low potential which prevents the clumping of silver grains to form a mottled image.

Fine-grained: Applied to a negative with very little granularity; one which may be enlarged from 7 to 10 diameters or more with satisfactory quality.

Fingerprint camera: A fixed-focus camera with built-in lights used to photograph fingerprints, stamps, and other small objects.

Fixation: The process of making soluble the undeveloped silver salts in a sensitized material by immersion in a hypo solution.

Fixed focus: A term applied to a camera in which the lens is set permanently in such a position as to give good average focus for both nearby and distant objects.

Flare spot: A fogged area on the developed negative due to the multiple reflection of a strong light source by the several surfaces of the lens elements.

Flash gun: The battery case, lamp socket, and reflector used with photoflash lamps.

Flashtube: A glass or quartz tube, usually wound in helical shape, containing two electrodes and filled with xenon or other inert gasses at a very low pressure; used as the light source in flash units and photographic stroboscopes.

Flat: The expression denoting lack of contrast in a print or negative.

Flatness of field: The quality of a lens which produces sharpness of image both at the edges and at the center of the negative.

Floodlamp: In general, any lamp or lighting unit producing a broad beam or flood of light; colloquially used as a contraction for photoflood lamp.

Focal length: The distance between the center of the lens and the point at which the image of a distant object comes into critical view. The focal length of a thick lens is measured from the emergent nodal point to the focal plane.

Focal plane: The plane at which the image is brought to a critical focus. In other words, the position in the camera occupied by the film emulsion.

Focal plane shutter: A shutter which operates immediately in front of the focal plane. A shutter of this type usually contains a fixed or variable-sized slit in a curtain of cloth or metal which travels across the film to make the exposure.

Focus: The plane toward which the rays of light converge to form an image after passing through a lens. (The most important function for the policeman or fireman to perform before snapping the shutter.)

Focusing cloth: A black cloth used to cover the camera while focusing so that the image on the groundglass may be more easily seen.

Focusing hood: A collapsible tube shading the groundglass of a camera so that a focusing cloth is not needed.

Focusing magnifier: A lens through which the image on the groundglass is viewed for critical focusing.

Focusing negative: A negative containing geometrical patterns which is temporarily substituted for the picture negative when focusing an enlarger.

Focusing scale: A graduated scale on a lens or a camera, permitting focusing on a given subject by estimating its distance from the camera and setting a pointer to correspond.

Focusing screen: A sheet of groundglass on which the image is focused.

Folding camera: A camera having a collapsible bellows so that it may be closed for carrying.

Foot-candle: The intensity of light falling on a surface placed one foot distant from a point light source of one candle power.

Forcing: Continuing development beyond the normal times in an effort to secure more detail.

Foreground: Generally, that part of a scene closer to the camera than the main subject.

Formula: A list of ingredients and quantities necessary to compound a photographic solution.

Fresnel lens: A lens consisting of a small central plano-convex lens surrounded by a series of prismatic rings; also known as an echelon lens.

Frilling: The detachment of the emulsion from its support around the edges; happens most often in hot weather or because of too much alkali in the developer.

Full aperture: The maximum opening of a lens or lens diaphragm.

Gallon: A unit of liquid measure used in the United States and the British Empire; an American gallon contains 128 ounces; the British Imperial gallon contains 160 ounces; abb.: gal.

Gamma: A numerical measure of the contrast to which an emulsion is developed.

Gamma infinity: The maximum contrast to which an emulsion can be developed.

Gas bells: Bubbles forcing the emulsions from the support, caused by strong chemical action and resulting in minute holes in negative.

Gelatin: A jelly-like by-product produced from bones, hoofs, horns, and other parts of animals.

Ghost: The reflection of an image on one or more lens surfaces caught by the negative.

Ghost images: The reflection of the light from a bright subject, by the elements of the lens or its mounting, to form a spurious image.

Glossy: Applied to photographic papers which are heavily coated with gelatin so that they may be ferrotyped.

Glycerin sandwich: A means of making prints from scratched or damaged negatives; they are placed between glass plates coated with glycerin which temporarily fills in the scratches.

Gradation: The range of densities in an emulsion from highlights to shadows.

Grain: Used in speaking of individual silver particles or groups of particles in the emulsion which, when enlarged, become noticeable and objectionable.

Grain: A unit of weight. In the avoirdupois system, 437.5 grains (gr.) equal an ounce.

Gray scale: A monochrome strip of tones ranging from pure white to black with intermediate tones of gray. The scale is placed in a setup for a color photograph and serves as a means of balancing the separation negatives and positive dye images, and is cropped from the finished print.

Groundglass: A screen at the back or top of the camera upon which the image may be focused.

Groundglass screen: A translucent screen mounted in the back or top of a camera, upon which the image formed by the lens can be observed.

Gun: Any device for igniting flashlamps or flash powder; also, the gunstock for supporting small cameras with greater firmness.

H & D (Hurter and Driffield) System: A system for measuring film speed. Little used in this country.

Halation: A blurred effect, resembling a halo, usually occurring around bright objects; caused by the reflections of rays of light from the back of the negative material.

Halftones: A term used in speaking of the middle tones lying between the shadows and highlights.

Halides (or Haloids): A chemical term applied to binary compounds containing any of the elements, chlorine, bromine, iodine, and fluorine.

Halogen: Iodine, fluorine, chlorine, and bromine are known as halogens.

Hard: A term used to denote excessive contrast.

Hardener: A chemical such as potassium or chrome alum which is added to the fixing bath to harden the gelatin after development. Prehardening solutions may be used prior to development.

Hard-working: Applied to a developer which tends to give high contrast.

High-key: Applied to a print having the majority of its tones light grays and white.

Highlights: The brightest parts of the subject, which are represented by the denser parts of the negative and the light gray and white tones of the print.

Hold back: To shade portions of an image while printing in order to avoid excessive density; similar to dodge.

Hue: The name by which we distinguish one color from another: blue, red.

Hydrometer: An instrument used to find the concentration of a single chemical in water. Most common use is in mixing large quantities of hypo.

Hydroquinone: A reducing agent which is widely used in compounding developers for photographic materials.

Hyperfocal distance: The distance from the camera, such that if an object at that point is in sharp focus, then all objects from one-half this distance to infinity give satisfactory definition on the groundglass screen.

Hypo: A contraction of sodium hyposulfite (sodium thiosulfate). Hypo is used in compounding fixing solutions. These, in turn, are used to make soluble the undeveloped silver salts in an emulsion.

Hypo test: A method of checking the completeness of washing by running the drippings of wash water from the film or print into various testing solutions; also, commercial solution used to test strength of hypo.

Identification: A photograph showing the head and shoulders, both front and side views, of a person.

Illumination: The illumination at a point on the surface of a body is the intensity of light received, and is expressed as the number of lumens per square foot or the number of foot candles.

Image: The representation of an object formed by optical and/or chemical means.

Imbibition: Literally the act of absorbing. The process of dye transfer in the wash-off relief process of making color prints.

Incandescent: Glowing with heat (as tungsten filament in incandescent lamp).

Incident light: A meter reading designed to be held at the subject position, facing the camera, to measure light strength at the subject plane.

Index of refraction: The mathematical expression of the deviation of a light ray entering a given medium at an angle to its surface.

Inertia: Hurter and Driffield termed the exposure, indicated by the intersection of the straight-line part of the characteristic curve with the log exposure axis, the inertia. It is an inverse measure of the speed of the plate.

Infinity: A distance so far removed from an observer that the rays of light reflected to a lens from a point at that distance may be regarded as parallel. A distance setting on a camera focusing scale, beyond which all objects are in focus.

Infrared: Invisible rays of light beyond the red end of the visible spectrum.

Intensification: The process of building up the density of a photographic image by chemical means.

Interval timer: A laboratory clock that may be set to ring after a given time has elapsed.

Invasion phase: Refers to that part of the development process during which the developer penetrates into the emulsion.

Inverse square law: A physical law which states that illumination intensity varies inversely with the square of the distance from a point source of light.

Invisible rays: Those rays, such as X-rays, ultra-violet, and infra-red, which are not visible to the eye.

Iris diaphragm: A lens control composed of a series of overlapping leaves operated by a revolving ring to vary the aperture of the lens.

Keeper: An acid chemical added to two-solution developers to prevent oxidation of the developing agent.

Kelvin: A thermometer scale starting at absolute zero (-273° C. approximately) and having degrees of the same magnitude as those of the Celsius thermometer. Thus 0° = 273° K; 100° C = 373° K, etc.; also called the absolute scale.

Key: The prevailing tone of a photograph, as high-key, low-key, medium-key.

Kilo: 1000
Example: *Kilocycle*:   1000 cycles; abb.: kc
Kilogram: A unit of weight; 1000 grams; abb.: kg
Kilometer: A unit of length; 1000 meters; abb.: km
Kilowatt: 1000 watts; abb.: kw

Kodachrome: A commercial monopack produced by Eastman Kodak Company. It is processed by reversal to produce colored positive transparencies.

Kodalith: Trade-mark of the Eastman Kodak Company for its line of high-contrast photochemical films and developers. Fine for copying spot maps.

Land camera: Camera developed by the Polaroid Corporation about 1950 which makes finished photographs in about 10 seconds by the diffusion-transfer process; also known colloquially as "Polaroid" camera.

Lantern slides: Small transparencies, either 2x2, 3¼x3¼, or 3¼x4, intended for projection.

Latent image: The invisible image formed in an emulsion by exposure to light. It can be rendered visible by the process of development.

Lateral chromatic magnification: Refers to the formation of colored images of different sizes in the same plane, of an object removed from the principal axis of the lens.

Latitude: Exposure latitude is the quality of a film, plate or paper which allows variation in exposure without detriment to the image quality. Development latitude is the allowable variation in the recommended developing time without noticeable difference in contrast or density.

Leader: A strip of film or paper at the beginning of a roll of film which is used for loading the camera or projector.

Lens: An optical term applied to a piece of glass which is bounded by two spherical surfaces or a plane and a spherical surface. The term is also applied to a combination of several glass elements, such as a photographic objective.

Lens board: A detachable board carrying a lens and a shutter, which is fastened to the front of the camera.

Lens cap: A cover used to protect a lens from dust and damage when not in use.

Lens hood: A shade to keep extraneous light from the surface of a lens.

Lens paper: A fine soft tissue paper used for cleaning lenses.

Lens shade: A detachable camera accessory used to shield the lens from extraneous light rays.

Light fog: The fog produced over an image by accidental exposure of film to extraneous light.

Light trap: A system of staggered passageways or double doors so that a darkroom may be entered or left without light being admitted.

Line copy: Original material to be copied, containing only black and white areas or lines, without halftones.

Line screen: A finely lined glass screen used in photomechanical reproduction to produce a halftone negative. Often referred to as a halftone screen.

Liter: A unit of capacity.

Litmus paper: Paper impregnated with azolitmin, used for testing solutions; it turns red in acid solutions, blue in alkaline baths.

Local reduction: The reduction of certain densities of a negative by the local application of a reducer or by rubbing with an abrasive paste.

Long scale: A long scale or contrast negative is one in which the least dense portion will transmit 50 to 100 times more light than the densest portion. A long scale or soft printing paper is one requiring 50 to 100 times the barely visible tint exposure in order to produce the deepest black.

Low key: The balance of light or dark tones of a photograph. If light tones prevail with few or no dark tones, the photograph is said to be "high key"; if the opposite, "low key."

Lumen: A measurement of light equivalent to that falling on a foot-square surface which is one foot away from a point light source of one candle power.

Lumenized: A trademark of the Eastman Kodak Company for an anti-reflection coating applied to lenses and other glass surfaces.

Luminosity: The intensity of light in a color as measured by a photometer.

Lunar caustic: Silver nitrate.

Lux: Lumens per square meter.

Macrophotography: Close-up photography, taking of a picture greater than the size of the subject.

Magazine: The container holding the film feed and take-up spools of a motion-picture or still camera, also a device for holding and exposing from 12 to 18 sheet films or plates in succession.

Magenta: A reddish-blue (minus green) color.

Mask: A sheet of thin black paper, metal, or celluloid used to secure white margins on a photograph.

Masking: A corrective measure used in three-color photography to compensate for the spectral absorptive deficiencies in pigments, dyes, and emulsions. This compensation improves the accuracy of color reproduction.

Matrix: A gelatin relief image used in the wash-off relief process of color photography.

Medium-key: Applied to a print having the majority of its tones medium grays, with only a small proportion of solid black or pure white.

Megacycle: 1,000,000 cycles, abb.: mc.

Meniscus lens: A positive or negative, crescent shaped, lens consisting of one concave and one convex spherical surface.

Meta-: A prefix to chemical names indicating substitution in the 1 and 3 positions in the benzene ring.

Meter: A unit of length, abb.: m. U.S. equivalent 39.37 inches.

Metol: A popular reducing agent, which is sold under trade names such as Elon, Pictol, and Rhodal. The Chemical name is monomethylparaminophenol sulfate.

Microdensitometer: A special form of densitometer for reading densities in very small areas; used for studying astronomical images, spectroscopic records, and for measuring graininess in films.

Micron: A unit of length; 1/1000 of a millimeter; abb.: F.

Microphotography: Taking a photograph through a microscope. Not necessarily using the lens of the microscope, but the lens of the camera.

Mil: 1/1000 of an inch.

Milky: Applied to the appearance of incompletely fixed films or plates; also of incorrectly prepared fixing baths.

Milligram: A unit of weight; 1/1000 of a gram; abb.: mg.

Milliliter: A unit of capacity; 1/1000 of a liter; approximately (but not exactly) equal to 1 cubic centimeter; abb.: ml.

Millimeter: A unit of length; 1/1000 of a meter; abb.: mm.

Millimicron: A unit of length; 1/1,000,000 of a millimeter, or 1/1000 of a micron; abb.: m.

Miniature camera: A term more or less generally applied to a camera using film 2¼x3¼ inches or less in size.

Minim: A unit of capacity; 1/480 of a fluid ounce or approximately 1 drop.

Modeling: Applied to the representation of the third dimension in a photograph by the controlled placement of highlights and shadows.

Monochromatic: A single color.

Monopack: Another name for integral tripack.

Montage: A composite picture made by a number of exposures on the same film, by projecting a number of negatives to make a composite print, or by cutting and pasting-up a number of prints and subsequently copying to a new negative, or by any of a number of similar processes.

Mordant: An etching bath used on metal; also a chemical which causes a dye to become insoluble and prevents its washing out.

Mottling: Marks which appear on negatives or prints which have not been sufficiently agitated during processing.

Mount: The cardboard or paper support to which a print is fastened for display.

Mounting tissue: Thin sheets of paper impregnated with shellac and used for attaching prints to mounts by application of heat.

M-Q developer: A developer containing Metol (Elon, Pictol, Rhodol, etc.) and hydroquinone (Quinol).

Mug shot: A photograph showing head and shoulders, both side and front views, of a criminal.

Multiple camera: A camera which makes a number of small photographs on a single large film or plate.

Multiple printing: Repeated printing of the same image on successive coatings of sensitizer on one sheet of paper, usually in the gum-bichromate process, to secure greater contrast.

Multiplying back: A sliding back for view cameras designed to make a large number of negatives in rows on a single plate or film.

Negative: A photographic image on film, plate, or paper in which the dark portions of the subject appear light and the light portions appear dark.

Negative paper: A paper base coated with a negative emulsion, used mainly by photoengravers.

Neutral: Without color; gray; chemically, a solution which is neither acid nor alkaline.

New coccine: A red, water-soluble dye used for dodging negatives.

Nicol prism: A type of prism used to produce polarized light.

Nitrate base: The term used to designate a photographic film base composed of cellulose nitrate. Highly inflammable.

Nodal points: The points on the axis of a thick lens, such that a ray traversing the first medium, passing through one nodal point, emerges from the second medium in a parallel direction, and appears to originate at a second point.

Non-halation: A light-sensitive material the back of which is coated with a light-absorbing substance which tends to reduce halation.

Objective: A lens that is used to form a real image of an object.

Opacity: The resistance of a material to the transmission of light.

Opal glass: A white, milky, translucent glass used as a diffusion medium in enlargers.

Opaque: Refers to an object which is incapable of transmitting visible light. A commercial preparation used to block out certain negative areas.

Optical axis: An imaginary line passing through the centers of all the lens elements in a compound lens.

Original: In copying, that which is to be reproduced.

Ortho: An abbreviation for orthochromatic.

Orthochromatic film: A film, the color sensitivity of which includes blue, green, and some of the yellow. Not sensitive to red.

Orthochromatic rendition: The reproduction of color brightness in their relative shades of gray.

Orthonon: Refers to a film whose color sensitivity includes ultraviolet and blue. Often referred to as "color-blind" film.

Overdevelopment: The result of permitting film or paper to remain in the developer too long, resulting in excessive contrast or density.

Overexposure: The result of too much light being permitted to act on a negative, with either too great a lens aperture or too slow a shutter speed or both.

Oxidation: The loss of activity of a developer due to contact with the air.

Pacifier (flattener): A term for a mixture of water and glycerin used to avoid curling of prints.

Packard shutter: A trade name for a type of shutter, operated by a rubber bulb and tube, much used on studio cameras.

Pan: An abbreviation for panchromatic.

Panchromatic film: A film that is sensitive to all colors of the visible spectrum.

Panoramic head: A revolving tripod head, so graduated that successive photographs may be taken which can be joined into one long panoramic print.

Parallax: The apparent displacement of an object seen from different points. Commonly encountered in photography in the difference between the image seen in the view finder and that actually taken by the lens.

Pentaprism: A five-sided prism used in single-lens reflex viewing hoods to turn the image right-side-up and laterally correct.

Perspective: The illusion of three dimensions created on a flat surface.

pH: The acidity of alkalinity of a solution expressed in terms of the hydrogen ion concentration. A neutral solution has a pH of 7.0; an acid solution below this value; and an alkaline solution above it.

Phot: A unit of luminance; one lumen per square millimeter.

Photochemical action: A chemical action induced by exposure to light.

Photoengraving: A method of producing etched printing plates by photographic means.

Photoflash lamp: A light bulb filled with aluminum wire or shreds in an atmosphere of oxygen; the heating of the filament ignites the primer which in turn fires the aluminum, giving a short brilliant flash of light.

Photoflood lamp: An electric lamp designed to be worked at higher than normal voltage, giving brilliant illumination at the expense of lamp life.

Photogrammetry: The science of mapping by the use of aerial photographs.

Photogravure: A method of making an intaglio engraving in copper from a photograph, using the gelatin image as an acid resist.

Photomacrography: Enlarged photography of small objects by the use of a long bellows camera and a lens of short focal length.

Photomicrography: Photography through a microscope.

Photomontage: A picture composed of several smaller pictures.

Photoregression: The gradual disappearance of the latent image which has not been subjected to development.

Photosensitive: Material which is chemically or physically changed by the action of light.

Photostat: The trade name of a camera which makes copies of documents, letters, drawings, etc., on sensitized paper; also the copies made by means of this camera.

Phototopography: The mapping or surveying of terrain by means of photography.

Pincushion distortion: A term applied to the pincushion-shaped image of a square object obtained when the diaphragm is placed behind the lens.

Pinholes: Tiny clear spots on negative or positive images, caused by dust, air bells, or undissolved chemicals.

Plate back: An attachment to certain rollfilm cameras such as the older Kodaks, the Rolleiflex, etc., permitting the use of plates or sheet film; incorrectly used as a description of a camera primarily designed for use with plates; such cameras are plate cameras, not plate-back cameras.

Plate holder: A lightproof holder in which sensitized plates are held for exposure in the camera.

Pola screen: A screen which transmits polarized light when properly oriented with respect to the vibration plane of the incident light. When rotated to a 90 degree angle it will not transmit the polarized light.

Polarized light: Light which vibrates in one manner only—in straight lines, circles, or ellipses. Light is commonly polarized by passing a light beam through a Nicol prism or a polarizing screen.

Positive: Meaning the opposite of negative. Any print or transparency made from a negative is termed a positive.

Pre-exposure: Exposure of a sensitized material to light either during manufacture, or by the user before exposure in the camera, as a means of intensifying the latent image, particularly in shadowy areas.

Prefocused: Applied to a lamp having a special type of base and socket which automatically centers the filament with respect to an optical system.

Preservative: A chemical—such as sodium sulphite—which, when added to a developing solution, tends to prolong its life.

Primary color: Any one of the three components of white light—blue, green, and red.

Printing frame: A frame designed to hold a negative in contact with paper, under pressure, for the purpose of making prints.

Printing-out paper: A photographic paper forming a visible image immediately on exposure, without development. It must be fixed, however, for permanence of the image; abb.: P.O.P.

Process lens: A highly-corrected lens used for precise color-separation work.

Processing: The chemical treatment of exposed film to form a permanent visible image.

Projection printing: A method of making prints by projecting the image of the negative on a suitable easel for holding the sensitive paper.

Proof paper: Usually a printing-out paper (P.O.P.) which is exposed in contact with the negative to any bright light and does not require a developing solution to make a visible image. The image must be observed in subdued light or it will become dark and eventually disappear.

Proportional reducer: A chemical reducing solution which reduces the silver in the shadows at the same rate as that in the highlights.

Props: Accessories used to add interest or provide variety in an illustration or a portrait.

Quart: A unit of liquid measure, 32 ounces (American) or 40 ounces (British); abb.: qt.

Quartz lens: A special lens used for ultraviolet photography.

Racking: Moving either the lens board or the camera back to and fro while focusing.

Radiant energy: A form of energy of electromagnetic character. All light which causes a photochemical reduction is radiant energy.

Ratio: The degree of enlargement or reduction of a photographic copy with respect to the original.

Reagent: A chemical used to produce a desired reaction.

Reciprocity law: A law which states that the blackening of photosensitive materials is determined by the product of light intensity and time of exposure. Thus intensity is the reciprocal of time and, if one is halved, then the other must be doubled to obtain the same blackening.

Rectilinear lens: A lens corrected so that it does not curve the straight lines of the image.

Redevelopment: A step in the intensifying or toning procedure when a bleached photographic image is redeveloped to give the desired results.

Reducer: A chemical solution used to decrease the all-over density of a negative or print.

Reducing agent: The ingredient in a developer which changes the sub-halide to metallic silver. Usually requires acceleration.

Reflection: The diversion of light from any surface.

Reflector: Any device used to increase the efficiency of a light source. Examples are flashlight reflectors and tinfoil reflectors for outdoor pictures.

Reflex camera: A camera in which the image can be seen right side up and full size on the groundglass focusing screen.

Refraction: The bending of a light ray when passing obliquely from one medium to a medium of different density.

Replenisher: A modified developer solution which is added in small portions to a working developer to keep its properties constant.

Resolving power: The ability of a lens to record fine detail or of an emulsion to reproduce fine detail.

Restitution: Projection printing for the purpose of reducing the variation in the scale of prints.

Restrainer: Any chemical—such as potassium bromide—which, when added to a developing solution, has the power of slowing down the developing action and making it more selective.

Reticulation: The formation of a wrinkled or leather-like surface on a processed emulsion due to excessive expansion or contracting of the gelatin caused by temperature changes or chemical action.

Retouching: A method for improving the quality of a negative or print by use of a pencil or brush.

Reversal: A process by which a negative image is converted to a positive. Briefly, a negative is developed, re-exposed, bleached, and redeveloped to form a positive.

Rollfilm: A strip of flexible film, wound on a spool between turns of a longer paper strip, for daylight loading into rollfilm cameras.

Rollfilm holder: An accessory permitting the use of rollfilm in sheet-film cameras.

Safelight: A light, the intensity and color range of which are such that it will not affect sensitive materials.

Safety film: Film with a cellulose acetate base; so-called because it burns very slowly.

Safety shot: An unordered, duplicate exposure, made in case of damage to one negative in processing.

Scale: Scale is the ratio of a linear dimension in the photograph to the corresponding dimension in the subject.

Schiener Scale: A European system of speed ratings for films. It is little used in this country. Abbreviation is Sch.

Scum: A surface layer which forms on pyro developers, and occasionally on chrome-alum fixing-hardening baths.

Secondary colors: Colors formed by the combination of two primary colors. Yellow, magenta, and cyan are the secondary colors.

Selective absorption: The capacity of a body for absorbing certain colors while transmitting or reflecting the remainder.

Sensitizer: Dyes used in the manufacture of photographic emulsions. Sensitizers can be of two types: one to increase the speed of an emulsion; the other to increase its color sensitivity.

Sensitometer: A device for producing on sensitized material a series of exposures increasing at a definite ratio. Such a series is needed in studying the characteristics of an emulsion.

Sensitometric strip: A series of densities in definite steps.

Separation negatives: Three negatives, each of which records one of the three colors — blue, green, and red.

Sepia toning: A process which converts the black silver image to a brownish image. The image can vary considerably in hue, depending on the process, the tone of the original, and other factors.

Set: An interior or exterior scene or part of a scene, together with furniture or natural objects, built in a studio for photography, or on a motion-picture lot.

Shadow area: The darker portions of a picture or the lighter portions of a negative.

Shadows: A term applied to the thinner portions of a negative and the darker parts of a positive slide or print.

Sheet films: Individual films loaded into separate holders for exposure; usually on a heavier base than rollfilms and film packs.

Shoot: To make an exposure.

Short-stop bath: A solution containing an acid which neutralizes the developer remaining in the negative or print before it is transferred to the fixing bath.

Shutter: On a camera, a mechanical device which controls the length of time light is allowed to strike the sensitized material.

Silhouette: A photograph which shows only the mass of a subject in black, against a white or colored background.

Single weight: Applied to a photographic paper with a lightweight stock; abb.: SW.

Siphon: A bent tube or similar device used to empty containers of fluid by atmospheric pressure.

Skylight: A large window, usually inclined and facing north, used as principal light source in certain photographic studios.

Slide: A positive print on glass, or a film transparency bound between glasses for projection; also the removable cover of a sheet-film plate, or film-pack holder.

Sliding back: A camera so arranged that half the film may be centered in front of the lens, so that two pictures may be taken on a single sheet of film.

Sludge: A chemical precipitate or impurities which settle to the bottom of the container.

Sodium thiosulfate: Sodium hyposulphite, commonly known as hypo.

Soft: A term used in describing prints and negatives which have low contrast.

Soft-focus (adj.): Applied to a lens which has been deliberately undercorrected to produce a diffused image; also applied to pictures made with such a lens.

Soft-focus lens: A special type of lens, used to produce a picture with soft outlines. Such lenses are well adapted to portrait work.

Solarization: The production of a reversed or positive image by exposure to a very intense light.

Spectrogram: A photograph of a spectrum, made by the use of a spectrograph.

Spectrophotometer: An instrument for comparing the intensities at the corresponding wavelengths of two spectra.

Spectrum: A colored band formed when white light is passed through a prism or a diffraction grating; it contains all the colors of which white light is composed; plural, spectra.

Speedgun: A device to ignite flashlamps in synchronism with the opening of the camera shutter.

Spherical aberration: A lens defect which causes rays parallel to the axis and passing near the edge of a positive lens to come to a focus nearer the lens than the rays passing through the center portion.

Spool: The reel on which film is wound for insertion into a camera.

Spot lamp: A type of mushroom-shaped electric lamp having an integral reflector and producing a narrow, concentrated beam of light.

Spotting: The removal of small blemishes in photographic negatives or prints.

Squeegee: A strip of flat rubber set in a handle; used to remove excess moisture from prints before drying; as a verb, to press surplus moisture from prints.

Stereo camera: A camera having two lenses or the equivalent through which the pair of pictures making up a stereogram may be taken simultaneously.

Stereoscope: A device containing lenses, prisms, or mirrors, through which a stereogram is seen as a single, three-dimensional picture.

Stills: Photographs as distinguished from motion pictures.

Stirring rod: A glass, Bakelite, or hard-rubber rod used to stir photographic solutions.

Stock solution: A concentrated solution which is to be diluted with water for use.

Stop: A lens aperture or a diaphragm opening such as f/4, f/5.6, etc.

Stop bath: Preferred term for an acid rinse used following development of paper and films to neutralize them before placement in fixing bath; also incorrectly referred to as short stop.

Stop down: To use a smaller aperture.

Straight: Not retouched; applied to negatives or prints.

Strobe unit: An electronic unit which can be used many times for flash photography.

Subtractive process: A process in color photography, using the colors magenta, cyan, and yellow. Contrasted with additive color process.

Subtractive reducer: A reducer which affects the shadows in a negative without noticeably affecting the highlights.

Sunshade: A hood placed over a lens to keep stray light from its surface; similar to lens hood.

Superproportional reducer: A reducing solution which lowers the highlight density faster than it affects the shadow density.

Supplementary lens: An attachable lens by which the focal length of a camera objective may be increased or decreased.

Surface development: A characteristic of some fine-grain developers, which tend to develop the image mainly on the surface of the emulsion.

Swing back: The back of a view camera which can be tilted in both vertical and horizontal planes.

Synchro-flash: A term applied to flash photography in which a flash bulb is ignited at the same instant that the shutter is opened, the flash bulb being the primary source of illumination.

Synchro-sun: A term used in flash photography where flashlight and sunlight are used in combination.

Synchronizer: A device for synchronizing the shutter of a camera with a flashlamp so that the shutter is fully opened at the instant the lamp reaches its peak intensity.

T-number, T-stop: A system of marking lens apertures in accordance with their actual light transmission, rather than by their geometrical dimensions as in the f-stop system.

Tangent of an angle: The ratio of the length of the opposite leg to the adjacent leg of a right triangle.

Tank: A container or mechanical device in which films or plates may be processed, sometimes without the need of a darkroom.

Telephoto lens: A lens of long focal length having a separate negative rear element; it is used to form larger images of distant objects; it is similar in results to a telescope.

Tessar: A trade name for a type of anastigmat lens composed of two pairs of lens elements; one pair is cemented together, the other pair is separated by an air space.

Test strip: An exposed strip of bromide or chloride paper containing several different exposures used to determine the correct exposure for printing.

Texture: Applied to showing an object's surface roughness or smoothness in a photograph; often achieved by using light from a direction almost parallel to the surface of the object.

Thin: Applied to a weak negative lacking in density in the highlights and detail in the shadows.

Three-quarter: Applied to a portrait pose, standing or seated, including the figure approximately to the knees.

Tilt-top: A device attached to a tripod head to permit the camera to be set at various angles in elevation.

Time exposure: An exposure in which the shutter is opened and closed manually with a relatively long interval between.

Time-gamma-temperature curve: A curve of developing time plotted against developed contrast or gamma. The contrast for any given time may be read directly from the curve, or vice versa. The curve applies only for one particular developer and emulsion.

Timer: A special darkroom clock giving audible or visible indication of various time intervals.

Tone: In photography this usually applies to the color of a photographic image or, incorrectly, to any distinguishable shade of gray. To change the color of a *photographic image* from its natural black to various colors, either by means of metallic salts, or by mordanting certain dyes to the image; *such dyes do not stain the gelatin*; note the difference from tinting.

Toning: A method for changing the color or tone to an image by chemical action.

Translucent: A medium which passes light but diffuses it so that objects cannot be clearly distinguished.

Transmission: The ratio of the light passed through an object to the light falling upon it.

Transparency: An image on a transparent base, which must be viewed by transmitted light. Also refers to the light transmitting power of the silver deposit in a negative and is the opposite of opacity.

Tray siphon: A device for washing prints which projects a stream of water into a tray, and simultaneously siphons off an equal amount of hypo-laden water from the bottom of the tray.

Trimming board: A device consisting of a board, a hinged blade, and a rule placed at right angles to the blade; used for trimming prints.

Triple extension: Applied to a camera whose bellows extension approaches three times the focal length of its lens.

Tripod: A three-legged stand used to support a camera.

Tripod socket: A threaded opening in the base of a camera used to fasten the camera to the tripod head.

Tungsten: A metallic element of extremely high melting point used in the manufacture of incandescent electric lamps. In photography, tungsten is used to refer to artificial illumination as contrasted to daylight. For example, film emulsion speeds are given both in tungsten and daylight.

Ultraviolet filter: A filter which transmits ultraviolet light, as used for photography by the reflected ultraviolet light method.

Ultraviolet rays: Rays which comprise the invisible portion of the electromagnetic spectrum just beyond the visible violet. Ultraviolet wavelengths are comparatively short and therefore disperse more easily than visible wavelengths. This is a factor to be taken into account in high altitude photography since these rays are photographically actinic.

Underdevelopment: Insufficient development; due to developing either for too short a time in a weakened developer or, occasionally, at too low a temperature.

Underexposure: The result of insufficient light being allowed to pass through the lens to produce all the tones of an image; or of sufficient light being allowed to pass for too short a period of time.

Uniform System: A system of marking diaphragm aperture used until recently, in which an f/4 lens was marked U.S. 1; f/5.6 was equal to U.S. 2; f/8 equal to U.S. 4; f/11 equal to U.S. 8, etc.

Unipod: Similar to tripod but with only one telescoping leg; it is compact and easily portable.

Universal developer: A developer which will give satisfactory results on films, plates, and photographic papers.

Vernier Scale: A device used on a camera to indicate distance.

View finder: A viewing instrument attached to a camera, used to obtain proper composition.

Vignetting: Underexposure of the extreme edges of a photographic image; occasionally caused by improper design of lenses or too small a sunshade; also sometimes intentionally done in portraiture.

Visible light: The small portion of electromagnetic radiation which is visible to the human eye. Approximately the wave lengths from 400 to 700 millimicrons.

Weak: Applied to a negative which is thin due to underexposure or under-development.

Wide-angle lens: A lens of short focal length and great covering power used to cover a larger angle of view than a normal lens will include from a given viewpoint.

Working solution: A photographic solution which is ready to use.

Zoom lens: A lens which can be varied in apparent focal-length while maintaining focus on a given object; it gives the effect of moving to or from the subject when used on a motion-picture camera.

BIBLIOGRAPHY

The Challenge of Crime in a Free Society, a report by the President's Commission on Law Enforcement and Administration of Justice, United States Government Printing Office, Washington, D.C., February, 1967.

Crime Investigation, by Paul L. Kirk. Interscience Publishers, Inc., Fourth printing, February, 1966.

Criminal Investigation, by Charles G. Vanderbosch. International Association of Chiefs of Police, Professional Standards Division, 1319 18th Street, N.W., Washington, D. C.

Criminalistics, by William W. Turner, Consulting Editor, and the editorial staff of the Bancroft-Whitney Company, San Francisco, California. Aqueduct Books, a division of the Lawyers Co-operative Publishing Company.

Developing, Printing and Enlarging, by Al and Devera Bernsohn, Little Technical Library. Ziff-Davis Publishing Company, Chicago, Illinois.

3 Dimensional Photography, Principles of Stereoscopy, by Herbert C. McKay, F.R.P.S. Jones Press, Inc., Minneapolis, Minnesota.

The Encyclopedia of Photography, Greystone Press, New York, N. Y.

Enlarging is Thrilling, by Don Herold, Federal Manufacturing and Engineering Corporation, 199-217 Steuben Street, Brooklyn, N. Y.

The Evidence Handbook for Police, by Franklin M. Kreml, Director, Northwestern University. Published by Northwestern University, Evanston, Illinois.

Fire Administration and Technology, by Captain Robert McGannon, N.Y.C.F.D. (retired). Published by Arco, 219 Park Avenue South, New York, N.Y. 10003.

The Fireman's Responsibility in Arson Detection, prepared by the Fire Service Training Committee of the National Fire Protective Association. Third reprint (1966), published by National Fire Protection Association International, 60 Batterymarch Street, Boston, Mass. 02110.

Forensic Science, by H. J. Walls. Published by Frederick A. Praeger, 111 Fourth Avenue, New York, N. Y. 10003.

Fundamentals of Criminal Investigation, by Charles E. O'Hara. Published by Charles C. Thomas, Springfield, Illinois.

Homicide Investigation, by LeMoyne Snyder. Second edition, published by Charles C. Thomas Company, Springfield, Illinois.

Homicide Investigation, by S.R. Gerber and Oliver Schroeder. Published by The W.H. Anderson Publishing Co., Cincinnati, Ohio.

Installation and Maintenance of Aerial Photographic Equipment, Air Force Manual Number 95-3, Department of the Airforce, Washington, D.C. 20015, June, 1964.

An Introduction to Criminalistics, by Charles E. O'Hara and James W. Osterburg. Published by the MacMillan Co., New York, N. Y.

Modern Criminal Investigation, by Soderman and O'Connell. Revised by Charles E. O'Hara. Fifth edition, published by Funk and Wagnalls Company, New York, New York.

N F P A Handbook of Fire Protection, by Crosby-Fiske-Forster. Eleventh edition (1954), published by National Fire Protective Association, 60 Batterymarch Street, Boston, Mass.

New Leica Manual, by Willard D. Morgan and Henry M. Lester. Published by Morgan and Lester, New York, N. Y.

NIKON F NIKKORMAT Handbook of Photography, by Joseph D. Cooper and Joseph C. Abbott. Published by Amphoto, New York, N. Y.

Omega Enlarger Guide, by Dr. Kenneth S. Tydings, S.M.P.T.E. Published by Chilton Company, Philadelphia, Pa. and New York, N. Y.

Photo Lab Index, by Morgan and Morgan, Inc., Hastings-on-Hudson, New York, N. Y.

Photographer's Mate 1 & C, Rate Training Manual, prepared by Naval Personnel, Navpers 10375-B, United States Government Printing Office (1969), Washington, D.C.

Photographer's Mate 3, prepared by Bureau of Naval Personnel, Navy Training Courses, Navpers 10373, United States Government Printing Office (1958), Washington, D. C.

Photographer's Mate 3 & 2, Bureau of Naval Personnel, Navy Training Courses, Navpers 10355, United States Government Printing Office, Washington, D. C.

Photographic Evidence, by Charles C. Scott. Second edition, West Publishing Company, St. Paul, Minnesota.

Photography, Volume I, prepared by Bureau of Naval Personnel, Navy Training Courses, Navpers 10371-A, United States Government Printing Office (1953), Washington, D. C.

Photography and the Law, by George Chernoff and Hershel B. Smith. American Photographic Book Publishing Company, 33 West 60th Street, New York, N.Y. 10023

Photography for Scientific Publication, by Alfred A. Blaker, Principal Photographer, Scientific Photographic Laboratory, University of California, Berkeley, California. W. H. Freeman Company, San Francisco, California and London, England.

Photography in Crime Detection, by J. A. Radley, M. Sc., F. R. I. C. Chapman and Hall Ltd., London, England.

Photography the Amateur's Guide to Better Pictures, by Wyatt B. Brummitt, R. Will Burnett, Ph. D., Herbert S. Zim, Ph. D. Sc. D. Golden Press, Western Publishing Company, New York, N. Y.

Photolamp and Lighting Data Pamphlet, by General Electric Company, revised 1968, Cleveland, Ohio 44112.

Police and Crime Photography, by Burt Murphy. Verlan Books, New York, N. Y.

Police Guidance Manuals, a Philadelphia model, by Louis B. Schwartz and Stephen R. Goldstein, University of Pennsylvania Law School. Printed by the University of Pennsylvania Printing Office, Philadelphia, Pa. (1968).

Rollei Handbook, by Alec Pearlman, FIBP, FRPS. Published by Fountain Press, London, England, Rayelle Publications, Philadelphia, Pa.

The Speed Graphic Guide, including Crown and Century cameras, by Kenneth S. Tydings, S. P. E. Greenberg and Ambassador Books Ltd., New York, N. Y. (1952).

The Stereo Realist Guide—Stereo Made Easy for Everyone, by Dr. Kenneth S. Tydings, Pod. D., Ph. G., S. P. E., Photographic Consultant and Inventor; Instructor in Photography at Long Beach Peoples' College. Published by Greenberg, New York, N. Y. (1951).

Stereo Realist Manual, by Willard D. Morgan and Henry M. Lester. Published by Morgan and Lester Publishers, New York, N. Y.

The following books and pamphlets published by the Eastman Kodak Company, 343 State Street, Rochester, New York 14650.

Applied Infrared Photography, No. M-28, 10-68.

Basic Police Photography, No. M-7, 1964.

Copying, No. M-1, 6-65.

How to Make Good Pictures, Eighteenth edition.

Infrared and Ultraviolet Photography, No. M-3, 11-63.

Kodak Color Dataguide, No. R-19.

Kodak Color Films, No. E-77.

Kodak Films, No. F-1.

Kodak Master Photoguide, No. AR-21, 1966.

Photo Chemistry, No. W-39, 12-57.

Photography in Law Enforcement, 1948.

Photography in Law Enforcement, 1959.

Photography Through the Microscope, No. P-2, 6-66.

Photomacrography, No. P-53, 11-66.

Processing Chemicals and Formulas, No. J-1, 5-54.

Ultraviolet and Fluorescence Photography, No. M-27, 12-68.

AUDIO VISUAL

The Eastman Kodak Company has a 35 mm slide presentation called Law Enforcement Series. It is available to you by writing to the Eastman Kodak Company, Kodak Audio-Visual Service, Rochester, New York 14650.

The slide presentations available are:

(1) General-Evidence Photography
(2) Color Photography in Police Science
(3) Principles of Flash Photography
(4) The Importance of Perspective in Police Photography
(5) Fire-and-Arson Photography
(6) The Use of X-Rays in Criminal Investigation
(7) Identification Through Radiography
(8) Photography as a Tool of the Arson Investigator
(9) Accidental Fires and Explosions
(10) The Silent Witness—16 mm film (25 minutes)

INDEX

Figures and charts are indicated by italic type; text often also appears on these pages.

PHOTO CREDITS

EXERCISE 1—CHAPTER 2

1. Identify the parts of this simple camera and explain the purpose of each part.

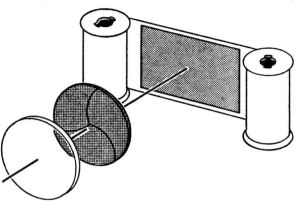

What essential part of the camera is missing from this drawing?

2. For this exercise, you will need a simple camera and a roll of film (if you have an adjustable camera, set the aperture at f/8, the shutter at 1/60 of a second, and the focus at 12 feet. Leave it there—it will be the equivalent of a simple camera.)

Put a roll of Kodacolor II film into the camera and shoot the entire roll, following the rules on page 8 of this book. Pick subjects that will yield interesting photos: friends, landscapes, animals, etc. Then have the film developed at a neighborhood drugstore or camera store.

Attach the best and the worst of your photos on this sheet. Explain why you feel that the one is good and the other is bad.

EXERCISE 2 — CHAPTER 3

1. On the back of this page, make a simple drawing of your camera from the front, side, top, back, and bottom. Identify each part of the camera. Then fill in the spaces below.

   Make of camera:
   Film size:
   Focal length of lens:
   Shutter speeds:
   f/stops:
   Closest distance on which I can focus:
   Type of viewing system:
   Lenses available for the camera:
   Lenses which I have:
2. What kind of exposure meter are you using?

EXERCISE 3 — CHAPTER 4

1. The ease of transporting and using a camera and handling film to be exposed is inversely proportionate to the ease with which the exposed film can be handled in the darkroom. Below, draw a graph which demonstrates this ratio. Include all fine basic film sizes.
    For the police photographer, which is more important: ease of handling camera and fresh film, or ease of handling film in the darkroom? Why?

2. Should departments send their films to a professional processing laboratory? Why or why not?

3. Study the chart on page 24. In which film size are the greatest variety of film types available? The least?

4. What is the difference between sharpness and acutance?

5. How might grain affect a photograph to be used for a courtroom exhibit?
    How does speed affect grain?

6. Purchase a roll of black and white film for your camera. After removing the film, cut and flatten the box it came in. Tape it to this sheet. Circle every word, phrase, or number on the box which tells you something about the film. Then label each circle, explaining what the word, phrase, or number means.

7. Load the film into your simple camera, or a camera set for f/8 at 125 and 12 feet. Take photographs similar to those you took for exercise 1. If possible, take photographs of the same subjects from the same angles when the film is filled, remove it from your camera. Save it. You'll be developing it in exercise 3.

EXERCISE 4 — CHAPTERS 6 & 7

1. Develop the film which you exposed in Exercise 2. With luck, you will have a batch of good negatives. Make a proof sheet, as explained in chapter 7. Attach the best and worst proofs below (if you are using a 4 x 5 camera, the proofs can be stapled to this sheet.)

     Is your judgment of best and worst proofs based on negative quality, composition, or something else? Explain your judgment.

2. Enlarge as many of your negatives as your instructor suggests. Choose the best and worst of the enlargements and attach them to this sheet. Are they from the same negatives as the best and worst of your proof sheet? Does enlarging change the quality of your negatives?

EXERCISE 5 — CHAPTER 8

1. Load an adjustable camera with black and white film. ASA____(fill in). Outdoors, place a subject in sunlight. Frame the subject and focus. Set the shutter speed at 1/100 or 1/125. Photograph the subject at f/16, f/11, f/8.5, f/5.6, f/4. Now set the aperture at f/11. Shoot the same subject at 1/30, 1/60, 1/125, 1/200, 1/500. Move into shade and repeat the above exposures, preferably with the same subject at the same distance. Develop the film and make a proof sheet. Attach the proof sheet to this page. Which were the best combinations of aperture and shutter speed for sunlight and shade? (Get into the habit of noting the exposure for each photograph you take, e.g: "cactus growing from man's ear — f/11 at 125".)

   If possible, repeat this exercise with a faster or slower film. The results will be notably different.

2. Using a fresh roll of film, try using the f/16 system in several kinds of light: sunny, cloudy, shade. Attach the prints to this sheet. How well does the system work?

Name _____

Instructor _____

EXERCISE 6 — CHAPTER 8

1. Find two subjects which are ten feet apart. Stand fifteen feet from the nearest subject and line both subjects up so that they are framed in your viewfinder, the nearer subject to the right. Focus on the distant subject. Calculate the correct exposure and shoot several pictures, beginning with a large aperture opening and fast shutter speed. With each successive shot, stop down one stop and lengthen the shutter speed. Note each exposure.

   Develop the film and enlarge each negative. Attach the prints to this page. Is the closer subject (the one on the right) in focus in each photograph? Why or why not? Which exposure produced the best over-all photograph?

Name _____

Instructor _____

EXERCISE 7 — CHAPTER 8

1. For this exercise, you will need a flash attachment which can be held away from the camera. Take one photograph of a subject with the flash attached to, or held next to, the camera, and directed at the subject. Take a second photo of the same subject from the same distance, this time directing the flash at the ceiling. Now hold the flash as far away from the camera as possible. Aim the flash at the subject and shoot. Hold the flash at the same distance from the camera, but direct the flash at the ceiling. Attach prints of all four exposures to this page. Which was the best exposure? Why?

EXERCISE 8 — CHAPTER 10

1. In your school parking lot, *carefully* place two cars hood-to-hood to give the appearance of a head-on collision. Photograph the scene. Attach the prints to this page and explain each angle and view.
2. Lift the hood of an automobile and photograph the engine, once in daylight and once with fill-in flash. Is there a difference between the two photographs?
3. Repeat number two, but photograph the dashboard of the vehicle.

EXERCISE 9 — CHAPTER 11

1. Have a friend lie on the floor with his eyes closed. Shoot the scene as if it were a homicide. Attach the prints to this page and explain each angle and view.

EXERCISE 10 — CHAPTER 12

1. Make a shoe impression in soft dirt, sand, or snow. Photograph it from several angles, using direct lighting and oblique light. Choose your best print, attach it to this page, and explain why it is a successful photograph. Be sure to include a data sheet.
2. Find a doorjam with scratches and marks. Photograph the jam, trying to bring out the marks. Attach the best print to this page and explain why it is a successful photograph.

EXERCISE 11 — CHAPTER 13

1. Using an ink pad, make several fingerprints on this page. Photograph them and attach the prints to this page. Are the enlargements comparable in detail to the original prints? Why or why not?

EXERCISE 12 — CHAPTER 14

1. On this page, make several different samples of writing. Obliterate each sample. Use the methods discussed in Chapter 14 to photograph each sample so that it is recognizable.